COUNSELING
AS A
PROFESSION

Nicholas A. Vacc, Ed.D.
Professor and Chairperson
of Counselor Education
The University of North Carolina
Greenboro, North Carolina

Larry C. Loesch, Ph.D.
Professor
Dept. of Counselor Education
University of Florida
Gainesville, Florida

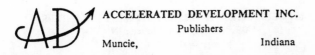

ACCELERATED DEVELOPMENT INC.
Publishers
Muncie,   Indiana

COUNSELING AS A PROFESSION

Library of Congress Number: 87-70348

International Standard Book Number: 0-915202-66-2

© Copyright 1987 by Accelerated Development Inc.

Technical Development: Tanya Dalton
                        Judy McWilliams
                        Marguerite Mader
                        Sheila Sheward

ACCELERATED DEVELOPMENT Inc., PUBLISHERS
3400 Kilgore Avenue, Muncie, IN 47304
(317) 284-7511

To

Jennie Vacc

and

Katherine Loesch

our first and most caring

teachers and counselors

PREFACE

The tremendous growth and vitality of professional counseling and its increasing interaction and fusion with other human-service professions have created an identity crisis of sorts. As a result, professional counselors are internally seeking to assert themselves among other professional mental-health service providers and, in so doing, to distinguish themselves from counseling psychologists or clinical psychologists, psychotherapists, psychoanalysts, or social workers by the different activities undertaken and services provided. Externally, professional counselors are seeking to convey to the public that they are effective providers of mental-health services and that they have knowledge and skills specifically suited to identifiable and unique needs in society.

Recent professional emphases within the counseling profession on areas such as professional counselor certifications and licensures, preparation program accreditations, and continuing professional development have helped to alleviate the identity crisis. However, its resolution is not yet complete because there remains considerable confusion and misunderstanding about what a professional counselor *is* and what a professional counselor *does*. This situation continues to exist, for the most part, because of an obvious void in the professional counseling literature; specifically, an organized and clear presentation of the nature and activities of the professional counselor. Needed are descriptions of the distinctive characteristics of professional counselors, the differences between professional counselors and other providers of mental-health services, and the approaches, methods, and activities used by professional counselors to alleviate the problems for which they render help. Our hope and intention is that this book fulfills these needs, and therefore helps to fill the void in the professional counseling literature.

Accreditation standards for programs preparing professional counselors stipulate that new students should receive a "professional orientation;" that is, they should be educated early in their programs about the professional counselor's roles and functions, the knowledge and skill bases for professional counseling, and the professional and ethical guidelines for professional counseling. Unfortunately, this orientation traditionally has consisted of an academic experience that emphasizes establishing a foundational knowledge base for, and development of, so-called basic counseling skills. Even more unfortunately, this academic experience has typically been comprised of "bits and pieces" from a variety of professional sources, and therefore has failed to provide a coherent introduction and has digressed substantially from the *orientation* purpose. Counselor trainees have been expected to develop a "professional orientation" and to act as "professionals," but many have not had benefit of an effective explanation of these expectations in terms of activities, behaviors, and guidelines. Thus, far too often counselor trainees have emerged from this experience with the *mis*understanding that having good counseling skills is the sum and substance of being a "professional" counselor.

Our purpose is to provide a professional resource which describes comprehensively what a professional counselor is, what a professional counselor does, and where and when a professional counselor works. Of course, other resources are available with the same *stated* purpose. However, our experience has been that those resources too often overemphasize the "how and why" of professional counseling and, in so doing, diminish the emphasis on the "what and where" of professional counseling.

Such resources typically focus on teaching how and why to conduct particular counseling activities, and therefore give only cursory attention to the what and where of these activities. We believe that, given the diversities and complexities of professional counseling activities, substantive "how and why" preparation is not possible from a single resource; such preparation is best accomplished through other, more specialized academic or other experiences. We further believe that the purpose of a "professional orientation" is to emphasize what, where, and when; not how and why. Therefore, our emphasis is orientation to professional counseling, with the key term being "emphasis." However, some discussion of "how and why" is necessary for understanding the "what, where, and when" of professional counseling.

Although we expect that this book will be used primarily by persons who are integrally involved in the counseling profession (e.g., counselor trainees, educators, or practitioners), we also intend for it to be useful to other professionals. That is, we hope that this book will provide an effective "explanation" of professional counseling for professionals who interact and associate with professional counselors, but who are not themselves professional counselors.

The counseling profession and professional counselors are indeed "coming of age" as a distinctive faction among professional mental-health service providers. We hope that this book will serve to facilitate and further enhance the evolution of counseling as a profession and to promote the professional counselor.

Nicholas A. Vacc

March 1987

Nicholas A. Vacc, Ed.D.

Larry C. Loesch

Larry C. Loesch, Ph.D.

CONTENT

LIST OF FIGURES

Chapter **1**

PROFESSIONAL COUNSELING: A POINT OF VIEW

[Counseling is]...the fusion of many influences. It brings together the movement toward a more compassionate treatment of mental health problems in mid-nineteenth century France, the psychodynamic insights of Freud and psychoanalysis, the scientific scrutiny and methodology of the behavior approach, the quantitative science of psychometrics, the humanistic perspective of client-centered therapy, the philosophical bases of existentialism, and the practical insights and applications that evolved from the vocational guidance movement. (Belkin, 1984, p. 19)

Belkin's description of counseling is appropriate because it captures the comprehensiveness of the activity known as counseling and, broadly speaking, all counseling specialities work with principles and theories of behavior. To help clients enhance their lives, professional counselors apply knowledge, skills, and techniques derived from the areas of human growth and development, the social and behavioral sciences, and from counselor education. Their work may involve individual interpersonal relationships, social or small-group interactions, or community-wide involvements. They also may be involved with personal, social, familial, or vocational concerns. And finally, they may be involved with either direct or indirect service delivery.

Attempting to delineate the broad counseling specialities (i.e., mental health counseling, school counseling, and student personnel in higher education) as being distinct from one another is difficult because professional counselors with different specialities have much in common; primarily, all are concerned with helping people with problems, with prevention of difficulties, and with acceleration in development. As members of a group of mental health professionals, counselors distinguish themselves by the applied nature of their work. Some focus on mental-health counseling, while others are concerned with student personnel in higher education or school counseling. However, regardless of specialty, a common bond exists among professional counselors; the goal of helping people to "cope" and to find effective solutions for problems that can arise at any point in the lives of otherwise primarily normal people.

Mental-Health Counseling

Mental-health counseling emphasizes the provision of services in the community, business or industry, or in private practice. Within these settings, professional counselors are involved in the provision of many types of mental-health counseling services. For example, they may provide family, adult, adolescent, or child counseling services; administer preventive mental health programs; provide consultation services; or help people find and achieve appropriate vocational goals and placements.

Student Personnel in Higher Education

Student personnel in higher education is based on the recognition that undergraduate and/or graduate students' problems and development have to be considered in the context of the total college or university environment. Professional counselors in higher education settings have special concern for the university community and its problems. They may be occupied with recruitment (admissions), managing a counseling program, student residence life, career planning and placement, student mental health, student activities (e.g., fraternities and sororities), special student groups (e.g., students with handicaps, foreign students, and students requiring educational opportunity programs), student discipline, retention, advising, or student development in general.

School Counseling

Professional counselors in this specialty area view the school as a unique "community" that must be studied and understood if the people in that environment are to be assisted with their educational, personal, and social development. All people working in the school (i.e., administrators, supervisors, teachers, cafeteria workers, secretaries, custodians, volunteers, and teacher aides) are viewed as important contributors to the achievement of educational goals and to the quality of life in a school. However, the professional counselor in the school setting specializes in facilitating the development of children and adolescents, with emphases on interactions among children, school personnel, and parents.

Student personnel in higher education and school counseling share a concern for understanding the settings in which behavior occurs. Professional counselors in these settings bring their knowledge, skills, and techniques to the situations, and apply them to problems, situations, and opportunities presented within these special environments (i.e., unique places in which people live, work, and study).

DIFFERENCES BETWEEN PROFESSIONAL COUNSELORS AND OTHER MENTAL-HEALTH SPECIALISTS

Mental-health professionals, other than counselors, include counseling and clinical psychologists (applied and academic), social workers, marriage and family therapists, and psychiatrists. *Applied psychologists* focus primarily on psychological pathology, or what is commonly viewed as abnormal, illness, or disease. They are typically involved in the diagnosis of personality problems with an emphasis on personality reorganization (rebuilding the structural and functional effects of a person's personality), and are concerned with maladaptive behavior (i.e., psychopathology). Applied psychology is usually subdivided into school, counseling, clinical, industrial, and community psychology. In contrast, *academic psychologists* are primarily concerned with areas in basic psychology (e.g., perception, history, physiology, and experimental psychology). Typically, academic psychologists conduct research in laboratory settings on the many factors that influence animal and human behavior, with careful control of variables or factors extraneous to those being investigated. Psychologists who work in academic settings are typically concerned with obtaining data that help the understanding of human and animal behavior and that lead to generalizations.

Social workers have a special concern for community problems that may lead to psychopathology; e.g., intrafamily problems, unemployment, poverty, "urban decay." Emphasis is placed on the complex social system and the delivery of social services, usually in the context of the medical model (i.e., remediation of existing problems). Two major focal points in social work are (1) "social advocacy" (i.e., social program delivery and planning) and "clinical practice" that typically eminates from comprehensive community mental health hospitals and centers, and (2) mental health consultation to community organizations, families, and individuals. In the latter context, social workers often gather and interpret pertinent information about a patient's personal history and social situations; information that may assist physicians with diagnoses and treatments.

Marriage and family therapists, a more recently developed specialty, have much in common with social workers because of their interest in the family as a unit of the community. However, they tend to be primarily occupied with family psychotherapy.

Psychiatry is frequently confused with applied psychology because professionals in these two areas direct their interest toward the diagnosis and treatment of psychopathology. Psychiatrists, however, are medical specialists who study the characteristics of people and explore such topics as abnormal behavior, motivation, drives, and anxiety, and the medical and psychological conditions that affect these dynamics. Typically, psychiatrists conduct their work in hospital settings. In sharp contrast to psychologists, psychiatrists often use psychopharmacological drugs (i.e., medications) in the treatment of psychopathological disorders.

Although distinguishing completely among various mental-health professionals is impossible, differentiation on the basis of commonly held perceptions is possible. For example, mental health problems may be conceptualized along a continuum from rather minor "adjustment problems" for otherwise normal people to "abnormal behavior" (i.e., severe psychopathology). Similarly, the "work orientations" of mental-health professionals may be conceptualized as being on a continuum from scientist with an emphasis on theory and research to practitioner with an emphasis on affective interactions. A combination of these continua forms a quadrant system based on descriptions of the extremes.

Mental health professionals may be placed in the quadrants as illustrated in Figure 1.1. Presently, insufficient research data exist for determining which quadrant placement would be best for a given profession, but the figure may be used to convey general, relative positions of several of the professions discussed.

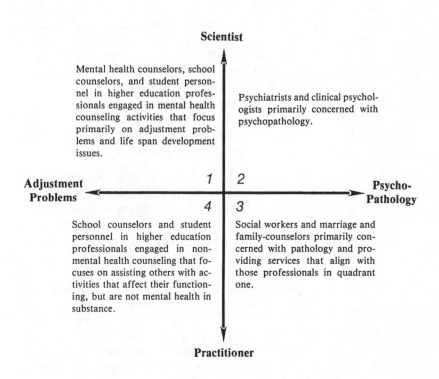

Scientist

Mental health counselors, school counselors, and student personnel in higher education professionals engaged in mental health counseling activities that focus primarily on adjustment problems and life span development issues.

Psychiatrists and clinical psychologists primarily concerned with psychopathology.

Adjustment Problems ← 1 | 2 → **Psycho-Pathology**

4 | 3

School counselors and student personnel in higher education professionals engaged in non-mental health counseling that focuses on assisting others with activities that affect their functioning, but are not mental health in substance.

Social workers and marriage and family-counselors primarily concerned with pathology and providing services that align with those professionals in quadrant one.

Practitioner

Figure 1.1. Mental-health service delivery continuum.

Illustrative Case—Keith

The approach to a given problem varies by specialty and can be best explained through an example. Consider Keith, who is a 27 year-old male struggling unsuccessfully to advance himself within in a large retail firm. According to his wife, he is very nervous and becomes tense when he leaves for work. He does not concern himself with responsibilities in the home, and he annoys his wife with unprovoked verbal assaults on their six-year-old son. Keith appears unhappy at work and his wife is unhappy about her inability to comfort him. Despite the necessary oversimplification of this example, it can be used to illustrate certain distinctions among the various mental-health specialties.

A social worker would most likely view Keith's presenting problem in the context of the occurrence of various factors in a population. Consideration would be given to the kind of neighborhood in which Keith resides, his income, his educational background, and whether or not his wife works (i.e., socio-economic factors). Also of interest to the social worker would be elements of the couple's lifestyle such as possessions, what is being purchased on installment plans, club memberships, religious affiliations, childhood history, and past individual medical or psychological problems. The social worker might believe that a referral is necessary, or might view the particular problem as solvable through meetings with the couple to discuss family dynamics.

Based on this information, the *social worker* might refer Keith to a psychiatrist and would provide the latter with a picture of generalities based on his/her knowledge of family dynamics and adult behaviors. An important role for the social worker is to contribute to the understanding of a problem by providing information about the social-psychological variables in Keith's life.

Marriage and family therapists would also consider demographic and contextual variables. However, the primary focus of their concern would be intra-family dynamics. The therapist would arrange an interview with the couple, perhaps including the child, and would focus attention on whether their problems are with interpersonal relationships within the family or with social situations with other groups of people. The marriage and family therapist would focus primarily on the problems of adjustment as they relate to the interpersonal relationships of the family. During therapy, the marriage and family therapist would have cogent and useful advice to offer Keith and his wife on how to improve their interpersonal relationships, based on the premise that Keith's improved interactions would be a benefit in helping his entire life.

The *psychologist* would probably interview Keith and perhaps administer a battery of psychological tests. The psychologist might view Keith's problem as hostility toward authority figures, or that he has not matured sufficiently to maintain adequate control of his impulses. Keith also could be viewed as anxious because he is not achieving to the level of expectations held for him by himself and/or others. From the psychologist's perspective, these factors may be contributing to a low level of self-esteem or valuation which creates feelings of unworthiness. This interpretation of Keith's situation is based on psychoanalytic-personality theory, but psychologists are not confined to this approach in viewing people's problems. Another psychologist might base the problem on the work of the behavioral psychologist B.F. Skinner, using knowledge from learning theory and what are known as behavior modification techniques.

The *psychiatrist,* like the psychologist, is concerned with diagnosis and would arrange for an interview with Keith. In addition, both would more than likely request information from significant others in Keith's life. For example, demographic information, as well as information on family interactions and past occurrences of problems (i.e., family history), could be gained from a social worker, and a psychologist could provide results of clinical psychological tests. The psychiatrist would be interested mainly in determining causes or reasons or, at the very least, gaining a good understanding of the symptoms for Keith's behavior with the intent of prescribing treatment. The treatment might be medication to reduce the anxiety and general implusive behavior, or therapy with the psychiatrist or, more typically, with a social worker.

The *professional mental-health counselor* working with Keith would consider the same data as the other mental-health service providers, but would apply the data to lifespan development (i.e., vocation, career, family, childrearing, interpersonal and intragroup relationships, and the person's context of a quality life). The professional counselor knows the type of environment in which Keith is employed and the values associated with it. Like the social worker and marriage and family therapist, the professional mental-health counselor would try to understand family dynamics. The counselor would depart from the procedures of the other professionals by perhaps deciding jointly with Keith to administer a battery of psychological, interest, and educational tests. However, testing would be avoided if the counselor and Keith have sufficient information as a result of their interviews. The professional counselor might conclude that Keith and his wife could benefit from joint counseling, or that a referral is needed because of the severe degree of pathology present with Keith. Whether or not a referral is made, the professional mental-health counselor would conduct counseling sessions with Keith to help him formulate an appropriate plan of action (i.e., proper referral or continued counseling).

In sharp contrast to the other specialists, the *professional school counselor's* involvement with Keith and his family would begin with the son. The assumption is made that the family dynamics have affected a change in the child's behavior (e.g., the child is exhibiting learning difficulty or acting-out behavior in the school) and his teacher has sought help from the school counselor. Although the focus of concern is the child's behavioral changes, the school counselor must work closely with the teacher in order to help the child. The school counselor utilizes the same data as that considered by the mental-health counselor, but it is applied to the school situation. A school counselor tries to understand a student from the child's perspective, prior knowledge of the school and the teachers, observations of the child in the classroom, interviews with the child, and data contained in the child's cumulative school file. The latter usually includes group achievement and intelligence test data, general family information, and previous teachers' comments and grades. However, the school counselor may not believe that sufficient information is available and subsequently may decide that an interview with the parents could be beneficial. In this situation, interviewing Keith and his wife might aid the school counselor in determining that (1) the "core" problem of the child's school learning and/or overt-behavior problems is due to interpersonal problems at home, and (2) the parents could benefit from counseling. The school counselor would focus primarily on improving the child's behavior and performance in school, but would also help the child to cope with problems at home.

Of course, many areas of overlap exist among mental-health service providers, and the illustrations and distinctions cited above are not as clear-cut as described. For example, social workers and marriage and family therapists may be knowlegeable of and have skills in career development and testing, and some professional counselors may function as psychologists. However, what professional counselors have in common are knowledge and skills in human growth and development, social and behavioral sciences (especially psychology), helping relations, group interactions, assessment and appraisal, research methodology, and a profound respect for the scientific approach.

ASSUMPTIONS FOR PROFESSIONAL COUNSELORS

The counseling profession is based on certain assumptions, some of which are definitive and fully agreed upon by professional counselors. Others, however, are implicit, not specifically stated or readily acknowledged and, in many instances, not clearly perceived. Two factors which most professional counselors view as important to successful practice are the professional counselor's knowledge and skills and the professional counselor's personality. Without useful knowledge, a professional counselor is unable to practice effectively. Likewise, in order to practice, the professional counselor needs to be able to respond to clients in ways that promote their willingness to profit from the counselor's efforts. Relatedly, a professional counselor must exhibit personality characteristics that allow clients to be receptive to the counselor's efforts.

Knowledge

A professional counselor needs to be knowledgeable of those aspects of mental health that relate to the development, relief, and solution of an individual's emotional or career concerns which are associated with quality of life. In addition, the professional counselor must be aware of the effect biological and societal influences may have upon an individual's behavior. Knowledge development should include preparation in eight areas:

1. human growth and development;

2. social and cultural foundations;

3. the helping relationship;

4. group dynamics, processes, and counseling;

5. life style and career development;

6. appraisal of the individual;

7. research and evaluation; and

8. professional orientation.

These are the "core" areas recognized by the Council for Accreditation of Counseling and Related Educational Programs (1986).

Human Growth and Development. This area involves an understanding of the nature and needs of individuals at all age levels. Included are studies in human behavior, personality theory, and learning theory.

The focus of human growth and development permits the professional counselor an opportunity to gain an understanding of how psychological, sociological, and physiological factors influence behavior at all developmental levels.

Social and Cultural Foundations. Included in this area are studies of change, ethnic groups, subcultures, sexism, changing roles of women, urban and rural societies, population patterns, cultural morés, use of leisure time, and differing life patterns. Knowledge of traditional disciplines such as the behavioral sciences, economics, and political science is emphasized.

The Helping Relationship. Knowledge of the helping relationship comprises counseling and consultation theory, development of self-awareness, and an understanding of how and why clients do what they do. Development of helping relationship skills for the successful practice of counseling is emphasized.

Group Dynamics, Processes, and Counseling. Theories of group behavior, group practices, methods for working with groups, group dynamics, and observational and facilitative skills, are included in this area.

Life Style and Career Development. Vocational-choice theories, the relationship between career choice and life style, sources of occupational and educational information, approaches to career decision-making processes, and approaches to career exploration comprise this area of knowledge development. The intent is to enable the professional counselor to be of assistance to clients in their personal, social, emotional, and vocational choices and/or with the activities in their daily living.

Appraisal of the Individual. The particular knowledge, skills, and experiences necessary to enable a professional counselor to gather information to use in making judgements about clients and environmental settings comprise this area. Included are methods for gathering and interpreting data (i.e., use of tests), individual and group testing, observation techniques, and general skills necessary for the assessment and appraisal of individuals' behaviors.

Research and Evaluation. Effective functioning as a professional counselor necessitates a knowledge base in the areas of statistics, research design, and development of research and demonstration proposals. Professional counseling practitioners, regardless of specialty, must be able through research to contribute to the body of literature in the profession.

Professional Orientation. This area includes knowledge of the basic components of the counseling profession; i.e., professional organizations, codes of ethics, legal considerations, standards of preparation, certification, and licensing. In addition, the role identity of the professional counselor and other human-service specialists is explored.

Personality

Even the most knowledgeable and well-trained professional counselor will be unable to help others if certain personality characteristics are not evident, thus causing clients to be unreceptive to the professional counselor's behaviors. Although the qualities of personality that promote effective counseling are elusive, researchers have identified several personality characteristics that are important in promoting a productive counselor-client relationship. Three personality qualities that are considered essential for a professional counselor to be effective are security, trust, and courage (Belkin, 1984).

Security. Prerequisites to security are self-confidence, self-respect, and freedom from fear and anxiety. Anxiety is associated with the diminished ability to attend to the client during an interview (Milliken & Kirchner, 1971). Secure counselors feel comfortable about themselves and therefore provide healthy models for their clients. The professional counselor who is suspicious and who questions everyone's motives is unlikely to be of help to others.

As a personal quality, a secure counselor is more likely to allow clients to be themselves. Counselors who are comfortable with themselves do not seek to satisfy their own needs by "shaping the client in their own image." They have the capability to allow clients to develop at their own rates and in their own directions.

Trust. Trust, in its most elementary form, is to be able to give, receive, and depend on others, a quality that is highly important in determining the professional counselor's attitude toward people. According to Belkin (1984), trust, which develops during the early stages of life, is difficult to learn if not acquired when young. In counseling, the absence of trust may cause a counselor to act in ways that do not benefit clients.

Courage. All human beings appear to have an innate desire to be loved, recognized, and respected. Professional counselors, however, must be able to put aside their own needs within the context of counseling in order to find gratification. For example, the professional counselor must be willing to absorb a client's anger, and to accept a sense of "aloneness" as the client progresses and becomes autonomous from the counselor. Analogous to professional counselors working with clients is parents allowing their growing children to mature and develop. During a counseling relationship, the client initially relies upon the counselor, shares personal thoughts, aspirations, and behaviors which are rarely made public, and seeks direction and order in his/her life. Subsequently, counselors must be emotionally capable of relinquishing their clients' dependency and allowing them to gain control of their own lives.

In summary, professional counselors need to have enough self-security, self-trust, and courage to relinquish a part of themselves when helping others.

Bardon and Bennett (1974) found that particular personality qualities of helping professionals affect their behavior when making judgements about clients. They suggested that professionals working with clients need to possess personality qualities that include genuiness, positive skepticism, and empathy. These qualities also are important and relevant to professional counselors.

Genuineness. As Truax and Carkhuff (1967) indicated, genuineness involves a concern for what happens to people. To understand the importance of this quality, reflect upon the role professional counselors play in the lives of their clients. Counselors are empowered to tell others what to do. They have great authority because they are viewed as experts. Such power in relationships with their clients can only be regulated or controlled by a sincere and over-riding concern for the welfare of others, a value that is integral to preventing potential misuse of authority.

Positive Skepticism. Another important personality quality is an attitude of positive skepticism. Skepticism, as viewed by Bardon and Bennett (1974), reflects an understanding of the imperfections of the current state of knowledge, instrumentation, and methods. Unfortunately, professional counselors often have to act without the security offered by the exactness available in other disciplines (e.g., the "hard sciences"). However, because of the nature of their involvement with real-life situations that require assistance, and because better alternatives typically are unavailable, professional counselors must act. A cautious, skeptical, and yet critical approach that makes use of past successes and failures, must be an abiding value of professional counselors when assisting clients. The adjective "positive" has been included to suggest that skepticism should be linked with a willingness to persist and try new approaches. This is most important because professional counselors will have disappointments, immediate results may be lacking, and occasionally, clients may be uncooperative. Therefore, an optimistic outlook, despite discouragement, is required.

Empathy. Empathy is the ability to identify with others (Truax & Carkhuff, 1967). Professional counselors on many occasions work with people whose values and life experiences are very different from their own. Also, clients often enter a counseling relationship being extremely antagonistic toward the counselor; the counselor is perceived as "threatening" and reflective of the troublesome social system that most likely prompted their seeking assistance. Functioning well can be difficult when people are hostile, angry, and negative. Professional counselors, however, must develop an understanding of how their clients feel and must be able to respect those feelings even when they appear to be making the counselor's job difficult.

Summary. Although the personality qualities presented above are not explicit, they are highly important in determining how the professional counselor functions. Perhaps the personality qualities are more reflective of the attitude professional counselors take toward the nature of their work as opposed to their knowledge. Knowledge, of course, is the base upon which the practice of counseling is built, but it is ultimately more useful for professional counselors to approach the problems that confront them regarding human behavior, when they possess the various personality variables suggested by Belkin (1984), Bardon and Bennett (1974), and Truax and Carkuff (1967).

The Counselor as Scientist

A final assumption about professional counselors, the *sine qua non,* is that the professional counselor is a scientist; a view that is consistent with the earlier assumption of positive skepticism as a desirable characteristic of the professional counselor. If an individual's behavior can be altered and the individual is capable of making that change as a result of the counseling relationship and process, then the professional counselor must observe the effects of his/her procedures as they affect individuals by carefully measuring and evaluating change. Professional counselors are continuously being confronted with measuring the effects of their counseling in order to derive specific conclusions. Therefore, a scientific aspect of the practice of counseling exists.

The practitioner as scientist has been described by Barlow, Hayes, and Nelson (1984) as involving three interrelated activities or roles. First, the practitioner is a consumer of research findings reported in professional journals and at professional meetings. The information gained involves either initial or re-examined assessments of approaches for the practitioner to put into practice. In the second role, the practitioner is an evaluator and appraiser of approaches that use empirical methods that would increase effectiveness and accountability. Third, the practitioner is a researcher who produces and analyzes data, and who reports these data to the scientific community at professional meetings and in professional journals.

Conceptually, the research basis for practice or professional activities and judgements of counselors is illustrated in Figure 1.2. A majority of what is known about human behavior derives from research in the social and behavioral sciences, much of which is conducted under circumstances that are less than ideal. With repeated replications, however, the scientific credibility of research findings is enhanced and enables the scientist to draw conclusions. When professional counselors try to determine something about a client's behavior, they must take into account many factors or variables, some of which cannot be ignored such as developmental stage, age, gender, situational events, attitudes, personality, personal habits, and cultural considerations. Literally, the professional counselor is confronted with an almost limitless number of confounding variables when counseling.

Illustrative Case—John. To illustrate, consider John, an adolescent whose behavior alienates others because it is offensive. To understand John's behavior and to help him alleviate his inappropriate behavior, the professional counselor must understand what is known about adolescent behavior, how behavior is changed, how John perceives what is happening to him with regard to others and different aspects of his life, and other special problems John brings with him when interacting with others. The professional counselor, who is working with John, must help using two resources at once. One is the existing data that have been derived by other practitioner-scientists and then accumulated to the extent that laws or rules have been established for people in general. The other is existing data specific to John, his behaviors, and his life situation. The

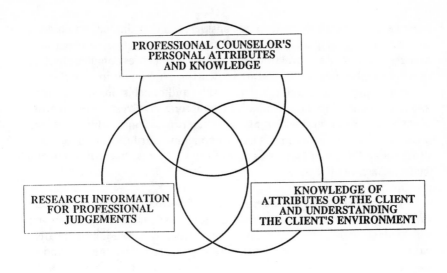

Figure 1.2. The influence of research and practice as they affect the outcomes of a professional counselor working with clients.

former is termed nomothetic which pertains to general laws and principles, while the latter is termed idiographic or that which is characterized as individual laws of behavior in order to explain individual cases.

THE PROFESSIONAL COUNSELOR
AS A PRACTITIONER-SCIENTIST

Professional counselors, to be most effective in helping individuals, must integrate information, reconcile differences, and view themselves as scientists. All evidence needs to be considered and evaluated, and a decision derived through distillation of all available knowledge, information, and experiences. As a practitioner-scientist, the professional counselor, in a very real sense, is engaged in a scientific experiment in which questions are raised and examined, and results and conclusions are changed as new evidence becomes available. Counseling involves a series of formative evaluations and action plans. When professional counselors take a course of action or discuss what is happening during counseling, they must judge the probability of the validity of change made in a client's behavior against the data.

To understand how a competent professional counselor practices, one must recognize that practice is scientific; it takes place when knowledge, both nomothetic and idiographic, is filtered by a professional counselor. Competent professional practice is also the interaction between the professional counselor and knowledge in a setting; an interaction designed to foster helpful behavior. Ultimately, professional counselors are only as useful or as valuable as is the amount of knowledge they've gained. This book is dedicated to the assumption that *the content of counseling is never removed from scientific methods.*

In addition to knowledge and techniques, effective counselors must have skills in scientific inquiry, not only to enable counselors to be fully functioning professionals, but to establish counselors as self-regulating professionals. This viewpoint is neither original nor new; the scientist-professional model has long been used by counselor preparation programs approved by the American Psychological Association (APA) (Hock, Ross, & Winder, 1966).

Adoption of the APA training procedures is not being suggested for professional counselors, but the practitioner-scientist viewpoint, as opposed to the scientist-practitioner approach, makes considerable sense for the future of professional counseling. Moreover, this viewpoint is consistent with the existing Ethical Standards of the American Association for Counseling and Development (1986). In these Standards are stipulated that counselors must gather data on their effectiveness and use the findings to guide them in the counseling process. The spirit of scientific inquiry therefore must pervade the perspectives of professional counselors, with the manifestation of the spirit being the common rule rather than the exception.

Inherent in the practitioner-scientist approach is viewing scientific inquiry in counseling from a much broader perspective than has been characteristic in the past. As mentioned earlier, the core of this view is the professional counselor's development of a habitually inquiring, critical attitude about practice. Thus, scientific methods are equated with inquiry as well as traditional methods of normative data gathering. This means that professional counselors must continually engage in careful, scientific review of all their activities. Common to both scientific inquiry and practice is the necessity for a questioning attitude, a method of problem solving, a high regard for evidence, and methods for self monitoring and improvement. The practitioner-scientist approach, then, is more than just data gathering and analysis; it is a way of approaching all professional activities.

The distinctive feature of the practitioner-scientist approach is the need for professional counselors to have competent training in knowledge and techniques associated with counseling and research methods. Being a professional counselor, therefore, means being competent in facilitating science as well as human development. While a major part of a professional counselor's time is spent in practice or direct service, a part of the direct service must be devoted to the improvement of and subsequent changes in services as determined through scientific inquiry. An important element of the practitioner-scientific approach is that it encourages professional counselors to examine and compare client behaviors for decisions about counseling goals, intervention strategies, and effectiveness of the counseling process. The approach guides the professional counselor to promote sensitive counseling that is uniquely suited to each client.

Many people view the scientific approach as a "one-time" activity. However, counseling and data gathering are continuous processes throughout a relationship with a client; activities which in fact establish direction for the counseling process. The scientific approach is a means for obtaining and using information to generate and establish counseling goals and intervention strategies, and to determine the effectiveness of counseling.

The focus of this ongoing process is *not* to find the "truth" for working with people, but rather to use information in a way that helps clients develop. In this respect, the professional counselor can be viewed as an experimenter who is continually assessing and conceptualizing the relationships among the information obtained, counseling goals, and counseling approach. The effectiveness of the professional counselor is therefore maintained by the counselor's ability to gather data in a scientific manner and to use it for making ongoing modifications to the counseling process. Without the scientific component, the counseling process becomes merely an "act of faith."

Chapter 2

EVOLUTION OF THE COUNSELING PROFESSION

To fully characterize the history of an entity as nebulous as a profession is impossible. However, some understanding of the history of the counseling profession is necessary if its current status and future are to be understood effectively. Although heritage is not destiny, destiny is in part contingent upon heritage. The question is, how can the history of a profession be explained? One possibility, and the one of choice here, is to review the history of an organization that has long served as a representative of a profession. In the current context, the American Association for Counseling and Development (AACD) (formerly the American Personnel and Guidance Association; APGA) is such an organization.

Counseling professionals, who view themselves solely as "psychotherapists," might suggest that the history of the counseling profession dates at least to Sigmund Freud, and probably farther back to the earliest "psychological healers." However, that view is parochial and inconsistent with the perspective of the counseling profession taken in this book. More typically, the history of the counseling profession traces its beginnings to approximately the turn of the twentieth century. That was

when education professionals began to realize that young people in society needed help in making effective vocational decisions. The visionary efforts of professionals such as Frank Parsons and Mrs. Quincy Adams
Shaw were particularly notable. In brief, they and their colleagues began
a series of significant activities designed to enable teachers to help
students with vocational planning and decision-making. The significance
was twofold. One, the activities marked the first attempt at formally providing *psychologically-based* services for "normal" people (i.e., the use
of "psychological" services for persons without severe mental illness).
Two, through the Vocational Bureau of Boston, they sought to train a
"new" professional with the title "Teacher-Counselor" (Smith, Engels,
& Bonk, 1985). Thus, they associated the title "counselor" with the provision of helping or counseling services for people who were not seriously
disturbed.

As interest and activities in "vocational counseling" grew during the
early 1900s, those involved soon recognized that a national organization
would be beneficial to those sharing a common professional interest.
Therefore, the National Vocational Guidance Association (NVGA) was
formed in 1913, primarily as a result of the efforts of Jesse B. Davis who
served as the first NVGA Secretary. NVGA retained its original name
until 1985 when it became the National Career Development Association
(NCDA).

Other professionals did not lag far behind those interested in vocational counseling in deciding that "normal" people had needs other than
educational or psychotherapeutic assistance. For example, the needs of
students on college and university campuses, and those of the professionals who addressed student needs, were recognized in the second
decade of the twentieth century. The National Association of Deans of
Women (NADW) was formed in 1913. Soon after, the National Association of Student Personnel Administrators (NASPA) was formed in 1916.
At about the same time, college and university placement officers, then
called "appointment secretaries," determined that their particular professional needs and interests were not being met effectively by NVGA
and that their work represented a broader professional perspective than
that reflected in either NADW or NASPA (Johnson, 1985). They,
therefore, established the National Association of Appointment
Secretaries (NAAS) in 1924. NAAS continued to broaden its professional scope and eventually evolved in 1929 to the National Association
of Placement and Personnel Officers (NAPPO), and then to the
American College Personnel Association (ACPA) in 1931.

The historical association between counseling and education has also been reflected in other ways. For example, the Teachers College Personnel Association (TCPA) was established in 1931, with the intent of focusing on testing and research activities. This focus, however, was not unanimously agreed upon within the organization and TCPA existed both as a separate organization and as an affiliate division of the American Association for Colleges of Teacher Education (AACTE) during its first twenty years. In 1951, TCPA changed its name to the Student Personnel Association for Teacher Education (SPATE). One year later it separated from AACTE and became one of the founding divisions of APGA. In 1974, SPATE restructured its professional perspective and became the Association for Humanistic Education and Development (AHEAD) (Wilson & Robinson, 1985).

The value of professional supervision and preparation also has been evident throughout the history of the counseling profession. This importance was first formally recognized with the founding of the National Association of Guidance Supervisors (NAGS) in 1940. Although NAGS was originally composed exclusively of counselor supervisors, it soon attracted counselor trainers. Thus, in 1952 the name was changed to the National Association of Guidance Supervisors and Counselor Trainers (NAGSCT), and the organization became one of the founding divisions of APGA. Nine years later, NAGSCT changed its name to the Association for Counselor Education and Supervision (ACES).

"Strength through unity" was a common theme in the United States in the early 1950s as reflected by the relationships among the counseling professions. In 1952, NVGA, ACPA, NAGSCT, and SPATE joined together to form the American Personnel and Guidance Association. Herr (1985) aptly summarized the nature of this founding:

> The intent of these four associations was to create a unified structure that would have the collective strength to pursue goals impossible to achieve for smaller, special interest groups, as were the founding divisions at the time.
>
> In creating the confederation known as the American Personnel and Guidance Association, however, it was apparent that the founders were not ready to completely surrender the autonomy of their individual associations.... They sought common cause within the larger association umbrella, but did so with an intent to retain the capability to advance the special interests of their divisions. (p. 396)

The "common bond but individual identity" theme remained evident as APGA (AACD) grew in terms of both members and divisions.

Vocational guidance continued as the major focus of "counseling" services in American schools for approximately four decades prior to World War II. However, the post World War II era fostered an awareness that "traditional" vocational counseling services were not appropriate for a growing segment of the school population; students planning to attend college. During the late 1940s, therefore, a large number of school counselors turned their attention to college-bound students. This schism in the professional focus of counselors working in schools prompted the need for a professional organization that was better suited to counselors who were less oriented to vocational counseling in schools. The result was the formation in 1953 of the fifth APGA (AACD) division, the American School Counselor Association (ASCA) (Minkoff & Terres, 1985).

Recognition of the counseling needs of persons with disabilities also increased in the post World War II era, and incited the passage of the (Federal) Vocational Rehabilitation Act (VRA) in 1954. The VRA not only symbolized the importance of the needs of persons with disabilities, it also provided funds for training counselors to assist with those needs. During this same time period, a growing number of members within APGA (AACD) were becoming involved in rehabilitation counseling activities. These factors melded together during the early 1950's and led eventually to the formation of the Division of Rehabilitation (DRC) within APGA (AACD) in 1958. In 1962, the DRC became the American Rehabilitation Counseling Association (ARCA) (DiMichael & Thomas, 1985).

Although what might be referred to as a "subliminal affection for empiricism" had long been present in the APGA (AACD) membership, it did not fully emerge until the mid-1960s. A number of professionals, most of whom were already APGA (AACD) members, moved to form a division specifically for professionals with interests in measurement and evaluation. Their efforts resulted in the 1965 origination of the Association for Measurement and Evaluation in Guidance (AMEG), the seventh APGA (AACD) division. However, formal incorporation of this division did not occur until 1968 (Sheeley & Eberly, 1985). In 1984 AMEG changed its name to the Association for Measurement and Evaluation in Counseling and Development (AMECD) to be consistent with the name change of the parent organization.

The recurrent vocational counseling emphasis in APGA (AACD) re-emerged with a new focus in 1966 with the formation of the National

Employment Counselors Association (NECA). The new focus was on employment counseling as a specialty area within the more general field of vocational counseling. Similar to AMECD, most of the original members of NECA were already members of other existing APGA (AACD) divisions (Meyer, Helwig, Gjernes, & Chickering, 1985).

The late 1960s and the early 1970s were times of "social consciousness raising" in the American society and APGA (AACD) was not untouched by this movement. A large number of professionals within the association believed a need existed to recognize specifically the needs and talents of ethnic minority persons. However, opinions differed considerably about how the recognition should be manifested within a professional organization. Eventually, in 1972, the disparate ideas came together in the formation of the Association for Non-White Concerns in Personnel and Guidance (ANWC) (McFadden & Lipscomb, 1985). ANWC changed its name in 1985 to the Association for Multicultural Counseling and Development (AMCD) in order to reflect more accurately its current professional orientation.

Although the Association for Religious and Values Issues in Counseling (ARVIC) traces its history in APGA (AACD) to 1973, the seminal activities for the division began in 1951 with the formation of the Catholic Guidance Council in the Archdiocese of New York (Bartlett, Lee, & Doyle, 1985). That beginning lead to the 1961 formation of the National Catholic Guidance Conference (NCGC) by members of APGA (AACD). The evolution from NCGC to ARVIC reflected change in the nature and purposes of the division. Bartlett, Lee, and Doyle (1985) stated that:

> As an organization, ARVIC has experienced a metamorphosis. It no longer attempts to serve solely as a Catholic professional organization; rather, it attempts to fill a void within the AACD structure by providing a forum for the examination of religious and values issues in counseling. (p. 449)

Throughout most of the early history of the counseling profession, the emphasis was on "one-to-one" counseling interaction between the counselor and client. However, maturation of the profession brought with it a realization that work with groups is not only effective but also economically more efficient. This realization prompted APGA (AACD) professionals who were interested in all facets of group dynamics and processes (including counseling) to form the Association for Specialists in Group Work (ASGW). It became an APGA (AACD) division in 1973 (Carroll & Levo, 1985).

A unique example of the counseling profession's responsiveness to the multifaceted needs of society is found in the Public Offender Counselor Association (POCA), which officially became an APGA (AACD) division in 1974. POCA was created to be responsive to the specific professional needs and interests of counselors who work with public offenders (Page, 1985).

The rapid growth of the American Mental Health Counselors Association (AMHCA), which officially became an APGA (AACD) division in 1978, perhaps knows no equal in the history of professional organizations. From its beginnings in 1976, AMHCA has expanded until it holds the largest AACD divisional membership (Weikel, 1985); in excess of 12,000 members. AMHCA's growth reflects the fact that a considerable number of professional counselors now work in other than educational settings.

The Military Educators and Counselors Association (MECA), although not a formally recognized AACD division, is an organizational affiliate of AACD. MECA was created to be responsive to the professional needs and interests of counselors who work with military service personnel and veterans, their dependents, and civilian employees of the military services (Cox, 1985).

The Association for Adult Development and Aging (AADA) is another organizational affiliate of AACD. Members of AADA have as their primary professional interest counseling persons at all stages of adult development. However, the greatest emphases are given to midlife, pre-retirement, and gerontological counseling specializations.

An emerging "special interest" group (SIG) within AACD is comprised of marriage and family counselors. While professional counselors in this group focus on the nuclear family, their interest extends to marital and sibling problems, family subsystems, and external societal influences that affect the family system.

In 1983, APGA changed its name to the American Association for Counseling and Development. The change was symbolic of the evolving professional orientation among AACD members, and indeed within the counseling profession. As Herr (1985) stated:

> [T]he overriding issue was that the term guidance was essentially used only in elementary and secondary school settings and was becoming an archaic and

vague term even there. Although such a perception of the term guidance is questionable, the primary argument for the name change was that association members were increasingly being found in settings other than education and that what these persons did was *counseling,* not *guidance.* (p. 395)

Today, the total AACD membership has surpassed 51,000 and continues to grow steadily. Literally every facet of the counseling and human development professions and all types of professional counselors are represented within this organization.

LESSONS FROM HISTORY

Clearly the history of AACD is not a complete history of the counseling profession. Nonetheless, a professional organization, because it is composed of members of a profession, reflects the issues and trends within the profession represented by the organization. Therefore, a number of inferences about the counseling profession can be drawn from the history of AACD. And as Oliver Wendell Holmes, Jr. noted, "A page of history is worth a volume of logic."

Lesson 1: Professional counselors are identifiable and unique

Unfortunately for professionals who refer to themselves as counselors, the title "counselor" has been used in a wide variety of contexts in the American society. The media are replete with "legal counselors," "real estate counselors," "financial counselors," "travel counselors," and the like. Overexposure to the title counselor has served to desensitize the public to the title in general, and to its application to a type of mental health professional in particular. However, regardless of the overuse of the title, a group of professionals exists who may be accurately and validly referred to as counselors. Further, the application of the title is more than "self-annointment" by those who refer to themselves as counselors. At least nineteen states now have licensure laws for "professional counselors" (or corresponding titles that include the word counselor), and similar laws are being considered in approximately 27 other states. Thus, the use of the title professional counselor to refer to a particular type of mental health professional is, and continues to be, grounded in law. Relatedly, although this specific use of the term counselor has not yet become commonly understood by the general public, such understanding is rapidly increasing.

Professional counselors are also uniquely identifiable within the counseling profession. Of course, a number of different types of professionals exists who do "counseling" (e.g., clinical and counseling psychologists, clinical social workers, psychoanalysts, and psychiatrists). However, professional counselors are not "mini-psychologists," "closet psychoanalysts," "imitation social workers," or "pseudo-shrinks." Nor are they people who only give advice, tell students what courses to take, or tell people which jobs to pursue. They are, simply, professionals whose primary vocational activity is the provision of counseling and closely related mental-health services.

Lesson 2: Counseling professionals may be differentiated in a variety of ways

Why is differentiation necessary and/or appropriate among professional counselors? An effective answer must encompass two components, one theoretical and one pragmatic. With regard to the former, there are those in the counseling profession who have alledged that "counseling is counseling is counseling" regardless of the nature of the persons receiving the counseling services, persons providing the services, location of services, and how or with which set of techniques the services are being provided. This perspective belies the complexities of people in society and the counseling profession, as well as the widely varying places and circumstances in which counseling services are rendered. In an "age of specialization," the needs for and benefits of specialization within the counseling profession are readily evident. To suggest that counseling is "an" activity that is applicable regardless of clientele or location is to deny the effectiveness gained from years of research and development of specialized counseling activities.

With regard to the second component, the simple fact of the matter is that counselors work in relatively easily differentiated settings and/or with relatively easily differentiated clients. What follows then is that professional counselors can maximize their effectiveness by developing specialized skills specifically applicable in the settings in which they work and/or to the clients with whom they work.

To differentiate among professional counselors is prudent. One way would be on the basis of title, as presented in Chapter 1. Another differentiation can be made on the basis of type of setting in which counseling services are provided, type of counseling service provided, and type of primary professional interests and activities. By relating this to the

AACD history presented previously, one can note that the various AACD divisions also may be clustered along three dimensions. For example, ASCA and ACPA clearly relate to particular settings. Similarly, ARCA, NCDA, NECA, ASGW, POCA, AMHCA, and MECA relate to types of counseling service, while ACES, AHEAD, AMECD, AMCD, and ARVIC relate to primary professional interests and activities.

Unfortunately, neither the three differentiation bases presented nor the divisional titles listed are sufficient to differentiate completely among counseling professionals because complete differentiation actually is not possible. For example, school counselors quite obviously engage in and are concerned with vocational counseling and working with ethnic minorities. Similarly, other professional counselors are involved with and concerned about matters and activities beyond their *primary* professional activities. Thus, professional counselors tend to be multifaceted in terms of professional concerns and involvements. Nonetheless, to differentiate among them often is expedient for purposes of communication clarity.

Lesson 3: Professional counselors fulfill societal needs not fulfilled by other professionals

One example of the validity of this statement is POCA. Page (1985) stated that, "POCA is unique because it emphasizes the importance of providing counseling services to public offenders.... Other professional associations such as the American Correctional Association place emphasis on correctional concerns rather than on rehabilitation concerns" (p. 455). Other examples are also readily available. School counselors, as represented by ASCA, are the primary (and in many cases the only) providers of mental-health services to students in schools. Similarly, employment counselors, as represented by NECA, are the primary (and again in many cases the only) providers of counseling assistance in governmental employment agencies.

Lesson 4: Professional counselors fulfill societal needs also being fulfilled by other professionals

The provision of many counseling services is not restricted to professional counselors. For example, marriage and family counseling services are provided by many mental-health counselors, as represented by

AMHCA, but they are also provided by professionals such as social workers, counseling and clinical psychologists, and marriage and family counseling specialists. Similarly, many ACPA members provide counseling services to college and university students, but so do other professionals such as counseling and clinical psychologists. Thus, many of the professional activities performed by professional counselors are also offered by other professionals (as was illustrated with the case of Keith presented in Chapter 1). This overlap helps to associate and involve counselors with other professional specializations, and allows them to benefit from the knowledge gained from the work experiences and research of other professionals.

Lesson 5: The counseling profession reflects needs and trends in society

The beginning of the counseling profession, vis-à-vis the earliest vocational counseling activities, is testimony to this lesson. The counseling profession literally came into existence because of societal needs which were not being met in other ways. If young people had not had a need for assistance with vocational concerns, or if such a need had been fulfilled through other means, Parsons, Adams, Davis, and others would not have found it necessary to act as they did to begin the counseling profession.

Current examples are also obvious. The formation and rapid growth of AMHCA reflects the widespread need for mental health services for (other than seriously disturbed) people in society. Problems such as those relating to interpersonal and family relations, stress management, lifestyle management and development, and vocational and personal adjustments are common to "normal" people. Counselors help people with the various manifestations of these problems, and professional concern about these problems is reflected in the professional activities of counselors and professional organizations.

The counseling profession's efforts to meet the needs of society are also reflected in the many new settings and situations in which counselors are now working. For example, the last decade has seen a tremendous growth in the number of counselors working in business and industry settings, residential facilities for older persons, abused-person shelters, medical facilities, and various other places where, historically, counselors have not worked. Perhaps most importantly, because of the counseling profession's responsiveness to the needs of society, the expansion of the number of settings and situations in which counselors work continues to increase.

Lesson 6: The counseling profession sometimes seems to act in opposition to trends in society

Concerns about the rights and responsibilities of and respect for individuals have a long history in the American society. However, in the so-called modern era, these concerns were most evident in society during the 1960s and early 1970s. In general, those were times in which attention was given to "individuality" as the essence of the human condition. Relatedly, they were times when empiricism, as applied to human characteristics, traits, and behaviors, was decried in society at large. However, during the same times, a resurgence of interest was in empiricism in the counseling profession. This phenomenon was reflected in the formation of AMEG (AMECD) in the mid-1960s. Another fact to be considered is that AMEG (AMECD) had its largest membership during the late 1960s and early 1970s, but as society's emphasis on "individuality" ebbed, so did the AMEG (AMECD) membership.

The above situation was not the paradox it seemed to be; rather, it was an example of a professional response to current conditions in society. As society clamored about "individuality," counseling professionals sought to understand better both "individuals" and "individuals within society." The counseling profession sought to gain this understanding through application of proven scientific methods. Such methods incorporate, and indeed emphasize, empiricism. Therefore, although the counseling profession appeared to be antithetical to the trend in society, it was in fact attempting to be effectively responsive to that trend. Those activities in turn lead to development of many "empirical" methods and resources from understanding individuals. As those methods and resources became available and common, ostensible interest in empiricism among counseling professionals waned.

Lesson 7: The counseling profession has a flirtatious relationship with empiricism

At various times throughout its history, the counseling profession has been wavering between being enamored with empiricism (vis-á-vis rigorous diagnosis, assessment, and research) and being disenchanted with empiricism (vis-a-vis almost totally unstructured approaches to counseling). The history of AHEAD (formerly TCPA and SPATE) is a classic example of this phenomenon. Originally conceived as an organization dedicated to research and evaluation, it evolved into an organization for counselors primarily interested in humanistic perspectives. Humanism and empiricism are certainly not totally separate, but just as certainly empiricism is not a major focus within humanistic perspectives.

Other evidence of the fluctuating relationship between the counseling profession and empiricism can be found through a review of the contents of professional counseling journals. For example, the contents of AACD's *Journal of Counseling and Development* (formerly the *Personnel and Guidance Journal)* show that the journal, at times, was almost completely devoted to research but at other times was almost totally devoid of research.

In more recent times, the counseling profession has sought a "balanced" relationship with empiricism. On one hand, the counseling profession has acknowledged the need for and benefits of empiricism, an acknowledgement reflected, for example, in training and ethical standards adopted within the profession. On the other hand, the counseling profession has not mandated that empirical perspectives be adopted within the profession and indeed has gone to some lengths to insure that it is not considered mandatory (also as reflected in the training and ethical standards). In general, the counseling profession seems to have taken the position that empiricism is important, but only for those counselors who deem it important.

THE COUNSELING PROFESSION TODAY

A rapidly growing understanding of, and demand for, positive mental health is evident in the American society in a number of ways. For example, "self-help" mental-health books are setting sales records, businesses and industries are allocating substantial fiscal and physical resources to employee well-being, communities are acting to alleviate various types of physical and mental abuse, prominent campaigns have been launched against drug and alcohol abuse, and "wellness" activities are being sought by millions of people. Collectively, these and other activities similar to them signify society's realization that positive mental health is desirable, and more importantly, achievable.

Counseling and Mental Health

Society's concern with mental health is reflected in the counseling profession; reciprocal impacts exist between the mental-health movement in society and the counseling profession. For example, the movement has fostered the realization that in order for positive mental health to be achieved, it must be present both within and across people's lives. People have come to understand that positive mental health cannot be attained in one aspect of their lives without being achieved in other aspects of their lives as well, and also that positive mental health should be achieved at all age levels. This realization has in turn created demand for counseling services that relate to many different facets of people's lives. The direct effect on the counseling profession has been a greatly increased need for professional counseling services, and relatedly for professional counselors.

The counseling profession has impacted the positive mental-health movement in society by literally providing more services than are sought. A fact is that many counseling services are provided to help people with existing problems, the typical view of the purpose of counseling. The counseling profession, however, takes a much broader perview of the situation and seeks to foster and promote positive mental health in a number of other important ways. For example, professional counselors engage in many developmental and/or preventive activities intended to help people to be able to cope with certain types of problems before they occur. Additionally, professional counselors frequently provide consultation services to help people helping other people with problems and concerns. And finally, the counseling profession has extended its service provision settings to many places where people would not typically expect to find them (e.g. health care centers, government agencies, religious institutions).

These mutual impacts have resulted in the counseling profession having a rapidly growing recognition and appreciation in society. Most counselors readily acknowledge, however, that the counseling profession has not yet achieved a complete or fully recognized place in society. The counseling profession is therefore acting within itself to enhance its identity within society. These activities include trends such as development of new counseling theoretical bases and techniques, increased use of technology, promotion of professional standards, improvement of training methods, expansion of political involvements, extension of service areas, promotion of public awareness of the counseling profession, and increased attention to accountability.

Counseling and Theories

The counseling profession has long been grounded in a relatively few basic counseling theories (e.g., client-centered, existential, behavioral, rational emotive, gestalt) and has worked diligently to establish effective techniques based on those theories. However, the counseling profession also has been receptive to new theoretical perspectives (e.g., cognitive-behavioral and social learning theory) that have evolved from the fields of psychology, sociology, education, and other related disciplines. True to the history of the profession, it is also working hard, through research, professional discourse, and experimentation, to develop effective new techniques based on these newer theories. As a result, professional counselors have before them ever expanding sets of theoretical perspectives and techniques upon which to base their counseling activities. These trends have added to the identity of the counseling profession by allowing counselors to provide more and better services to an increasing number of people.

Counseling and Computers

The counseling profession also has begun to capitalize on modern technological advancements. This trend is perhaps most evident in the area of vocational counseling where a number of relatively sophisticated computer systems are regularly used to enhance vocational development and counseling activities. Integration of technology is also evident in other parts of the counseling profession. For example, more and more counselors are using computers for data and information management in their "normal" counseling activities. However, the use of computers to assist counseling processes and activities is by no means universally accepted or practiced. Ekstrom and Johnson (1984) aptly summarized the current situation:

> Computers are a topic that counselors can no longer ignore. Computers are now being utilized to provide course and client scheduling; to improve counseling office management; to create, administer, score, and interpret tests; to provide information about careers and colleges; to assist individuals in making educational and occupational choices; to provide instruction and remediation; to provide personal and mental health counseling; as tools for research; and as aids in writing reports or papers. All of the indications point to computers being even more widely used in counseling in the future. (p. 132)

The use of computers and other so-called modern technology contributes to the identity of the counseling profession primarily by expediting the work of counselors, and therefore allowing them to provide better services to more people.

Counseling and Ethical Standards

Two major types of professional standards are currently being emphasized within the counseling profession. One is ethical standards: standards of behavior voluntarily adopted by the members of a profession to insure the welfare of service recipients. The primary ethical standards for professional counselors are those developed and maintained by AACD. AACD's Ethical Standards were developed by the membership over a period of approximately thirty years and are periodically updated to reflect new needs and circumstances. Adherence to ethical standards is voluntary because they have no basis in law. The vast majority of professional counselors diligently strive to adhere to them because such behavior enhances society's view of the counseling profession as one which cares deeply about the welfare of its service recipients. However, if a counselor engages in unethical behavior, the counselor's behavior may be subjected to peer review. For example, if an AACD member is alledged to have engaged in unethical behavior, AACD's Ethical Standards Review Committee will investigate and review the situation. Professional sanctions, such as loss of AACD membership, may be imposed on AACD members found guilty of unethical behavior.

Counseling and Counselor Preparation

The other set of standards currently receiving considerable emphasis within the counseling profession is that related to preparation practices. These "Standards of Preparation" will be discussed at greater length in Chapter 3. The important points as they apply to this discussion are that counselor training standards exist and that they are widely implemented within the counseling profession. Approximately 450 counselor preparation programs exist in the United States and its territorial possessions (Hollis & Wantz, 1986). Standards of preparation are necessary to insure that counselor trainees receive appropriate and effective training regardless of the preparation program in which they participate. The implementation of standards of preparation is also particularly important in a "mobile" society where both counselors and clients frequently relocate; standardized counselor preparation helps to insure effective counseling services regardless of location. Such standardization also helps to enhance society's perception of the counseling profession as one which carefully monitors its own activities.

In addition to the implementation of standards of preparation, the counseling profession continually seeks other ways to improve counselor training. Professional journals focusing on counselor preparation are replete with research on current training practices as well as innovative ideas for new training methods. Professional meetings for counselors also heavily emphasize new approaches to counselor preparation. Collectively, these are indicators that the counseling profession is striving, in many different ways, to improve the effectiveness of counselor preparation. This effort is being put forth because the counseling profession realizes that effective preparation has a direct result in effective services and an indirect result in enhancement of society's perceptions of the profession.

Counseling and Political Involvement

Another major thrust in the counseling profession is increased involvement in the political system. The most obvious example of this phenomenon is the widespread and increasing passage of state level counselor licensure laws. However, professional counselors are also becoming active in other political arenas. For example, state and national counselor organizations frequently employ lobbyists to promote legislation that benefits not only the counseling profession but also the people who receive counseling services. The situation is effectively summarized by Solomon (1982) who wrote that:

> Counselors and other human service providers are in a pivotal position to effectively communicate the concerns of people they serve to policy makers at local, state, and national levels of government. They are in an even better position to shape legislative initiatives, bills, and laws to more appropriately address counseling issues that directly impact the counseling profession as well as the people they serve. Most of the political successes that affect the counseling profession will depend largely on counselors themselves. (p. 580)

Political awareness and sophistication are rapidly increasing within the counseling profession, with one result being an enhanced public perception of the profession.

Counseling and Public Relations

Counselors are also working hard to facilitate public awareness of the counseling profession and its benefits to people in society. Historically, counselors and other mental health professionals were relatively "low key" in public relations activities. Now however, counseling professionals have realized that effective public relations is an important part of the establishment of a favorable identity. Counselors are therefore systematically undertaking public relations activities (e.g. public service announcements and media promotions) to increase society's awareness of the services and benefits provided by counselors.

Counseling and Accountability

Awareness of the need to be accountable is increasing in the counseling profession. Professional counselors realize that the benefits of their activities are not "self-evident" to persons outside the profession. Counseling is, for most people, a very private matter. Even those who benefit greatly from counseling services are not likely to share their experiences with others because of the (perceived) stigma of having had a need for counseling. Thus, few people outside the counseling profession are "singing the praises" for counselors. Professional counselors are aware that their responsibility is to prove that what they do is helpful, effective, and desirable, therefore they have intensified their efforts to be accountable. A major thrust is being made to show that counseling results in *behavior* change among counseling service recipients. Clearly this thrust is consistent with the practitioner-scientist perspective presented earlier. More generally, however, it reflects the fact that demonstrating an ability to produce positive behavior change provides the strongest basis for the positive identity of the counseling profession within society.

In summary, public awareness of the counseling profession is rapidly improving. Collectively, professional counselors provide an amazingly large array of services in an equally amazingly large number of settings and situations. Perhaps most importantly, this situation shows every sign of continuing because professional counselors are working hard to improve, extend, and increase the services they provide and the audiences they serve.

Chapter 3

PROFESSIONAL PREPARATION OF COUNSELORS

The preceding chapters have illustrated that neither singular nor simple answers exist to the questions "What is a professional counselor?" and "What does a professional counselor do?" Also, neither a singular nor a simple answer exists to the question "How should professional counselors be prepared?" Indeed, the question, "What should be done to produce a good counselor?" has been a source of continuous debate since the inception of the counseling profession. Given the current complexities of the counseling profession, a response to this question must necessarily be multifaceted. Further, underlying issues must be addressed before the responses can be understood.

ISSUES IN COUNSELOR PREPARATION

Historical perspective, research, and common sense reveal that professional counselors are differentially effective in their counseling activities, or more simply stated, some counselors are better than others.

Yet while the effect is readily acknowledged, the causes of the differentiation remain issues of concern in the counseling profession. Some of the major issues involved can be best stated and addressed as questions.

1. Are professional counselors born or made?

The vast majority of professional counselors like to conceive of themselves as warm, caring, concerned, hopeful, and loving people whose primary goal in life is "to help other people." Relatedly, research generally shows that the greater the extent to which counselors possess these characteristics and others, such as those discussed in Chapter 1, the more effective they are in their professional counseling activities. Accordingly, considerable concern exists in the counseling profession about the "personal characteristics" of potential professional counselors. At issue is whether potential counselors must have certain types of personal characteristics before beginning counselor preparation or whether appropriate characteristics can and must be developed in potential counselors during their counselor-preparation programs.

A substantial portion of the professional counseling literature has focused on the determination and/or specification of counselor characteristics associated positively with counseling effectiveness. This effort was based on the potentially significant implication of whether such associations can be definitively established. If particular personal characteristics can be shown as being definitively and positively associated with counseling effectiveness, then those characteristics could be used as selection criteria for persons to enter counselor preparation programs. Applicants possessing the given set of characteristics to the greatest extent would be admitted while those possessing the characteristics to a lesser extent would be denied admission, and therefore presumably denied access to the counseling profession.

The search for characteristics associated positively with counseling effectiveness has covered an amazingly large and diverse array of personal attributes and a multitude of apsects of counseling effectiveness, and has involved use of an equally diverse set of measurement and evaluation instruments and techniques. However, even though substantial effort has been invested, clear and definitive results have not been found. For example, Rowe, Murphy, and DeCsipkes (1975) conducted a comprehensive analysis of the 1960 to 1974 professional literature on the relationships between counselor characteristics and counselor effectiveness, and concluded that further search for such relationships should be discontinued because the results of previous studies were "generally disappointing, often contradictory, and only tentative" (p. 241). Conversely, however, Wiggins and Weslander (1986) concluded that:

> This study demonstrated some definite differences between groups of [school] counselors rated as effective or ineffective. Ineffective counselors are rated low by the supervisors, are dissatisfied with their jobs, have low self-esteem, have a low level of tolerance for ambiguity, and are not correlated significantly with the Holland environmental code for counselors. Effective counselors are rated high by the supervisors, are happy with their jobs, have high self-esteem, have a high level for tolerance for ambiguity, and have congruent Holland codes. (pp. 34-35)

Thus, the best statement that can be made is that some professionals believe that definitive, positive associations have been established between personal characteristics and counselor effectiveness while others believe associations have not been determined. Relatedly, while many counselor preparation programs use evaluations of applicants' personal characteristics for selection purposes, many others do not. The search continues.

The alternative side of this issue holds that appropriate personal characteristics are developed within the context of counselor preparation programs. Again, however, conflicting evidence exists about whether desirable changes actually take place. For example, Zahner and McDavis (1980) concluded that "The results [of their study]...indicate that training for both the professional and paraprofessional groups [of counselors] has minimal influence on moral development of its current or past students" (p. 248). Conversely, Schwab and Harris (1981) concluded that "The results [of their study] suggest...that counselor trainees do change and grow toward being more self-actualizing from the time they enter to the time they graduate from their counselor training program" (p. 222). The fact is generally accepted that counselor preparation programs do change the personal characteristics of the people who participate in them. However, the exact nature and extent of these changes have not yet been fully determined.

The debate about whether good counselors are "born or made" has been deemphasized in counselor preparation practice today because most programs attend to both sides of the issue. Most counselor preparation programs give attention to "personal characteristics" of applicants although the nature and extent of the attention given varies. Procedures employed range from the use of specific, multifaceted evaluations (e.g., "personality" inventories and personal interviews) to the use of global indicators of applicants' personal characteristics (e.g., reference letters and applicant goal statements). Most counselor preparation programs also incorporate activities that are intended to enhance participants' personal characteristics. Again, these procedures vary from very specific (e.g., "sensitivity" group activities to improve self-disclosure abilities) to general activities (e.g., lectures on professional commitment). Thus, a major theoretical issue has been deemphasized through actual practices.

2. What selection criteria are important?

Counselor preparation programs are similar to other professional preparation programs in that they are primarily graduate-level (i.e., post baccalaureate) curricula. However, a distinguishing feature of counselor preparation programs is the lack of a commonly associated undergraduate-level (i.e., baccalaureate) curriculum. For example, persons aspiring to be physicians typically must first complete a "pre-med" undergraduate curriculum and persons aspiring to be lawyers must complete a "pre-law" undergraduate curriculum. Similarly, persons aspiring to be counseling or clinical psychologist typically must first complete a "psychology" undergraduate curriculum. By comparison, no "standard" undergraduate curriculum typically must be completed before persons can enter counselor preparation programs. Institutions with undergraduate-level counselor preparation curricula do exist, but they are extremely rare. Therefore, the undergraduate programs completed by applicants to counselor preparation programs are diverse. In fact, students in counselor preparation programs represent extremely varied previous academic preparations, including those in the areas of the "social" and "hard" sciences, liberal arts, fine arts, and business. This situation has had, and continues to have, significant implications for the selection of students for counselor preparation programs.

During the early years of the counseling profession, as described in Chapter 2, most professional counselors worked in educational institutions, primarily as secondary-school counselors. Persons seeking entry to counselor preparation programs usually held baccalaureate degrees in education and were working as teachers. In addition, many counseling professionals then viewed previous training and experience in "teaching" as "necessary" for becoming an effective school counselor and, relatedly, most state departments of education required prior teaching experience for certification as a school counselor.

As the counseling profession has evolved and become diversified, the relevance and importance of prior training and experience in teaching has been deemphasized for several reasons. First, the proportion of professional counselors who work in schools has decreased significantly and, therefore, the potential relevance of prior teaching experience has decreased proportionately. Second, a considerable number of states now certify persons to work as school counselors who have not had teaching experience but who complete school-counselor preparation programs. Finally, research has not shown that school counselors with previous training and experience in teaching are more effective than school counselors without teaching experience; no empirical basis exists for suggesting that teaching experience is particularly beneficial to being an effective counselor. Even in light of these considerations, however, a substantial portion of professional counselors have completed baccalaureate curricula in education. One reason is that school counselors still constitute a significant portion of professional counselors in general, and many of them have had prior training and experience in teaching. Another is that most counselor preparation programs are housed in schools or colleges of education within institutions of higher education, and so undergraduate education majors typically have a greater probability than other undergraduate students of becoming familiar with counselor preparation programs.

When school counseling and the associated prerequisites were preeminent in the counseling profession, counselor educators (or trainers) could hold reasonable, relatively common assumptions about the previous academic and experiential backgrounds of students in counselor preparation programs. More importantly, they could build upon those assumptions in the construction of counselor preparation curricula. Today, however, to make generalized assumptions about students' prior training and experiences are not possible, and counselor preparation programs must be constructed to accommodate students with widely varying backgrounds.

Academic performance and aptitude are perhaps the most widely used selection criteria for entry into counselor preparation programs. Undergraduate grade point average is the most commonly used indicator of applicants' academic performance. The most commonly used indicator of applicants' academic aptitude is their score(s) on graduate-level academic aptitude tests. For example, in reference to counselor preparation programs Hollis and Wantz (1986, p. 55) indicated that "the most frequently used standardized test as a selection instrument is the

Graduate Record Examination (GRE)." The Miller Analogy Test (MAT) is another frequently used instrument. Because counselor preparation programs are graduate-level curricula, students in them must have sufficient academic skills and aptitude to satisfactorily complete the academic requirements. However, research generally shows that these indicators are neither substantially related to nor particularly good predictors of counseling effectiveness. Therefore, academic performance and aptitude indicators continue to be used because they help to identify students who will successfully complete counselor preparation academic requirements and not because they are good predictors of counseling effectiveness.

Counselor preparation programs generally require applicants to have letters of reference submitted with their applications for evaluating an individual's "character," "potential for academic success," "potential for success as a counselor," or any combination of these factors. Hollis and Wantz (1986) indicated that 2.8 letters of reference is the average requirement used by counselor preparation programs. Unfortunately, research shows that evaluations provided in reference letters usually add little if any discriminative power in the prediction of either academic success or counseling effectiveness. Thus, while the practice is common, the actual benefits of requiring applicant reference letters are few.

Some counselor preparation programs require applicants to submit a "goal(s) statement" that includes a brief explanation of what the applicant intends to do upon graduation from the program. Goal statements are used in evaluating the extent to which applicants have made decisions about their vocational aspirations. Generally, the more focused the applicant's goal statement, the more favorable is its evaluation because it is typically easier to define appropriate preparation activities for specific goals (i.e., specific work settings and/or counseling activities). Unfortunately, the nature of the counseling profession and counselor preparation programs detract from the usefulness of goal statements. Many people are unaware of the many different aspects of the counseling profession until after they have been admitted to counselor preparation programs (in part because of the lack of undergraduate programs). Thus, applicants' goal statements typically reflect a restricted knowledge base, which in turn restricts the goals they espouse.

Beyond these commonly used selection criteria (i.e., academic performance, letters, and goals) as well as the frequent use of personal interviews of applicants to counselor preparation programs, there is only diversity. Indeed, additional selection criteria are almost as varied as are counselor preparation programs. That is, additional selection criteria are typically unique to particular programs. For example, some selection criteria are related to requirements for counselor certification or licensure, others are related to specific theoretical orientations held by program faculty, and still others are related to specific intended job placements for program graduates. Thus, no universal credentials exist that applicants to counselor preparation programs must possess. Even the few commonalities that are shared relate to academic success rather than counseling effectiveness. However, this situation should not be construed as bad or even negative. Rather, it is an appropriate reflection of the diverse nature of the counseling profession. Various professional counselors fulfill many different roles and functions, and appropriately people aspiring to be counselors should have equally varied credentials as they prepare to assume those roles.

3. How much academic preparation is necessary?

The delicate balance between efficiency and effectiveness is difficult to define, and even harder to achieve in many aspects of the counseling profession. For example, professional counselors always strive to provide the best possible services for their clients in the shortest possible time periods and with the least possible disruptions to and/or discomforts in clients' lives. In brief, professional counselors try to obtain for each client the best results as quickly and as easily as possible. An analogous situation exists for counselor preparation. The goal is to prepare effective professional counselors expeditiously. The issue is how?

The lack of a "standard" undergraduate preparation as it relates to selection criteria is also an important factor when considering the length or amount of counselor preparation. Because students enter counselor preparation programs with widely varying backgrounds, these programs must build upon an uneven foundation; therefore, establishing a "starting point" for counselor preparation is difficult. If the starting point includes excessive pre-program requirements, many persons who otherwise might have entered counselor preparation programs will not do so because of the perceived "extra" work necessary just to start the programs. Conversely, persons who have had relatively extensive prior preparations may find the initial counselor preparation work to be mundane or redundant, and thus demotivating. Typically, counselor preparation programs respond to this situation by incorporating a few "preprogram" requirements. These are usually a few courses, such as those covering personality theories, human growth and development, abnormal psychology, learning theories, or basic statistics, that most applicants to the program have already completed. Students who have completed the pre-program requirements begin the "basic" counselor preparation program curriculum upon admission. Students who have not completed the pre-program requirements are usually required to take them soon after admission and before they begin the "basic" counselor preparation program curriculum. Thus, counselor preparation programs attempt to "level the foundation" by creating a "happy medium" among the diverse backgrounds of program applicants.

The length of time and amount of credit hours needed for counselor preparation are also confounded by external forces pertinent to professional practice. To illustrate, state-level requirements for certification as a school counselor are typically less than counselor preparation program requirements. Because school-counselor certification requirements in most states are based on the assumption that school counselors will have had prior teaching experience, requirements for school-counselor certification in these states are listings of relatively specific courses as opposed to a requirement for completion of a fully integrated counselor preparation program. Conversely, in many of the states that have counselor licensure laws, requirements for being licensed as a counselor are greater than most counselor preparation program requirements. State legislatures have taken conservative approaches to "protecting the public welfare" in constructing their counselor licensure laws by including relatively extensive requirements. In addition to forces at the state level, national counselor certifying agencies have an influence on counselor preparation programs. These agencies typically have eligibility requirements approximating those of state licensure laws, and therefore tend to exceed those of the majority of counselor preparation programs. To summarize, some external forces act to influence increases in the length of time and amount of coursework for counselor preparation while others, in effect, act to influence decreases or, at least, maintenance of the status quo.

A third aspect of this issue relates to the academic bases for specifying the time length and/or coursework for counselor preparation. Typically, guidelines for counselor preparation have specified that programs should be a specified minimum number of academic credits. Although this approach allows for relatively easy *quantitative* comparisons of minimum requirements across counselor preparation programs, it is fraught with pragmatic difficulties. For example, although "quarter-hour" credits can be converted to "semester-hour" credits relatively easily, and vice versa, numeric conversions do not necessarily reflect content equivalence, even across courses having similar titles. Further, wide variations occur in minimum credit-hour requirements for similarly titled degrees across institutions within states and across states. For two counselor preparation programs to have essentially similar *content* (or course) requirements and to award similarly titled degrees, and yet have substantially different minimum credit-hour requirements is possible, and in fact quite common. This situation becomes even more confounded when variations in individual instructional styles and emphases are considered. That is, even when relatively specific guidelines have been presented for elements of counselor preparation programs, individual instructors have considerable freedom in interpretation and implementation of those guidelines and elements.

Partly in response to the difficulties in attempting to equate minimum credit hour requirements and partly for theoretical reasons, some counselor preparation guidelines specify enrollment in programs for a minimum period as well as a minimum of credit hours. The former requirement is based on the idea that the development of effective counseling skills entails more than the rote accumulation of knowledge. The belief is that effective counselors synthesize and apply knowledge learned in "typical" (i.e., didactic) courses, and that it then takes time and practice for counselor trainees to develop applied skills. Thus, the requirement of a minimum time period for enrollment is viewed as a way of "insuring" that counselor trainees have had sufficient time to synthesize and integrate knowledge before they attempt to apply it in the actual practice of professional counseling.

Current guidelines for counselor preparation programs attempt to be simultaneously responsive to a wide variety of factors. Accordingly, they reflect a series of compromises between what is theoretically desirable and what is practical, and between what is desirable and what is possible. Fortunately, the guidelines generally have been effective in achieving the delicate balances among these extremes, primarily through increasing the length of counselor preparation programs in general and the supervised field-experience components of those programs in particular (Hollis & Wantz, 1986).

4. What should be emphasized?

Two major issues are raised by this question. What content and skill areas should be emphasized and what method of instruction should be emphasized in counselor preparation programs?

Counselor Education and Supervision is a professional journal devoted in part to the presentation of ideas, research, and practices in counselor preparation. Perusal of issues of this journal, for even a relatively small time span such as a year, reveals extremely large and diverse sets of knowledge and skills with which counselors are supposed to be familiar and adept. The idea can be gained from this journal as well as from many others that professional counselors are supposed to know about everything, be able to do anything, and be able to work effectively with many, many different types of people. Quite obviously this is not possible, and more importantly, it is probably not desirable. Counselors, like most other professionals today, tend to "specialize," either in terms of clients to whom services are rendered or in terms of types of skills and activities used. Nonetheless, a commonly held assumption in the counseling profession is that a body of knowledge and a set of skills should be possessed by all counselors (at least at minimal levels) regardless of professional specialization. The counseling profession holds that a "generic" base of knowledge and skills must be learned and achieved by all professional counselors.

Considerable debate has always existed over the nature of the generic knowledge and skill base for professional counseling. The recommendations for the various knowledge and skill areas to be included in this generic base are far too numerous to be elaborated here; suffice here to state that knowledge of almost all aspects of human functioning and almost all counseling skills have at one time or another been proffered as being "essential" for all professional counselors. As a result, over the last several decades, counselor trainers and professional counselors have been engaged in an effort to achieve a degree of consensus about the nature of generic preparation for professional counselors. Although some of the results of this effort were alluded to in Chapter 1, they also will be discussed further in a later section of this chapter.

Somewhat less consensus exists about relative emphases given to different methods of instruction in counselor preparation programs. Debated is the amount of instruction which should be didactic compared with how much should be experiential. Didactic instruction involves the presentation of knowledge by an instructor through lectures and material resources to typically large groups of counselor trainees; i.e., typical classroom instruction. Experiential instruction, however, means that counselor trainees "learn by doing," typically under close supervision. Clearly agreement that some of each of these types of instruction should be incorporated into counselor preparation programs exists, because some knowledge areas are covered most effectively through didactic instruction and some skills are taught most effectively through supervised experiential instruction. However, the most appropriate method is not readily apparent in many areas. For example, generally an agreement is that all counselor trainees need to have good understandings of professional ethics. Didactic instruction is usually a good way for counselor trainees to learn the *contents* of various professional codes of ethics. However, the *applications* of professional ethics involve complex sets of intricate decisions and value judgements, and didactic instruction is probably less effective in this regard. Experiential instruction techniques, such as supervised "role-playing," are usually better for teaching counselor trainees how to *apply* professional ethics. But, the question remains, how much time should be devoted to each type of instruction? For the most part, the answer to this question has been left to the discretion of the counselor trainers in particular counselor preparation programs.

5. How should counselor preparation be evaluated?

The evaluation of counselor preparation program effectiveness has undoubtedly received the least attention of any of the major aspects of the counseling profession. While a considerable number of research investigations of the effectiveness of specific aspects of counselor training has been made, reports of total program effectiveness evaluations are almost nonexistent in the professional counseling literature. Ironically, this unfortunate state of affairs is in direct contradiction to increasing emphases on "personal" (i.e., individual) accountability for professional counselors. The professional counseling literature is replete with statements that professional counselors must be "accountable" for their professional and personal activities (see Chapter 8), but apparently counselor preparation programs are not holding themselves to similar standards.

In fairness, an acknowledgement should be made that significant obstacles to overcome in conducting evaluations of counselor preparation programs exist, not the least of which is determining appropriate criteria for effectiveness. Further, counseling professionals typically receive little or no formal preparation in program evaluation strategies or techniques (Wheeler & Loesch, 1981). Moreover, the counseling profession is not unique in these regards; few disciplines in the "social sciences" in general, or the "helping professions" in particular, have devoted time and effort to preparation program evaluation activities.

However, difficulties, lack of expertises, and common practice not withstanding, the fact remains that little evidence shows that counselor preparation programs achieve what they are supposed, or were set out, to do.

Professional counselors are frequently admonished to engage in individual accountability activities, and thereby have control over criteria for effectiveness, so as to avoid having criteria "imposed" upon them. This appears to be sage advice. However, the counseling profession apparently has not listened to its own advice, and with predictable results. "External forces" are having a significant influence on what constitutes effective counselor preparation. The most common "forces" in this regard are state and national counselor certification and licensure agencies. Professional counselor certification or licensure "eligibility" requirements literally define counselor preparation program effectiveness, at least for professional counselors seeking those credentials. A note should be made that professional counselors have had significant input into certification and licensure requirements, and therefore have had some say in what constitutes counselor preparation program effectiveness. However, also acknowledged should be that other persons (e.g., legislators and lay persons) have had significant roles in establishing certification and licensure eligibility criteria. As a result, the counseling profession has relinquished at least part of the control over definition and/or determination of counselor preparation program effectiveness.

A "hopeful" side to this situation remains. Concern about the nature of counselor preparation has been increasing during the last three decades, and in the early 1980s substantial investments of thought, time, effort, and resources came to fruition in the establishment of commonly accepted "standards of preparation" for professional counselors. The establishment and application of counselor preparation program standards of course is not synonomous with counselor preparation program evaluation. However, the standards of preparation serve to reflect the counseling profession's definition of what constitutes effective minimum counselor preparation. Thus, the movement toward application of the standards of preparation is a significant and necessary step toward evaluation of those programs.

STANDARDS OF PREPARATION

The preceding chapter described how the counseling profession evolved from a few individuals' rather inauspicious concerns about the vocational developments of adolescents into a comprehensive and complex profession that attempts to address the multitude of mental health services needs of literally all people in society. Current philosophies, practices, and trends in the preparation of professional counselors have evolved along an analogous course. In the early, formative years of the counseling profession, relatively little disagreement about the professional preparation of counselors existed, primarily because little differentiation among counselors was present and the vast majority of professional counselors worked in schools and had been teachers. They had common backgrounds and common vocational goals, and preparation was "simply" facilitation of transition from one role to another role in the school. However, as more and more distinct facets, roles, and functions emerged within the counseling profession, agreement about the nature of professional counselor preparation dissipated. In fact, considerable disagreement arose about the preferred nature of counselor preparation during the 1940s and 1950s. This situation prompted some members of the counseling profession to examine both what was happening and what should be happening in counselor preparation. Thus began the push for "standardized" professional preparation for counselors.

Historical Development

Similar to attempting to describe the evolution of the counseling profession in its entirety, to cover all the activities relevant to the evolution of current practices in counselor preparation is not possible. Therefore, the tactic of describing the evolution of one professional entity specifically concerned with counselor preparation will be used. That entity is the Council for the Accreditation of Counseling and Related Educational Programs (CACREP).

CACREP lineage can be traced to the the National Association of Guidance Supervisors (NAGS). One of the reasons for the founding of NAGS was to bring together individuals (i.e., supervisors and school guidance personnel) who had common concerns. Among those concerns was how to effectively supervise and administrate counselors whose roles and functions were changing and expanding and, concomitantly, whose preparations were becoming more diverse. This latter aspect prompted counselor trainers to become interested in and involved with the concern and, in part, led to the formation of the National Association of Counselor Supervisors and Counselor Trainers (NAGSCT) in 1952.

Throughout the nine-year life span of NAGSCT, concern about counselor preparation and the attention given to it were increasing. Relatedly, counselor trainers (educators) were becoming increasingly involved in the activities of the association, and eventually dominated its perspectives. This shift is partially reflected in the change of the name from NAGSCT to the Association for Counselor Education and Supervision (ACES), wherein counselor education/training and supervision are transposed.

The desirability of "standardizing" counselor preparation rose to prominence within ACES in the late 1950s and early 1960s, although the prominence was in fact fostered by a relatively small proportion of the ACES's membership. However, the ACES's membership was generally receptive to the idea of developing "standards of preparation," and in 1963 that division endorsed an initial set of standards of preparation that would, theoretically, apply to all (graduate-level) programs preparing professional counselors. Perhaps more importantly, it also committed to continue to develop the initial (ACES's) standards of preparation. An interesting note, however, is that while ACES *endorsed* the standards of preparation and their further development, ACES did not endorse a *requirement* that counselor preparation programs adopt and/or abide by those standards.

As attention to standards of preparation continued to increase within ACES, other professional associations also became interested in the issues involved and initiated their own activities. For example, the American School Counselor Association (ASCA) adopted a set of specific guidelines for preparation of secondary school counselors in 1967, and another specific set for elementary school counselors the next year. Similarly, the American College Personnel Association (ACPA) in 1968 adopted specific preparation guidelines for student personnel workers. Other associations did not formally adopt guidelines but instead increased their involvement through input and feedback to the members of ACES who were most involved in the development of the ACES's standards of preparation.

In response to the then relatively widespread interest in standards of preparation, the ACES's "Commission on Standards and Accreditation" was created in 1971. The significance of this event was two-fold. First, it was a reaffirmation of ACES's commitment to the development of standards of preparation. Second, and perhaps more important, it was the first formal acknowledgement of ACES's intent to establish procedures for accrediting counselor preparation programs. Thus, it signified ACES's commitment to implementing a plan wherein counselor preparation programs would be required to use and abide by the standards of preparation.

ACES's efforts relative to development of the standards resulted in the adoption of *Standards for Preparation of Counselors and Other Personnel Services Specialists* in 1973. This first set of standards delineated preparation guidelines for what is referred to as "entry-level" preparation; the minimum preparation necessary to assume a beginning position as a professional counselor. Typically, such preparation is incorporated into a master's degree program. Subsequently, in 1977 ACES adopted the *Guidelines for Doctoral Preparation in Counselor Education* to be applied to doctoral-level counselor preparation programs. Both of these sets of standards were revised and, in 1979, adopted by ACES as the *Standards for Entry Preparation (Master's and Specialists) of Counselors and Other Personnel-Services Specialists* and the *Standards for Advanced Preparation (Doctoral) in Counselor Education,* respectively. Concurrent with the adoption of the 1979 revised standards, ACES began to accredit counselor preparation programs according to those standards. ACES worked closely with the California Association for Counselor Education and Supervision (CACES) because CACES had already accredited a few programs in California using their own standards, which were very close to the ACES's standards.

The initiatives shown by ACES in the development of standards of preparation and the implementation of preparation program accreditation activities were generally acclaimed in the counseling profession, but they also severely taxed the resources of ACES. Thus, in 1980 the AACD Board of Directors voted to adopt both sets of ACES's standards, to support further work on the standards, and to establish and support an entity to conduct broad-scale activities relative to counselor program accreditation. This latter commitment led directly to the formation of the Council for the Accreditation of Counseling and Related Educational Programs (CACREP).

CACREP held its first official meeting in September of 1981, at which time it offically adopted the ACES/AACD entry-level and advanced-level standards of preparation, recognized and accepted the accreditations awarded by ACES (and therefore by CACES), and established ideological and procedural guidelines for its own accreditation process.

CACREP is currently an "organizational affiliate" of AACD. This means that it is a legally distinct (i.e., technically separate from AACD), not-for-profit organization which focuses solely on activities necessary for the accreditation of counselor preparation programs. However, while CACREP is legally distinct from AACD and is not directly involved in AACD's functioning, it does have non-technical linkages to AACD. For one reason, CACREP like most other accrediting agencies is not financially self-supporting and receives some financial support from AACD for its operations. For another, CACREP's membership is aligned with the AACD divisional structure; members of the "Council" are put there by AACD and AACD divisions. For example, in 1987, the Council included representatives from ACES, the Association for Measurement and Evaluation in Counseling and Development (AMECD), the American Mental Health Counselors Association (AMHCA), the American College Personnel Association (ACPA), the National Career Development Association (NCDA), the Association for Multicultural Counseling and Development (AMCD), the American Rehabilitation Counselors Association (ARCA), the Association for Specialists in Group Work (ASGW), and the Association for Humanistic Education and Development (AHEAD). Also a representative from AACD is on the Council (and therefore AACD is technically a *member* of the Council), a lay representative, and the CACREP Executive Director who serves as an *ex officio* member of the Council. Other AACD divisions are permitted to place representatives on the Council, but as of 1987, none had chosen to do so. This configuration allows CACREP to maintain close philosophical ties with the AACD. However, it also allows CACREP to function autonomously. For example, between 1981 and 1986, CACREP incorporated several relatively minor changes in the standards of preparation being applied as well as "guidelines" for several aspects of preparation without obtaining approval from AACD. Thus, today, CACREP has its own standards of preparation and accreditation processes, although they are philosophically aligned with the purposes and goals of AACD.

CACREP accreditation is program specific; it accredits individual preparation programs instead of the academic units (i.e., departments) in which the programs are housed. Because of the diversity of individual preparation program titles used in different academic units in different colleges and universities, CACREP accredits programs only under the four program titles it has adopted. The entry-level program titles used by CACREP are (1) *School Counseling,* (2) *Student Development in Higher*

Education, and (3) *Counseling in Community and Other Agency Settings.* The one advanced-level program title used by CACREP is *Counselor Education.* Within entry-level Student Development in Higher Education programs, one of three possible program emphases is identified: (1) *Counseling* (for persons intending to become counselors in colleges and universities), (2) *Administrative* (for persons intending to become administrators of college and/or university student services programs), or (3) *Developmental* (for persons intending to be providers of student services other than counseling, such as student financial aid, admissions, student residence life, or career planning and placement, for students in colleges or universities). Relatedly, commencing in 1988, a *Mental Health Counseling* emphasis may be identified within a Counseling in Community and Other Agency Settings program.

As CACREP's activities intensified and expanded as more programs sought accreditation, it received more and more suggestions from various professional groups about what ought to be covered in the respective sets of standards. The burgeoning amount of both solicited and unsolicited input about its standards of preparation prompted CACREP to adopt, in 1984, a moratorium on implementation of new standards and a plan for periodic "standards review and/or revision." CACREP therefore instituted a "five-year review cycle" for possible revision of its standards of preparation. This plan stipulates that changes in the standards can be submitted for consideration by CACREP at any time, but changes can only be adopted for use at the end of a five-year period. CACREP is, at the time of this writing, involved in a careful and extensive review of its current standards of preparation. The "new" (i.e., revised) CACREP standards resulting from this process are to be effective from July 1, 1988 until June 30, 1993. This procedure is intended to provide "stability" in the accreditation process; programs for which accreditation, or re-accreditation, is sought will have to contend with changes less frequently than in the past.

Accreditation standards, to a large extent, will determine program content. Accredited counselor preparation programs as well as other programs are considering accreditation bodies' standards to assure that their graduates have qualifications to compete in the labor market. Prior to the 1980s, faculty or programs decided what would be taught and to what extent. In the latter 1980s and 1990s, faculty members will be concerned with meeting accreditation standards as well as adding uniqueness to their respective programs to exceed the accreditation requirements.

Standards Format

The CACREP entry-level standards of preparation in effect until 1988 are subdivided into four sections: (I) Objectives, (II) Curriculum -Program of Studies and Supervised Experiences, (III) Responsibilities Concerning Students in the Program, and (IV) Support for the Counselor Education Program, Administrative Relations, and Institutional Resources. The related CACREP advanced-level standards of preparation in effect until 1988 also are subdivided into four sections: (I) Objectives, (II) Curriculum, (III) Responsibilities Concerning Students in the Program, and (IV) Support for the Counselor Education Program, Administrative Relations, and Institutional Resources. The nature and extent of specific content changes to be incorporated into the "new" CACREP standards of preparation are not known as of this writing. However, what is known is that the "new" entry-level standards will contain a reconfiguration of the standards into the following sections: (I) The Institution, (II) Program Objectives and Curriculum, (III) Clinical Instruction, (IV) Faculty and Staff, (V) Organization and Administration, and (VI) Evaluations in the Program. Also, three sets of specialization standards, identified as Appendices A, B, and C, will be built upon the other (so-called generic) entry-level standards: (A) Student Development in Higher Education Environmental and Specialty Standards, (B) School Counseling Environmental and Specialty Standards, and (C) Counseling in Community and Other Agency Settings Environmental and Specialty Standards for Specialization in Mental Health Counseling. The advanced-level standards will be contained in one section entitled, Doctoral Programs in Counselor Education. Because the reconfiguration of the subsections of the "new" CACREP standards will be adopted even though the specific standards within them have not yet been fully determined, the components of the CACREP standards of preparation will be discussed in terms of the reconfigured format.

Standards for Entry-Level Preparation

Section I. The first section of the proposed CACREP entry-level standards identifies requirements (for accreditation) for the institution and "academic unit" (i.e., department) in which the program for which accreditation is sought is housed. In general, this section specifies the needed "identity" of the program within the institution as well as the needed resources to conduct the program. The standards in this section reflect the belief that a counselor preparation program must be an "integrated program," with specifically assigned resources, rather than a "collection of courses" which students may take to obtain an academic degree. Some of the standards in this section relate to how the program is described in the institution's published materials (e.g., graduate school bulletin) and how the program is configured within the institution's organizational structure (e.g., department, school or college). A second group of standards relate to needed relationships between the program and other academic units and/or agencies with which the program is associated. Still others relate to needed financial support for the program operation and for the faculty specifically involved with the program. Standards also will be in this section that specify necessary program resources (e.g., computer and library facilities) for instructional and research activities associated with the program. Finally, a standard is included which stipulates that "counseling services" must be available to students in the program from other than program faculty. This latter standard is based on the belief that students in counselor preparation programs should have access to counseling services in ways that do not jeopardize their academic standings (as do other students in the institution).

Section II. The second section of the (proposed) standards incorporates several requirements directly related to some of the issues discussed previously. For example, one standard requires that the entry-level program extend over a minimum of two full academic years, defined as either four semesters or six quarters with a minimum of 48 semester hours or 72 quarter hours of graduate level credits required of all students. Students' participation in an activity intended to enhance their self-understanding, self-analysis skills, and interpersonal development is required in another standard. A third standard in this section stipulates that in cases where evaluations indicate that a student's participation and further continuation in the program are inappropriate, program faculty should assist the student to find a more appropriate academic or vocational placement. Finally, a standard is provided that relates to pre-program professional requirements and their integration into curricular requirements for the program. These standards are also in the current CACREP standards.

Other standards in the second section relate the necessity for having clearly defined and stated program objectives, and for distributing those objectives to students and others associated with the program. Similarly, standards exist relating to the development and distribution of instructional materials (e.g., course syllabi and reference lists) to students. Also, some standards in this section are intended to facilitate students' professional involvement beyond classroom instruction. For example, standards are included relating to students' participation in research activities with faculty and in extracurricular professional development activities such as workshops, seminars, and colloquia.

The major portion of the second section delineates the eight so-called "common core" areas of academic preparation. These are the same areas which were identified and defined in Chapter 1: Human Growth and Development; Social and Cultural Foundations; The Helping Relationship; Group Processes, Dynamics, and Counseling; Life Style and Career Development; Measurement (Appraisal of the Individual); Research and Evaluation; and Professional Orientation. The primary change in the proposed standards is that specific *knowledge* and *skill* requirements for counselor trainees are identified within each core area.

The requirement for an "environmental emphasis" within each student's counselor preparation program is also addressed in the second section. The environmental emphasis standards reflect the belief that (at least minimally prepared) counselors must be knowledgeable of the general workings of the professional settings in which they work as well as specific counseling techniques and clientele. Finally, this section contains standards relating to "specialized studies;" requirements which reflect the belief that counselors today "specialize" (i.e., focus on use of particular knowledge and skills with particular clientele) within their professional activities.

Section III. Because carefully supervised clinical practice has been, and is, at the heart of counselor preparation, the third section presents standards relating to clinical experiences and instruction for students. Some of the standards in this section relate to students' practicum and internship experiences. The practicum experience is viewed as the student's first experience with actual/real clients. Therefore, the standards call for students to have relatively limited but closely supervised counseling activities in practicum. The internship is viewed as an "advanced" clinical experience for students and is permitted only after the student has had at least one practicum experience. The standards stipulate that the student participate in the internship in a setting similar to the one in which the student intends to work. The setting for the student's internship is important because during this experience the student is supposed to perform the functions and duties of a "regular" employee of the setting. The standards also stipulate the required amount of students' contact time (in hours) with actual clients in their practica or internships.

The other standards in section three relate to the nature of clinical supervision for students in practicum or internship. The standards indicate that students in *either* practicum or internship must receive both individual and group supervision on a weekly basis. Individual supervision is a weekly meeting of at least one-hour duration between the student in practicum or internship and a program faculty member or another supervisor with equivalent professional credentials. Group supervision is a weekly meeting of at least one-and-one-half-hours duration between several (typically 5 to 7) students in practicum or internship and a program faculty member or another supervisor with equivalent credentials. In addition, a student in practicum or internship is required to have an on-site (i.e., "host") supervisor with whom the student meets according to a schedule they determine. Other related standards in this section stipulate the necessary professional credentials for supervisors and the needed interactions among supervisors and program faculty.

Section IV. Needed credentials of faculty and assignments to and within the program for which accreditation is sought are described in the fourth section of the proposed standards. For example, the standards indicate that an identified program leader or coordinator must be present, so that someone has "ultimate" responsibility for the program. They also stipulate that program faculty can only provide instruction in areas for which they have demonstrated expertise. Expertise, as used in this context, must be demonstrated through the program faculty members' recent involvement, respectively, in professional activities such as research, publication, consultation, and/or participation in professional organization activities.

Section V. The fifth section covers standards that address the operation of a program. Standards relating to required development and distribution of program informational materials and to program orientation activities for students are included. The need for clearly defined admissions policies and procedures is also addressed in some of the standards in this section. Of particular importance here are the standards relating to the specified minimum faculty-to-student ratio within the program and maximum faculty instructional loads. Finally, standards are included which relate to clear presentation and effective dissemination of students' requirements for matriculation through the program.

Section VI. The last section of the entry-level standards focuses upon various types of evaluations conducted within the program. One subset of standards in this section relates to required evaluations of students by program faculty. In general, the program faculty is charged with the responsibility for determining whether students are progressing satisfactorily in the development of their knowledge bases, skills, and professional orientation. Other standards in this section relate to required evaluations of instructional and clinical supervision activities by students and the dissemination of the results of those evaluations to program faculty. Another subset of standards in this section calls for periodic evaluation of the program by graduates of the program and dissemination of those evaluation results to all persons associated with the program. This latter subset is the only formal requirement for evaluation of the effectiveness of the program in the CACREP standards.

The standards in these six sections are applied by CACREP to all entry-level programs for which accreditation is sought; they in fact reflect the intent of "generic" preparation in entry-level programs. Concomitantly, the standards in the respective appendices reflect professional area specializations. For example, the standards in Appendix A relate to program specialization in Student Development in Higher Education. Those standards "supplement" the standards applicable to "generic" preparation so that graduates of a program in Student Personnel in Higher Education will be specifically prepared for work in student personnel areas. Similarly, the standards in Appendices B and C supplement the "generic" standards for graduates who intend to work as school counselors and counselors in community settings, respectively.

Standards for Doctoral-Level Preparation

CACREP uses the term "advanced-level" preparation to mean counselor preparation beyond entry-level preparation. Therefore, the CACREP standards for doctoral-level preparation are used *in addition to* the standards for entry-level preparation. A doctoral program in an academic unit can be accredited by CACREP even if no CACREP accredited entry-level program is included within the academic unit; however, the doctoral program must meet *both* the entry-level and advanced-level standards in order to be accredited. In general, the CACREP advanced-level standards extend the entry-level standards through greater emphases on supervised practice, research and statistics, and specific preparation in a professional specialization. The advanced-level standards also reflect the belief that preparation for "professional leadership" should be incorporated at this level. Therefore, specific standards are included that relate to activities presumed to facilitate development of professional leadership characteristics, abilities, and skills in doctoral students.

ACCREDITATION PROCEDURES

CACREP's accreditation process includes five "steps." First, the faculty, with assistance from students in some cases, conducts a "self-study" on the program for which accreditation is sought. The purpose of the self-study is to determine the ways the program meets, or does not meet, the applicable CACREP standards and to document the degree of compliance with each of the standards. This step involves substantial investment of time, effort, and resources because (1) each person associated with the program is supposed to be involved in the development of the self-study, (2) specific information is needed from each person associated with the program, and (3) collective, as opposed to individual, information and/or opinions about degree of compliance with each standard is required.

During the second step, the insitution's application materials and self-study are evaluated by a three-person review committee, composed of CACREP representative members, to determine if the program is ready for a site-team visitation. If the committee members reviewing the degree of compliance with each standard, as presented in the self-study, determine that the program (vis-a-vis the self-study) is not ready for a visitation by a site team, recommendations for needed changes and/or improvements are given and the self-study is returned to the institution. If the committee determines that the program is ready, the third step in the process (i.e., a visitation by a site team) is implemented.

CACREP site visitation team members are counseling professionals who have successfully completed training to act in accord with CACREP's accreditation procedures. The purpose of the site team visitation is to "validate" the institution's self-study; to determine if that which is contained in the self-study is accurate. Upon conclusion of the site visit, the team members compose a report of their findings based on their review of the program's self-study and their visitation to the institution.

In the fourth step, the CACREP Executive Director returns the site visitation team's report to the institution. The program faculty, in turn, review the site visitation team's report and respond to it. This response is made only in regard to the *accuracy* of the site visitation team's report, not in regard to any actions taken as a result of the site visitation team's report. This response is also delivered to the CACREP Executive Director.

In the last step, the CACREP council members review the institution's self-study, the site visitation team's report, and the institution's response to the site visitation team's report and make a decision about the accreditation status to be awarded to the program. One of three decisions may be rendered by CACREP about each program for which accreditation is sought: (1) Full Approval, (2) Provisional Approval (With Recommendations or With Commendations),or (3) Denial of Approval. Full approval extends over a period of seven years. Provisional approval extends over a period of two years and includes specific requirements about what the program must do to move from Provisional to Full approval. If the program does not fulfill the stipulated requirements within the two-year period, Denial of Approval is automatically assigned to the program. Conversely, the program may move from Provisional to Full approval in less than two years if the requirements are fulfilled earlier.

Historically, CACREP has rendered the decision "Denial of Approval" to programs on very few occasions. This should not be construed to mean, however, that CACREP approves almost all programs for which accreditation is sought or is lax in the application of its standards of preparation. Rather, it is a reflection of CACREP's "philosophy" and its operating procedures. Philosophically, CACREP is dedicated to the enhancement of the counseling profession by assisting counselor preparation programs to improve their effectiveness through adherence to and application of the (CACREP) standards of preparation. This philosophy is operationalized primarily in step two. The initial review of the program's self-study provides the institution with an opportunity to delay the application for accreditation of the program until the program "substantially" meets CACREP's standards of preparation. Thus, only those programs for which a high probability exists for at least Provisional Approval are processed through the subsequent steps in the CACREP accreditation process.

ACCREDITATION BY OTHER AGENCIES

Several agencies, other than CACREP, also accredit specific counselor preparation programs. For example, the American Psychological Association (APA) accredits doctoral-level counseling psychologist preparation programs, the National Council for Accreditation of Teacher Education (NCATE) accredits master's-degree-level school counselor preparation programs, the Council on Rehabilitation Education (CORE) accredits master's-degree-level rehabilitation counselor preparation programs, and the American Association for Marriage and Family Therapists (AAMFT) accredits master's-degree-level marriage and family counselor preparation programs. Although unique aspects to the goals and processes of each of these agencies are present, they are all philosophically similar to CACREP in that they desire to improve the counseling profession through implementation of standardized counselor preparation practices.

CONCLUSION

A strong movement exists within the counseling profession to improve counselor preparation through the application of "standards of preparation" within the context of program accreditation activities. For example, by the end of 1986, approximately 50 of the more than 450 academic units in the United States housing counselor preparation programs had CACREP approved programs. This may appear to be a relatively small proportion. However, it is substantial given that CACREP has had formal operations for only approximately five years. Moreover, applications to CACREP are increasing rapidly, indicating that the use of commonly supported and widely recognized standards of preparation is on the rise in the counseling profession. Perhaps more than any other current professional phenomenon, this movement stands to improve both professional counselors and the counseling services they provide.

Chapter 4

COUNSELING THEORY AND PRACTICE

Everyone has "problems" in their lives. However, a "problem" perceived as a major crisis by one person may be perceived as a minor annoyance by another. Consider the following examples. Joan cannot concentrate on her job during her husband's serious illness. Jack is confused about several career opportunities available to him. When the noise level of a class prevents Kim from hearing what the teacher is saying, she has difficulty learning. Jerry is having trouble adjusting to the requirements of fatherhood.

Most people are able to solve problems like the above through their own resources and activities, but others are unable to do so and seek a professional counselor's assistance. In addition to problem-oriented counseling, professional counselors help people by providing preventive and developmental counseling. Developmental and preventive counseling, which emerged in the 1950s in reaction to emphases on counseling for adjustment, focus upon exploring attitudes and values as they affect maturity. Developmental and problem-centered counseling differ in emphasis only; they do not differ in substance. Professional counselors help individuals with issues and concerns in a variety of ways, either on an individual (i.e., one-to-one) basis or in a small group. The professional counselor's assistance could be to (1) listen carefully and then offer suggestions and advice; (2) help persons understand the origins of their current concerns, thereby helping them to reconceptualize their past actions toward the goal of changing future behaviors; (3) offer support through empathic listening and attending to concerns; (4) establish and help persons implement a program of behavior modification; or (5) use a combination of approaches. Professional counselors vary widely in the ways in which they counsel clients, the kinds of client concerns with which they work, and the settings in which they conduct their work. Although, variation exists, commonalities are present in the counseling processes for all clients.

Among the general populace, counseling holds a variety of meanings because of the use of this term within different professions, e.g., "legal counselors," "real estate counselors," and "financial counselors." Moreover, even among professional counselors, definitions of counseling vary and range from those concerning the facilitation of wise choices to those promoting individuals' adjustments to society (Tyler, 1969). Approaches used by professional counselors also depend on their respective training and experience and are tempered by their personal beliefs and values, which are always involved in professional counseling, whether individual or group. Beliefs and values vary from counselor to counselor, although certain ones are universally held among counselors. For example, the worth, significance, and dignity of individuals must be recognized; individuals benefit from a particular form of the helping relationship; and personal autonomy and self-direction of individuals are valued.

Regardless of differences among counselors, both individual and group counseling require the use of identifiable communication skills and theoretical models as illustrated in Figure 4.1. Communication skills represent verbal and non-verbal techniques used by counselors to help people. Professional counselors distinguish themselves from other people and other professionals (e.g. media broadcasters) who use "communication skills" by applying a theoretical counseling model when working with clients. A counseling theory provides an integrated treatment of behavior and interpersonal relationships so decisions can be made about helping people. Accordingly, the counseling process necessarily involves use of both communication skills and counseling theory.

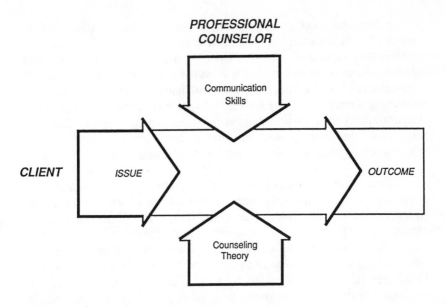

Figure 4.1. An illustrative diagram of the influence of communication skills and counseling theory upon a client's problem.

COMMUNICATION SKILLS

Several schema exist for delineation of individual (so-called "basic") communication skills that are used in counseling. For example, Carkhuff (1974) used Carl Rogers' presentations on psychotherapy and identified skills that need to be used by all counselors; Ivey (1971) reported a highly atomistic approach for training counselors in communication skills under the label "microcounseling;" and Kagan and Krathwohl (1967) and Egan (1986) developed "microskill" approaches widely used by counselors. Microcounseling and microskill are words used to describe an approach to teaching communication that simplifies the process of communication into basic skills. The process involves learning the basic skills of speech judged to be helpful and practical for more effective communication.

Each of the previous approaches, as well as others not mentioned, stresses the importance of using the communication skills such as clarification, reflection, use of "open" questions, concreteness, and summarization when counseling a client. To recognize that the use of communication skills does not in and of itself constitute professional counseling is important. These same skills are used by many indviduals in the community (usually under the aegis of being a good friend, having a good chat, or sharing with someone), but not necessarily in the systematic way they are used by professional counselors.

Two additional elements differentiate professional counseling from other forms of communication and conversation: professional training (including subsequent endorsement from the profession through certification and/or licensure) and subscription and adherence to professional standards. Thus, professional counseling is a process of communication which, in some ways, is similar to that used by many in society, but also is different because it is guided by an explicit theoretical rationale, is developed in the context of specialized training, and is conducted within the context of professional standards.

INDIVIDUAL AND GROUP COUNSELING

The use of communication skills is usually discussed within the context of training for or the practice of individual and/or group counseling. However, a very practical problem for professional counselors, particularly those working in institutional settings, is having adequate time to provide counseling services to all the people who desire them. When, for example, school counselors decide to see students for individual counseling, they make a substantial commitment of time (typically weekly or bi-weekly), and thereby decrease the time they have available for counseling services for others. The professional counselor has to decide whether such a large portion of time is appropriately spent working with individual students. An alternative is group counseling, which evolved from individual counseling as counselors realized they were limited in the amount of time available to individually reach all persons who desired help (Kemp, 1970).

Group counseling typically involves use of some of the communication skills employed in individual counseling. However, counseling more than one individual simultaneously makes some elements of the group counseling process much different from those of individual counseling.

Professional counselors doing group counseling must consider special and often additional issues that are of little or less concern when counseling a single client; e.g., selection of group members, size and composition of the group, initiation of the group, and duration of the counseling process.

Group counseling is often considered to be counseling *by* the group (i.e., rather than counseling *in* the group); forming a major difference between individual and group counseling. With group counseling, group members learn to accept responsibility for helping others within the group as well as themselves (Ohlsen, 1970). In this perspective, productive change can take place within individuals as a result of the behaviors of the individual, the group counselor, and the other group members. Trotzer (1977) referred to this composite phenomenon as constructive influence through harnessing the power of the peer group.

As with most small-group situations, powerful norms usually develop in the group. Group counselors strive to facilitate development (as opposed to imposition) of "helpful" norms within a group. One typically sought norm is "open communication" while another is "collaboration among group members" for the purpose of resolving problems. Thus, in group counseling not only are opportunities available for members of the group to be helped but also opportunities exist for members to be helpers for others, a condition rarely present in individual counseling. As members witness others giving and receiving help, they become more willing to do both themselves. This "spectator-type" counseling process increasingly enhances each group member's opportunities for feedback and assistance. Group members develop the ability to think and perform for the good of others and to ask for feedback for themselves, with the group leader reinforcing the right of and necessity for members to make their own decisions (Kemp, 1970; Trotzer, 1977).

Group and individual counseling are applied in many settings. However, practical considerations, such as time, resources, and costs, make group counseling particularly suitable for schools, businesses, and some community agency settings. Group counseling can be designed in a variety of ways to serve the needs of either homogeneous or heterogeneous groups. With the former, the group is comprised of similar individuals (e.g., adolescents, young adults, or single parents) who have a common concern (e.g., interpersonal relationship difficulties, self-development, or self-awarness). With the latter, different individuals (e.g., elderly people, adolescents, married couples, and the bereaved) with individual manifestations of their respective concerns are brought together for discussions. The counselor facilitates the development of common goals among members of a counseling group. Thus, a feeling of "safety in numbers" often develops in group members, along with the feeling that they and their concerns will be accepted by the group (Trotzer, 1977).

Because counseling groups consist of individuals with diverse backgrounds, interests, and life situations, each group becomes a social laboratory in which many beliefs, coping strategies, and practices are shared, compared, and examined. Through observation and experimentation under the leadership and facilitation of the group counselor, members of a group have the opportunity to learn and/or improve interpersonal, behavioral, and social skills that closely approximate those in society; e.g., caring, challenging, intimating, and refuting (Corey, 1981).

Group counseling is usually considered to permit the counselor to make more effective use of time by working with several people simultaneously. The rationale is that counselors are able to expand their sphere of influence beyond that which is possible in individual counseling by drawing upon the resources of group members and channeling them appropriately. Recognition must be made, however, that some situations and/or problems do not readily lend themselves to rectification through a group counseling process. In fact, individual counseling is by far the most predominant form of counseling used by professional counselors. It is often characterized by terms such as personal, face-to-face, and a relationship between two people. The major difference between group and individual counseling seems to be the number of persons (clients) being helped in a given block of time. In addition, all elements of what is thought of as counseling in groups take place within individual counseling except for interactions among members (clients). Individual counseling does have the advantage over group counseling of providing a setting which is perceived by many as "safer." Therefore, counseling may progress more quickly because the client has maximum personal contact with the professional counselor. In summary, both individual and group counseling are very important activities for professional counselors.

THEORETICAL MODELS

By virtue of professional preparation, a counselor beginning a counseling process has a theoretical model in mind no matter how vague, ill-formed, or undefined it may be. As clients' problems become clearer, so too does the theoretical model to be used by the counselor; the theoretical model provides direction for the counseling process. Although this "direction", initially, may be quite hazy, it exists in every counseling situation and ranges from a clearly articulated single model to one whereby the counselor has "forged" two or more models.

Several theoretical models describe the development of and are suitable for both individual and group counseling. Such models typically necessitate that professional counselors have comprehensive knowledge of personality and human development in order to use them. Equally effective counseling outcomes can result from many different theoretical models. However, no professional counselor is equally effective with each theoretical model. Moreover, little is known about how professional counselors can be most effectively matched with particular theoretical models in order to gain the greatest benefits; the selection of a theoretical model is at the discretion of the counselor. But, regardless of the model(s) selected, theories serve as maps for helping clients by providing direction and goals, clarifying the counselor's role, explaining what takes place during the counseling process, and evaluating the effectiveness of counseling.

Hopson (1982) discussed five "schools" of thought for classifying most of the theoretical models used by professional counselors: psychoanalytic, client-centered, behavioral, cognitive, and affective. The theories within each school that are used most frequently by professional counselors are briefly summarized.

Psychoanalytic Models

This model, in its general form, was historically the first, and approaches based on it concentrate on the past history of the client, understanding the dynamics of the person's personality, and the relationship between the client and the counselor.

Freudian Psychoanalytic Theory. This theory is based on the fundamental principle that an individual's behavior is controlled by desires to seek pleasure and to avoid pain, with the "mind" functioning as an expression of these conflicting forces. Freud (1911), the founder of the theory, referred to this concept as the "pleasure principle." It is viewed as operative throughout life, but experienced mainly during an individual's early years.

In Freudian psychoanalytic theory, an individual's present mental functioning is causally connected to past experiences, and current behaviors are determined by antecedent conscious and unconscious forces and/or events. Of importance are the effects which unconscious forces have upon an individual's mental processes and activities; mental elements are evaluated by their degree of consciousness or repression. The latter is important if an individual is repressing selected mental elements with the purpose of avoiding pain and displeasure. Consideration also is given to the manner in which libidinal (i.e., thought to be primarily sexual) drives interact with aggressive drives and the effect that this interaction has upon an individual's behaviors. Finally, the psychoanalytic approach indicates that an individual's behaviors can be traced to important experiences and events in childhood and subsequently generated fantasies, wishes, and dreams.

Proponents of Freudian psychoanalytic theory view a person's ultimate personality structure as influenced and determined by a culmination of biological factors and experiences. This includes the development of libidinal drives through the oral, anal, and phallic phases or stages of development, and the latency and adolescence periods of life. The oral phase, from birth to approximately 18 months of age, involves libidinal gratification through the mouth, lips, and tongue. Libidinal gratification during the anal phase (i.e., approximately 18 months to three years of age) involves activities related to the retention and passing of feces. During the phallic phase (i.e., approximately three to six years of age), the genitals become the central focus of libidinal gratification. Beginning with the latency period, which exists from the phallic phase to puberty and adolescence, the final development of an adult identity is initiated through socialization and education with significant others in the environment. Dominant within this developmental period are the *id* (i.e., the effect of libidinal and aggressive desires upon the mind), *ego* (i.e., the individual's self-identity), and *superego* (i.e., conscience).

Counseling based on the Freudian psychoanalytic theory empahsizes the client making rational responses and choices in response to unconscious conflicts, as opposed to the client responding automatically to them. Clients learn to control their lives through self-knowledge of their neurotic symptoms and behaviors which represent manifestations of their unconscious conflicts.

Counseling using this theory includes four main phases, all of which are related to transference: opening, developing, working through, and resolving. Transference involves feelings and expectations of the client that a counselor elicits by engaging the person in a therapeutic process. The client casts the counselor in a role (e.g., parent, spouse, or sibling) that meets the client's needs. A closely related phenomena is counter-transference, which occurs when the counselor's own needs become entangled in the client's needs. Countertransference may be reflected in the counselor's attraction for or dislike toward certain clients.

Adlerian Theory. Adlerian theory, which is also referred to as individual psychology, focuses upon the belief that behavior exists only as the process of individuals interacting with each other. Of importance in this theory are the concepts that behavior takes place in a social context and that individuals cannot be studied or understood in isolation (i.e., without understanding the social context of the individual). An individual's behavior may change throughout life depending upon the constancy of his/her life style and the alternatives with which the individual is confronted. Through self-determinism, individuals have choices about goals to be pursued. Heredity and environment, which are viewed in the context of how an individual uses them in reaching goals, do not cause a person's "being" or determine a person's behavior. Instead, individuals focus on "becoming" through striving for mastery and superiority in self-selected goals (Adler, 1972), completion (Adler, 1958), and perfection (Adler, 1964). Individuals face challenges through solving the "life tasks" of society, work, and sex with the key element being interdependency; for "the benefit of the society," individuals must learn "to work together" with members of the "other sex." In Adlerian theory, all individuals are *"mitmenschen,"* or equal, fellow human beings.

The Adlerian theory approach to counseling is based on the premise that individuals give their own meaning to life and behave according to their self-selected goals. As a result, they have control in shaping their respective internal and external environments and assume appropriate attitudes toward the outcomes of their selections. Individuals are also viewed as creative, self-consistent, and capable of change.

In Adlerian theory, the primary social environment for children is family constellation. By observing, exploring, and seeking feedback from their environment (i.e., home and family), individuals learn what is right and wrong, and what fosters their personal success. To be successful in attaining goals, an individual has to solve the aspects of life tasks, or compensate in some way for unresolved tasks. A counselor following the Adlerian approach examines with the client his/her "life style" and aims to change behaviors within the client's existing life style rather than changing the life style.

Analytical Psychotherapy. Developed by Karl Jung, analytical psychotherapy (counseling) focuses upon the relationship between the conscious and the unconscious. These two subsystems form the "psyche," a self-regulating system that controls an individual's behaviors. Analytical psychology emphasizes the need to become more aware of the conscious and one's "being" by developing a greater understanding of the unconscious. The unconscious subsystem is viewed as contributing greatly to providing direction and meaning and enabling one to be creative, but it also creates problems for the individual if neglected.

Jung advocated that an individual's behavior is both consciously and unconsciously motivated, with the two systems being compensatory to each other. If an individual consciously develops a strong attitude in a given direction, the counterpoint attitude becomes strongly developed in the subconscious. These differences become evident through observation of relationships with others, communication skills, work habits, and analysis and interpretation of messages from the unconscious provided through dreams.

Proponents of analytical psychotherapy believe that each individual experiences the instincts of hunger, thirst, sex, aggression, and individuation, which is striving to achieve a true self or the attainment of wholeness based on conscious and unconscious factors. A person's behaviors are influenced in part by current experiences and in part by what may happen in the future as a result of the present behaviors. While conscious forces are evident and available to an individual, unconscious forces are available only through symbols which are interpreted as guiding messages. During counseling based on this model, individuals experiencing difficulties or conflicts are helped by appropriate translations of the symbolic messages provided through their dreams.

Counseling from the analytical psychology perspective is concerned with the purposeful and prospective functioning of the "psyche," which is composed of the ego, personal unconscious, and nonpersonal unconscious. While past experiences are important in the development of personality and individuation because of the effect they may have upon present functioning, future outcomes also must be considered. Conscious elements are referred to as the ego. Previously conscious elements that can be readily retracted to consciousness are considered the personal unconscious. The final component of the psyche, the nonpersonal unconscious, is composed of factors (i.e., archetypes) that are unavailable to consciousness, but which affect behaviors. Examples of nonpersonal unconscious elements include the hero archetype, the Wise Old Man, rebirth, that which we do not want to be, feminine and masculine principles, and the need to experience meaning in life, centeredness, and wholeness.

Counseling within the context of analytical psychology is viewed as a process of helping clients find self-knowledge, achieve self-education, and/or reconstruct their personality. Individuals with conflicts experience unconscious messages that need to be addressed. After a complete analysis of an individual's consciousness, the unconscious is explored, mainly through dream interpretation, with a focus not only on antecedent causes, but on future behaviors as well. Enlarging upon given data through interpretation enables a client to perceive previously unconscious connections, motivations, and feelings. The goal is to make the client aware of the unconscious as much as is possible.

Client/Person-Centered Model

Person-centered counseling, which was originally termed client-centered counseling, focuses on developing "self-actualization;" an individual's inherent tendency to develop all capacities in order to maintain or enhance oneself. Developed by Carl Rogers during the 1940s, this model and its adaptations are based on an "if-then" principle and place substantial faith in the client's problem-solving abilities. If the counselor conveys genuineness, accurate empathic understanding, and unconditional positive regard, and the client perceives these attitudes, then the client will achieve beneficial change by moving toward self-actualization and overcoming self-internalized restrictions.

Counselors who use the person-centered theoretical approach to counseling assume the role of "being themselves" with their clients; their inner experiencing is permitted to be present during the counseling relationship with the client. Through the inner experiencing of the counselor's own feelings (genuineness), an understanding of the client's feelings is achieved (empathic understanding). This is accompanied by an acceptance or respect for the client's individuality (unconditional positive regard) which is derived from a trust in the self-directed capacity of the client. As the client's awareness of inner experiencing develops, positive changes come from within the client.

Within person-centered counseling, present experiencing is important and provides the resources for the client's personal growth and change. The counselor assumes the role of facilitator and helps clients establish and attach meaning to their inner experiencing. Any expression that could be interpreted as evaluative in nature is avoided by the counselor, as are probing questions and descriptions of the client.

Person-centered counseling fosters a relationship with the client that includes warmth and responsiveness from the counselor, freely expressed feelings influenced by a permissive climate, and the absence of coercion or pressure. In the relationship, the counselor is often referred to as the "helper" and the client is the "other."

An important assumption in person-centered counseling, as stated earlier, is that people are born with a tendency toward self-actualization; a basic motivation to enhance the organism. With growth, the client develops an ability to discriminate between positive and negative inner experiencing, and to acquire a sense of self. Thus, the client's self-concept and sense of self-regard develop. Self-regard is affected by the reactions of others and the introjections of conditions of worth. Conflict can arise when a client's self-regard is incongruent with his/her organismic needs and desires as they relate to the interactions with significant others in the environment. If negative organismic needs persistently prevail over self-regard needs, intervention may be needed. The intent of person-centered counseling, therefore, is to enable individuals who are experiencing conflict to incorporate previously denied organismic urges within their self-concept.

Behavioral Models

Within behavioral models for counseling, principles of learning and/or behavior modification are applied to the resolution of clients' problems. Two widely used approaches based on this model are behavior therapy and multimodal therapy.

Behavior Therapy. Changes in the principles of behavior therapy have been continually occurring since its beginnings in the 1950s, primarily because of updated research findings. As a result, four conceptually different approaches are used in behavior therapy (i.e., applied behavior analysis, neobehavioristic stimulus-response, social learning theory, and cognitive behavior modification). However, the primary hypothesis for behavior therapy remains unchanged; behavior modification techniques are used for treating all abnormal and/or maladaptive behavior. In contrast with previously discussed models, behavior therapy clients' previous thoughts are considered of little or no value in counseling, as are unconscious conflicts. Rather, current causes of behavior are the focal point, with treatment techniques varying according to clients' needs.

All behavior therapy is based on an educational model of human development as well as a commitment to scientific methodology. With the *applied behavior analysis* approach, behavior is viewed as a function of its consequences. Actual behavior rather than cognitive processes are of concern, with the behavor modification techniques of stimulus control, reinforcement, punishment, and extinction being emphasized. The *neobehavioristic stimulus-response* model of counseling focuses on anxiety. Intervention techniques involve systematic desensitization and covert conditioning for the purpose of extinguishing the underlying cause(s) of the anxiety. Overt behaviors and covert processes are assumed to follow the same laws of learning. Cognitive mediational processes, external stimuli, and external reinforcement are three focal points in counseling based on *social learning theory*. Current behaviors, cognitive processes, and environmental factors are viewed as interacting influences upon behavior. Cognitive processes, which are affected by environmental events, determine the treatment for environmental influences as they affect the individual. The client, however, determines what behaviors will or will not be changed, with behavioral change being directly related to the client's self-directed capabilities.

With the fourth approach, *cognitive behavior modification,* cognitive restructuring is emphasized. This involves using techniques for the purpose of gaining an understanding of individuals' interpretations of their experiences as they affect their respective behaviors. Alteration of irrational ideas, perceptions, and interpretations of significant individual experiences is emphasized.

Success within behavior therapy is dependent upon the client's willingness to make changes, and the interactions between counselor and client. The client is an active participant in the process and is encouraged by the counselor to be completely involved in determining and setting goals. The counselor's initial responsibility is to identify the existing concern. Toward this end, assessment techniques may be used, including psychological tests, behavioral observations, self-reports and self-monitoring, role playing, and imagery. Techniques used for treatment may include training in social skills and/or assertiveness, self-control procedures such as progressive relaxation and biofeedback, cognitive restructuring such as rational-emotive therapy, and real-life, performance-based techniques such as behavior modification programs used in classrooms.

Multimodal Therapy. Arnold Lazarus developed multimodal therapy during the 1960s and 1970s. With this model, behavioral psychology is extended to include assessment procedures and the interactions between sensory, imaging, cognitive, and interpersonal factors. Central to multimodal therapy is individual behavior which is determined through the "BASIC ID," an acronym for *b*ehaviors, *a*ffective processes, *s*ensations, *i*mages, *c*ognitions, *i*nterpersonal relationships, and *d*rug/biological functions. The component of "behaviors" involves an individual's activity level. Emotions and feelings, and reactions to these two elements are included under "affective processes." Personal awareness of reactions to bodily sensation (e.g., pain or pleasure) is considered under "sensations." Imagination is addressed through the "images" component, and an individual's analytical, planning, and reasoning skills are comprised in the "cognition" component. Relationships with others and the amount of emphasis placed on these by an individual are addressed by the "interpersonal relationships" component. Finally, the general health and physical well-being of an individual are addressed under "drug/biological functioning," which also includes biochemical/neurophysiological elements such as personal hygiene, exercise, diet, and medications used.

Multimodal counselors believe that a client's abnormal behavior is due to a multitude of problems (e.g., conflicts, unhappy experiences, and social deficits) that need to be treated using a multitude of intervention techniques (e.g., biofeedback, imagery, bibliotherapy, audiotherapy, assertiveness training, role playing). Likewise, because each individual is unique, therapy is approached through an individualized intervention plan based on the central hypothesis of "who or what is best for the respective individual." Of concern are the interactions among the modalities within the client's BASIC ID, as well as external influences upon behaviors. During the initial interview, a *Modality Profile* (i.e., list of problems and prospective interventions) is charted based on excessive and deficient modalities across the client's BASIC ID. Once the counselor determines problem areas, bridging and tracking procedures are employed. The counselor first addresses the client's preferred modality and then gradually bridges (i.e., leads/guides) the client into other modality areas that need attention. The direction of these bridges and the appropriate intervention technique to select for each problem are determined by tracking the preference order of modalities exhibited by a client. The preference order, referred to as *firing order,* varies across individuals and across situations. The counselor's role is to help clients understand influential antecedent factors affecting their respective behaviors and to use appropriate interventive techniques. The counselor also conducts an ongoing assessment of the client's progress and adjusts the Modality Profile accordingly.

Cognitive Models

Approaches based on a cognitive model focus on how clients conceptualize and cognitively organize their worlds. The common focus is to help clients change conceptualizations, and subsequently their associated feelings and behaviors. Three widely used approaches based on this model are rational-emotive therapy, reality therapy, and transactional analysis.

Rational-Emotive Therapy. Albert Ellis, who developed the theory of rational-emotive therapy during the 1950s, advocated that emotional consequences are mainly created by an individual's belief system and not by significant activating events. Within his theory, the focal point of an individual's intrapersonal and interpersonal life is his/her growth and happiness. An individual is born with an innate ability to create or destruct, to relate or remain isolated, to select or not select, and to enjoy or dislike; abilities that are affected by the individual's culture/environment, family, and social reference group. Primary goals in rational-emotive therapy are to help individuals (in rational and emotive ways) desire rather than to demand, work at altering elements of their being that they would like to change, and, with understanding, willingly accept aspects of their lives that are beyond their control.

Ellis indicated that several main propositions of rational-emotive therapy exist. He purported that individuals have innate abilities to be both self-preserving and self-destructive and to be rational as well as irrational. In addition, being influenced by others is most pronounced during the early years and therefore, individuals are greatly influenced by their early-life family environments. Because an individual is able to perceive, think, emote, and behave at the same time, cognitive, connotive, and motoric behaviors are also co-existent. Both normal and abnormal behavior are viewed as a function of perceptions, thoughts, emotions, and actions, and therefore, these elements are essential in any rational-emotive therapeutic relationship between the counselor and client. Also important is the need for the counselor to be accepting of a client and yet at the same time to be critical of the client's behaviors, pointing out deficiencies where necessary and strongly stressing self-discipline and autonomous functioning if the client remains dependent. Finally, the strong cognitive emphasis in rational-emotive therapy make it unnecessary to establish a "warm" relationship between client and counselor. With its purpose of helping individuals achieve deep-seated cognitive changes that could involve alterations in basic values, rational-emotive therapy uses a variety of methods, including didactic discussion, behavior modification, bibliotherapy, audiovisual aids, activity-oriented homework assignments, role playing, assertion training, desensitization, humor, operant conditioning, suggestion, and emotional support. Rational-emotive therapy includes a general form, which involves learning rationally appropriate behaviors, and a preferential form, which involves learning how to internalize rules of logic and scientific method while also learning how to dispute irrational ideas and inappropriate behaviors. Typically, general rational-emotive therapy is included as a part of preferential rational-emotive therapy. Eliminating emotional problems involves disputing disturbance-creating ideas through logical and empirical thinking. The "real" cause of an individual's problems are viewed as dogmatic, irrational, and unexamined beliefs that need to be exposed through objective, empirical, and logical evaluation. Individuals who are experiencing difficulty need to be made aware that the problem (1) is of their own making because of their beliefs rather than antecedent causes or conditions, (2) will continue unless addressed, and (3) can be extinguished or minimized through rational-emotive thinking and actions.

Rational-emotive therapy is a highly active-directive approach that views the client holistically, and stresses the biological components of personality development. When necessary, counselors strongly challenge a client's irrational beliefs. The major goal is to help individuals minimize their self-defeating outlooks through developing more realistic and acceptable philosophies of life. Identifying a client's basic irrational beliefs is of immediate importance to the counselor who then proceeds to expose the same and work with the client to develop more rational points of view.

Reality Therapy. Developed by William Glasser, reality therapy embraces the theory that the brain functions as a system that controls behaviors by fulfilling needs built into the environment. Individuals experiencing difficulties are doing so because they are unable to control or act upon elements in their environment in a satisfactory manner. The goal of reality therapy, therefore, is to help individuals focus upon choosing actions that are appropriate for satisfying the basic needs of staying alive, reproducing, having power, being free, and having fun.

Reality therapy views behavior as an integration of an individual's feelings, thoughts, and actions in consideration of personal needs and the behavior of others in the environment. Behavior is generated within the individual, dependent upon the needs to be satisfied, and antecedent experiences and outside forces are not of consequence since the focal point is present experiences and the client's awareness of how better choices of behaviors can be made. That each individual and society has a set of personal standards is a basic concept recognized by proponents of reality therapy and is an important consideration when helping clients who may be working contrary to society's or their own set of standards. Also of importance is teaching individuals to achieve more effective control of their environments; to choose more effective behaviors. In essence, reality therapy views teaching as therapeutic since the end result of therapeutic teaching should be greater fulfillment of the client's needs.

Eight basic steps are included in the practice of reality therapy. After establishing a relationship with the client and making friends, the counselor seeks input from the client as to what he/she is "controlling for" (i.e., what the client wants). The counselor then determines what the client is currently doing to achieve what he/she wants. The third step involves aiding the client to evaluate the effectiveness of what he/she is doing relative to achieving what is desired. This is followed by aiding the client in making a plan to achieve more effective control of the situation or environment. For the latter to work, the counselor gets a commitment from the client to follow through on the plan (step five) and then does not accept excuses from the client if the plan is not carried out (step six). Step seven concerns consequences, where possible, when a plan is not fulfilled. Involved are reasonable consequences such as temporary restrictions of freedom or temporary removal of privileges. The final (eighth) step in reality therapy is to not give up; to not allow the client to control the counselor. If a client is persistent in not following through on a plan, then the counselor helps the client attempt another plan which can be implemented, and the cycle continues until the client gains effective control of his/her life. Glasser acknowledged that gaining more effective control of life may take a long time. However, he believed that the process must eventually be successful because the individual controls the environment; the environment does not control the individual.

Transactional Analysis. Often referred to as TA, transactional analysis was developed by Eric Berne during the 1950s. The focal points of this theory are the child, the adult, and the parent; three independent and observable ego states that exist within every individual. These ego states are patterns of experiences and feelings that correspond to patterns of behavior. During the child ego state, an individual behaves like a child, emotionally, regardless of age. During the adult ego state, however, an individual reacts unemotionally to stimuli, primarily by using logic and factual data. The parent ego state involves behaviors that in essence replicate those exhibited by a parent. An individual's moral attitudes, beliefs, and values are the concern of the parent state. An individual in this state may attempt to influence, control, and/or evaluate the development of others.

A second important concept of TA is a transaction, or a unit of communication between individuals. Two levels of transaction are involved; the overt social level, and the covert psychological level. Diagramming transactions (a counseling function within transactional analysis) provides both the counselor and the client with a pictorial illustration of the latter's interactions with significant others in the client's environment. Circles containing a(n) P, A, or C to represent the respective ego states of parent, adult, and child, are connected by arrows according to the type of transaction involved. A solid-line arrow depicts a social transaction and a broken-line arrow represents a psychological transaction. In addition, three other types of transactions are utilized. During a complementary transaction (i.e., parallel arrows), an exchange is direct and overt; a definite communication between individuals. When a transference transaction (i.e., crossed arrows) occurs, exchanges are covert and discussion on a specific topic ceases immediately. The final form, an ulterior transaction (i.e., a solid-line arrow is parallel to a broken-line arrow and represents a dual-level exchange), involves an exchange between individuals during which both levels of transaction are actively and simultaneously in operation. With these "game"-type transactions, both the social level and the psychological message need to be used during interpretation and evaluation of an individual's behavior.

According to TA principles, social interactions between persons are based upon their respective needs for recognition, presented in the form of "strokes." *Strokes,* which are learned and are essential for growth, range from positive (i.e., approval) to negative (i.e., disapproval) to none at all (i.e., not caring), shape individual personalities, and vary from family to family. Individuals develop a system of stroking through their interactions with others, thus forming the basis to their acceptance of being OK or not OK and accepting others as OK or not OK. This developmental patterning is referred to as a *life script* and is illustrated with an *epogram*.

Five psychological forces are included in the epogram representing the critical-parent, nurturing-parent, adult, free-child, and adapted-child functions that comprise an individual's personality. Personalities are formed according to the differing contributions of each psychological force. The critical-parent finds fault, makes and enforces rules, and strives for individual rights. The nurturing-parent fosters growth and development. The adult is nonjudgmental, precise, and nonemotional. Spontaneity, eagerness, and creativity are some of the energies found in the free-child, whereas the adapted-child is conforming, flexible, and easy to get along with. A well-balanced energy system forms a bell-shaped epogram and is the goal of transactional analysis. Also included are the concepts of time and energy as extended in an ego state; if raised in one state, time and energy will be decreased in another state. A well-balanced energy system also exists in a bell-shaped epogram; the energy extended by the psychological forces is approximately normally distributed.

Affective Models

Approaches based on the affective model include Gestalt therapy and existential psychotherapy. They share the belief that problems accumulate and have to be discharged before the client can think clearly again.

Gestalt Therapy. Gestalt therapy, which was developed by Fritz Perls, focuses on the process of helping individuals become increasingly aware of the effect of their immediate, current experiences upon their current behaviors. Past and future experiences or behaviors are not emphasized. The process, undertaken individually but collaboratively by the counselor and the client, emphasizes the development of the client's self-awareness. Involved are the basic concepts of phenomenology, field theory, existentialism, and dialogue. The *phenomenological perspective* systematically analyzes only that which is currently being experienced by clients, with the intent being to help them become more aware of their own degree of awareness. With the *field theory perspective,* a behavior is viewed as a function of the person's life space or field. Meaning is given to a situation based on what is currently observed; the here-and-now which may include antecedent experiences if they affect related elements such as beliefs. The third perspective, *existentialism,* focuses on the individual who is doing the perceiving and the truth of the individual's relation to the environment. The fourth perspective is *dialogue and contact* with others in the environment are important. This perspective involves inclusion (i.e., experiencing another's situation as much as possible without losing one's own identity), presence (i.e., the counselor expressing his/her self to the client), commitment to dialogue (i.e., permitting contact to happen instead of making it happen and controlling the result), protecting the integrity of the client's experiences, and experiencing dialogue rather than talking about it.

Important to Gestalt therapy is holism and multi-dimensionality. Individuals exist with a clear boundary between themselves and others and, therefore, they need to understand themselves as a function of their environment. Abnormal behavior results from problems delineating the boundaries between one's self and others in the environment. The abnormal behaviors may be confluence (an absence of distinction between self and others), isolation, withdrawal, retroflection (a split between aspects of the self), introjection (lack of discrimination or assimilation of new information gained), projection (confusion of self and others), and deflection (avoidance of contact with others). Solutions to problem behaviors are achieved by dialogue and phenomenology concerning the client's present experiences. Therefore, a strong working relationship between the counselor and client is important, with the client assuming responsibility for "what is." The goals for the client are to develop complete self-awareness through direct contact with the counselor and self-regulation of a whole existence that is comprised of integral parts. Involved are the "good Gestalt" (i.e., the whole is clearly organized and in good form) and "creative adjustment" (i.e., a balance is established between self and the environment). Self-regulation, according to Gestalt therapy theory, can be achieved through phenomenology or here-and-now experiences and experimenting, dialogue through direct contact with the counselor, and awareness of the whole-field concepts of what is done as well as how and why it is done. The client focuses upon what he/she is aware of experiencing at the present time and then experiments with changes by using imagery, body techniques, or visualization.

Existential Psychotherapy. The focus of existential psychotherapy is for the client to find a true "sense of being." Authors closely associated with this theory include Victor Frankl, Irvin Yalons, and Rollo May. The approach is concerned with feelings of love, creativity, anxiety, despair, isolation, anomie, grief, and loneliness. A basic component is the

"I-Am" or ontological experience; realizing that humans are living and experiencing individuals who are able to choose their own being. When an individual's existence or values are threatened, anxiety is experienced. Therefore, existential psychotherapy emphasizes the reduction of anxiety and concentrates on aiding individuals to be tolerant of the to-be-expected anxieties normally experienced in daily being. Of major concern to the existential psychotherapist is the client's "neurotic anxiety," an anxiety that is inappropriate to a given situation. A second area of focus is the "neurotic guilt" experienced by a client due to fantasized transgressions, or self guilt due to an inability to live up to potentialities. As with anxiety, guilt also may take a "normal" form. The expectation is that individuals will experience some guilt in their daily being and therefore, need to be tolerant of this to-be-expected form of guilt.

According to existential psychotherapy theory, an individual's world is comprised of the *Unwelt,* or the biological (i.e., natural) world (also referred to as the environment), which addresses an individual's drives, needs, and instincts. The *Mitwelt,* or personal community, is concerned with interpersonal relationships. Self-awareness and self-relatedness are included in the third mode, *Eigenwelt,* which is concerned with one's relationship with self. The dimension of time is also significant in existential psychotherapy. Whether a client is able to recall important antecedent events is dependent upon his/her commitment to the present and future. Without the latter, past events have little relationship or effect upon the difficulties the person is experiencing. Relatedly, an individual's ability to transcend antecedent events to the present and future is important. Through *transcendere,* individuals are capable of continually emerging from the past to the present and the future; being able to transcend over time and space because of the ontological nature of human beings.

Difficulties can arise for individuals when they experience conflicts with the ultimate concerns of existing. Essential concerns or sources of anxiety include freedom or being responsible for one's existence, e.g., actions and choices. A second concern is existential isolation; a gap between oneself and the world and/or others. Death constitutes a third concern, while meaninglessness is a fourth. Of particular importance with meaninglessness is the development of values that provide an individual with a purposeful meaning for a direction to existing.

Existential psychotherapy counselors view their role as helping individuals to experience conflict in order to determine their unconscious anxieties and the maladaptive defense mechanisms being used, and to develop alternative strategies or mechanisms for coping with the problem. This entails identifying methods being used by a client as a means of avoidance when these instances occur, and helping the client to become aware of these situations and to make appropriate decisions for terminating a conflict for the betterment of his/her existence.

SUMMARY

This chapter defined the process of counseling first through a discussion of communication skills that are common to all helping and theoretical approaches for guiding professional counselors. Second, important concerns of individual and group counseling were presented, and finally, the more established counseling theories were reviewed. The point to be made is that several other existing approaches were not included in the review, some of which are "off-shoots" of the ones presented while others are highly unique. All have been designed to help people attain a higher level of personal competence. This quest for more autonomous and more self-competent individuals causes professional counselors to seek the most effective counseling theory and methods available. At this time, however, no single theory has been established as the quintessential approach to professional counseling.

Chapter 5

ASSESSMENT
AND
MEASUREMENT

The essential goal of assessment is to quantify a client's behavior and characteristics for the purpose of enabling the professional counselor to understand and help the client. Professional counselors, however, have given much less attention to assessment than they have to other professional issues in counseling. Yet, data obtained through assessment to quantify a client's behavior is important in helping a professional counselor make calculated decisions. For this important reason, an understanding of assessment is necessary for effective counseling.

A starting point for an introductory discussion of assessment is terminology. Accordingly, definitions of often-used terms as provided by Shertzer and Linden (1979), are presented below.

> **Assessment:** the methods and processes used in gathering data about, or evidence of, human behavior. This term is frequently employed when a professional counselor wishes to emphasize the distinction between the medical use of diagnosis with its connotation of abnormality, and the collection of information concerning the current state of human behavior.

Measurement: the act of identifying the amount or dimension of an attribute or distinguishing characteristic; an estimation of how much of a trait an individual displays or possesses.

Evaluation: the process of comparing measurements or relating them to other variables. For example, evaluation enables a professional counselor to form an opinion or to judge the adequacy or inadequacy of an attribute, trait, or object.

Appraisal: a term used synonomously with evaluation.

Interpretation: the act of interpreting the meaning or usefulness of behavioral data.

The goal of assessment in counseling is rather simple (i.e., to help the counselor and client). However, this goal becomes tremendously difficult to obtain if the data gathered are misused or misinterpreted. Incorrect interpretation or inappropriately used data result in wrong decisions, which adversely affects clients and limits their opportunities. Further, many counselors-in-training mistakenly view assessment merely as "paper-and-pencil testing," but assessment in counseling is a multidimensional process of which paper and pencil testing is only one component. The professional counselor needs to be interested in the results of a client's performance in a given situation in relation to the client's total functioning. Therefore, effective assessment procedures take into consideration not only the client's performance, but also the client's history, behavior, and environment. Because of this, assessment can be undertaken apart from the formal counseling process (e.g., through observations made by parents, loved ones, teachers, and/or employer).

Because good assessment is multidimensional, many areas within the process overlap. Yet, a dichotomy of functions exists; those that are involved within conventional assessment and those that are part of the assessment process which we shall refer to as empirical counseling. The discussion that follows is presented according to this dichotomy.

TRADITIONAL ASSESSMENT IN COUNSELING

The process of conventional assessment, which is based in the medical model, is diagnostic and evaluative in nature. The purposes of conventional assessment include diagnosis of traits and factors, assessment of strengths and weaknesses, classification, and selection for placement.

The outcome of conventional assessment leads to prescription which unfortunately tends to have as its focus the determination of what is "wrong" with a client. Its use in counseling dates back to the late 1930s, when the conventional- assessment model being used by psychologists was adopted with modifications by professional counselors (Williamson, 1939). The resulting model is referred to, in this text, as traditional assessment in counseling. In traditional assessment, the professional counselor assesses the individual development, and focuses on classifying or selecting people for training, educational, or vocational placement. Clients are expected to participate in assessment by reacting to the test results and the professional counselor's appraisal of their characteristics. However, a very highly skilled professional is needed to enable a client to be an active participant in the assessment process. Thus, a common concern with this model is that it often leads to prescription only as mentioned earlier. The process of conventional assessment too often provides answers, solutions, and advice rather than encouraging clients to take charge of their lives. When properly utilized, the traditional assessment model is an important element in professional counseling. Therefore, the essential components of this assessment process and their use are presented in the following material.

Purposes

In the traditional assessment model, tests are administered by professional counselors for a variety of purposes, but primarily because they provide information to assist the counselor and client in making decisions. The specific reasons for giving tests vary depending on the setting in which the professional counselor is working. Four reasons have been described by Cronbach (1970) and are presented.

Prediction or Planning. Tests are often given for the purpose of assisting professional counselors, clients, or administrators with decisions concerning future performance (e.g., the planning of an educational program for an individual or a group in business, industry, or school). Tests designed for this purpose provide measures of ability, achievement, or other human characteristics, and are used for making decisions.

Selection or Screening. A familiar use of tests involves the selection process employed by colleges and universities whereby individuals are accepted or rejected by an institution based, in part, on their performance on a standardized test. Tests also are used by many employers as a means of selecting individuals to fill vacancies in their work force. In a school setting, tests often are administered for the purpose of screening students with superior academic abilities, social problems, or academic difficulties.

Classification or Placement. Most states have laws which specify a criteria for certain educational programs. For example, standardized tests provide measures to be used for placing students in selective educational programs such as the academically gifted or beginning resource rooms and self-contained classrooms for students with specific learning problems. Also, tests are frequently used by the military or government for selecting individuals to participate or become eligible for benefits. In addition, tests can be used to classify students for individual or group counseling. Business and industry use tests for placement.

Many problems are apparent in the use of tests to make classification or placement decisions including problems with validity and reliability. Yet, most governmental regulations concerning people in public schools, the military, or agencies require that classification and placement decisions be based on test results.

Program Evaluation. In traditional assessment, a program, method, or treatment, rather than an individual, is being assessed. Suppose, for example, that High Point Hall, a drug rehabilitation center, decides to try an experimental aerobics program to help recovering substance-abuse users. Data would be needed concerning the effect(s) the experimental program might have upon the center's clients. The traditional treatment program would have to be evaluated followed by the implementation and evaluation of the experimental aerobics program. Typically, tests would be administered to each client before and after the traditional treatment program and the same pre-post testing procedure would be used during the experimental program. Clients' progress during the traditional program could then be compared with their progress during the experimental program for the purpose of evaluating each program's relative effectiveness.

Assessment of Individual Progress. An important use of tests not mentioned by Cronbach (1970) is the examination of client (or student) change or progress. Professional counselors' and clients' conclusions that progress is being made can sometimes be verified by the administration of standardized tests.

Standardized Tests

Professional counselors are required to administer, score, and interpret a multitude of standardized tests throughout their career. Because they also receive test information from colleagues and from a variety of other professionals outside the field of counseling, professional counselors need to have a working knowledge of standardized tests.

No one basic standardized test exists for counselors to use in assessment. Instead, they rely on a potpourri of instruments that can be classified into three categories of measurement: aptitude or general ability; achievement; and personality, vocational-interest, vocational-maturity, and attitude inventories. Also, certain types of tests are used more extensively by professional counselors in given professional settings. For example, tests purporting to yield information about vocational interest and maturity, personality, and attitude are more frequently used by the professional counselor who works with adolescents and adults.

The common characteristic of standardized tests is that they expose a person to a particular set of questions or tasks in order to obtain a performance that can be compared with that of individuals in a normative population. Another characteristic is their major strength of permitting tasks and questions to be presented in the same way to each person tested. Further, the responses are scored in a predetermined and consistent manner, thus permitting the performances of several individual test takers to be compared.

The actual scores achieved on a test are referred to as quantitative data; e.g., scoring at the 84th percentile on the verbal section of the Graduate Record Exam or earning an IQ score of 125. In addition to quantitative data, qualitative information can be derived from the administration of a standardized test. This information consists of non-systematic observations made while a client is taking a test and/or while the counselor is discussing the results of the test with the client.

Standardized tests used in traditional assessment can be classified into two principal categories: those assessing the cognitive domain and those assessing the affective domain. The major testing subcategories of the cognitive domain will be presented first.

Assessing the Cognitive Domain

The presentation of cognitive-domain assessment is divided into subcategories according to general ability measures, tests of general intelligence, aptitude tests, and standardized achievement tests.

General Ability Measures. Dictionary definitions of intelligence include the ability to learn and understand or the ability to cope with new situations. Mehrens and Lehmann (1984) reported that definitions of intelligence also include the capacity to learn, think abstractly, integrate new experiences, and adapt to new situations. Intelligence also has been used interchangeably with aptitude. Some test specialists, however, suggest that subtle shades of meaning distinguish these two terms. They consider intelligence as a general mental ability and aptitude as a specific ability factor. To illustrate this difference, the Stanford-Binet Intelligence Test would be considered a general measure of intelligence, whereas the Seashore Musical Aptitude Test would be viewed as a specific measure of aptitude. Historically, intelligence tests were assumed to measure innate characteristics that are not subject to change. As Mehrens and Lehmann (1984) reported, this assumption is invalid, and many test authors, in an attempt to avoid the implication of innateness, have instead adopted the term aptitude.

A helpful scheme for understanding apptitude tests is to categorize them as (1) individually administered instruments that provide a general measure of intelligence, (2) group administered tests that provide a general measure of intelligence, (3) group-administered, multifactor aptitude tests that provide multiple measures, and (4) group-administered aptitude instruments that provide a specific measure.

Individual Tests of General Intelligence. Although most schools, colleges, businesses, and industries use group tests of intelligence, having clinical information which can be gained most effectively through the administration of individual intelligence tests can be helpful in some situations. For example, the examiner sometimes needs to have an opportunity to observe the test taker's approach to problem solving, the amount of stress exhibited by the client during the test administration, and the client's test-taking behaviors.

The individual intelligence test has been considered the psychologist's basic tool (Bardon & Bennett, 1974). When correctly administered, individual intelligence tests provide a more reliable measure and a better understanding of the test-taker's behavior than do group intelligence tests. Correct administration, an important factor in obtaining a reliable measure, requires considerable training. In fact, many states mandate certain licensure, usually that of a psychologist, in order to use individual intelligence scores in any way that may affect a person's future. Instruments that require special qualifications to administer are referred to as "restricted," such as the Stanford-Binet and the various Wechsler tests (Wechsler Intelligence Scale for Children Revised, WISC-R, ages 6 through 16; Wechsler Pre-school and Primary Scale of Intelligence, WPPSI, ages 4 through 6 1/2; and the Wechsler Adult Intelligence Scale-Revised, WAIS).

Group Tests of General Intelligence. As graduates of American schools and colleges know, group intelligence tests are very much a part of an individual's educational life. For example, two tests widely used in predicting college success are the College Entrance Examination Board Scholastic Aptitude Test (SAT) and the American College Testing Program (ACT). At the graduate school level, widely used tests are the Graduate Record Examination Aptitude Test (GRE) and the Miller Analogies Test (MAT). Can you recall those times when you carefully and completely filled appropriate "bubbles" on an answer sheet with a heavy dark mark using a soft-lead pencil, for one of these tests?

Group intelligence tests are used much more frequently in educational settings than are individually administered tests; perhaps by a ratio as large as 20 to 1. Group intelligence tests are less expensive to administer because they can be given to a large number of individuals at one time. Also, they are not restricted tests and, therefore, are designed to be administered by non-licensed individuals. Their value and wide use, however, result generally from the fact that the data derived from them are comparable to those derived from the more time consuming individual tests. Many group tests of general intelligence report two subscores such as verbal and quantitative ability.

Although most group tests can be scored by hand, they are more often scored by a machine that produces raw scores, scaled scores, and percentile ranks. Group intelligence tests, if properly used, can be extremely informative to the professional counselor, particularly when assessing a client's overall functioning. But the results of group testing always should be used with caution. A case in point concerns the cultural-fairness of intelligence tests. People of different national origins and people in various diverse groups in America place different values upon verbal fluency and speed, factors which are important for performing well on intelligence tests. Also, educationally disadvantaged persons typically will be handicapped when intelligence tests are used to describe their functioning. No one intelligence test is best for all uses; care must be taken to select the correct test for a particular situation and population.

Multifactor Aptitude Tests. As mentioned earlier, differences of opinion are found on the value of multifactor aptitude tests in comparison to general intelligence measures. Supporters of multifactor aptitude tests believe that intelligence is composed of many specific abilities. Therefore, some professional counselors use multifactor aptitude tests for the practical reason that they facilitate vocational and educational counseling. They believe that differential descriptions of test results are helpful when discussing strengths and weaknesses with respective clients although, as Mehrens and Lehmann (1984) indicated, little data exist that support differential predictive validity.

Group Administered (Specific) Aptitude Tests. Specific aptitude tests usually measure the capacity to acquire proficiency in a specified activity. This type of test is typically used by professional counselors to help clients make vocational and educational selection decisions, and by institutions for placement decisions.

Standardized Achievement Measures. Professional counselors working in school settings are frequently involved with school-wide achievement-testing programs. They make arrangements for teacher administration and computer scoring, and they are often requested by other school personnel to assist with selecting tests. The latter function usually involves a decision made by a committee comprised of teachers, administrators, school psychologists, and professional counselors. The professional counselor who is involved with any test selection process should make certain that the instruments selected are valid for their respective purposes and possess other necessary psychometric properties.

Achievement tests are designed to measure an individual's progress or current knowledge as a result of education or training. How well does Mary read? Does Burt know the definitions for a list of words? After reading a paragraph, is Nancy able to recall its content? These are examples of questions that can be answered using data derived from achievement tests. Standardized achievement tests are seldom used by professional counselors working in non-educational settings with the exception of using achievement tests for purposes of screening or placement (e.g., typing, shorthand, computer proficiency, and similar knowledge or skill-based tests).

Assessing an individual's achievement level is useful because it enables the professional counselor to help plan successful experiences for others in learning and/or training. This is particularly important with students and clients concerned with career and educational planning. A professional counselor can assist these individuals with identifying their cumulative achievement, determining their strengths and weaknesses in academic performance areas, and comparing their achievement level with their ability or intelligence level.

Many standardized achievement tests are available ranging from assessments of general information (i.e., survey achievement tests) to assessments of a specific knowledge area (i.e., diagnostic tests). However, the current trend in educational settings is less emphasis on survey achievement tests and greater emphasis on those that assess specific kinds of functioning related to school achievement.

Survey Achievement Tests. Survey achievement test batteries consist of a group of tests, each assessing performance in a different content area. All tests in a survey battery are standardized on the same population, thus permitting meaningful comparisons of the results in the various content areas.

A general survey achievement battery (e.g., Stanford Achievement Tests or Iowa Tests of Basic Skills) is used when school personnel are interested in a student's academic progress in all subject areas because comparative information will be available (e.g., whether the student is better in arithmetic, spelling, or reading). However, if school personnel are interested in a student's specific strengths or weaknesses in a single-subject area, then a diagnostic test would be used.

Diagnostic Tests. This type of standardized achievement test is designed to identify a student's specific strengths and weaknesses in a particular academic area. Examples of standardized diagnostic tests are the Stanford Diagnostic Reading Test (SDRT), Diagnostic Tests and Self-Helps in Arithmetic, Metropolitan Readiness Tests, and Gates-MacGinitie Reading Test. The belief is that specific data enable teachers, principals, professional counselors, and school psychologists to decide what kinds of classroom activities will be most effective in helping a student learn, and to plan and organize future learning tasks that are appropriate for a student's developmental level.

In general, the age of the test taker and the kind of information desired determine the achievement test to be used.

Assessing the Affective Domain

This section is concerned with standardized noncognitive group inventories. The discussion will address tests that are concerned with individuals' interests, personality, and attitudes; assessing the affective domain.

The primary characteristics of standardized noncognitive tests are uniform administration and objective scoring. Most of the tests also have normative information that enables a professional counselor to make comparisons between a client and other individuals. With standardized noncognitive group tests, professional counselors can help answer questions such as what are Bill's interests? How does Ruth compare with other women concerning her interest in engineering? Is Tom abnormally aggressive? and Is Alice's concern about others atypical?

Many children and adults have difficulty with age-appropriate behaviors because emotional, interest, or attitude factors interfere with their cognitive functioning. In this regard, standardized noncognitive tests can help ascertain important information that can be of value during counseling. In addition, professional counselors occasionally use standardized noncognitive tests for identifying clients for group counseling (e.g., establishing group counseling for clients who show similar characteristics of high anxiety).

A number of standardized noncognitive instruments are available, making it possible for the professional counselor to assess noncognitive functioning in a variety of ways. However, disadvantages do exist in using group tests in this domain. In comparison to cognitive measures, noncognitive instruments are not well documented concerning their predictive validity; i.e., the ability to foretell what a person's behaviors will be in the future. Also, a client's responses can be affected by the influence of social desirability. Professional counselors need to be sensitive to the fact that most people are unwilling to provide, on paper-and-pencil tests, responses which are presumed to be different from the norm.

Another problem associated with all standardized noncognitive group tests is their susceptibility to client response sets; i.e., the tendency to reply in a particular direction, almost independent of the questions asked. For example, clients may be predisposed to remain in the "middle of the road" if a five-point, agree-disagree continuum is used, or they may have the tendency to select true for true-false items. Other problems with this type of test include (1) a reading level that may be above the client's reading achievement level, making the test beyond his/her ability, (2) a tendency for clients to guess in order to provide a response, and (3) the sacrifice of speed for accuracy, or vice versa.

As imprecise as standardized noncognitive group tests are, they do provide professional counselors with valuable information to use in helping clients. A point must be remembered, however, that while this information is helpful, it certainly is not definitive. In addition, most standardized noncognitive group tests also can be used with an individual. In fact, noncognitive tests are frequently administered to groups, but interpreted on an individual basis.

In summary, knowledge about a client's interests, personality, and attitudes is important in helping a professional counselor to communicate effectively during counseling and with other professionals. However, the use of these tests is not without limitations.

Personality Assessment. Personality assessment can be either a structured or unstructured self-report. Structured personality tests consist of questions that can be interpreted in relatively the same way by all clients. Unstructured personality tests, referred to as projective tests (e.g., Rorschach Inkblots Test), consist of ambiguous pictures or items to which clients respond according to their interpretation of the stimulus.

A variety of structured, self-report personality tests are widely used by professional counselors in numerous ways; the counselor is usually not dependent upon a single personality test. The vast majority of these tests are intended for use with adults. However, some can be administered to elementary- or secondary-school age students if the students' reading ability is adequate. The public appears opposed to the general use of personality tests in schools and therefore they are rarely used in school settings with groups of students. In some instances they may be used with a few select students with whom the professional counselor is doing individual counseling. Perhaps the ones most widely used across age levels are problem checklists and adjustment tests.

Attitude Assessment. Individual behavior is influenced by numerous confounding variables, many of which are extraneous to the person, but affect attitude. As research has demonstrated, individuals' attitudes are related to their behavior; they influence an individual's behavior concerning other people, activities, and objects. For example, if a group of students has an unfavorable attitude toward education, little learning will take place in the classroom. Accordingly, in order to know why Jim is behind in his college assignments and what can be done to help him improve his performance, or to know whether Jim is prejudiced, the professional counselor must develop an understanding of Jim's attitudes.

An important concern is that professional counselors understand that attitudes, which are not directly observable, are inferred from a person's verbal and nonverbal behaviors. To illustrate, prejudice cannot be seen as an object, but it can be observed, over a period of time, in the behavior of someone who is prejudiced.

Attitudes, which are learned, result from socialization and tend to be changeable, particularly with young people. The key to changing an attitude is to have knowledge of its status. This needed information can be gained through assessment using an attitude test or scale. As with all tests, the usefulness of any attitude scale depends upon its reliability, validity, and norms; the ease with which it can be administered and scored; and the meanings that can be derived from the data. However, perhaps more so than any other noncognitive assessment instrument, attitude scales have problems with psychometric properties. Typically, research correlations obtained between scores obtained using an attitude scale and observed behaviors are low. None the less, the information that a professional counselor and client can acquire from the client's performance on attitude tests makes them useful during counseling.

ASSESSMENT WITHIN EMPIRICAL COUNSELING

Empirical counseling, as used in this book, connotes the use of assessment for the purpose of determining goals, strategies, and effectiveness during the counseling process. For professional counselors to make decisions about a client's progress or services is becoming increasingly unpopular unless objective, systematically collected data can be amassed that bear directly upon those decisions. Collecting data at regular intervals during the counseling process provides direct information about the client's progress; the essence of assessment in empirical counseling. The following discussion presents the goals of assessment in empirical counseling; improvement of counseling and accountability.

Improvement of Counseling. Through assessment, the professional can determine whether the counseling procedures being used are producing desired results and can facilitate the revision of unproductive counseling procedures. Accordingly, professional counselors can determine whether they are wasting a client's or their own time on ineffective counseling procedures. If counseling is producing desired results, the professional counselor can with confidence continue with the counseling process.

Accountability. The second reason for professional counselors collecting quantified measures of their clients' progress is to respond to requirements for accountability. Within a school setting, for example, the professional counselor may have to demonstrate to the pupil-personnel director, principal and/or board of education that counseling processes are actually helping students. In student development in higher education, a similar situation exists with the professional counselor needing accountability data for his/her supervisor or the institution's vice-president for student affairs. Or, a business or industry may want to compare several methods of communication-skill training workshops if it is concerned about which method will do the best job. Accountability data for the professional counselor in community or agency settings are needed for insurance companies and third-party payers as well as for supervisors. For example, counselors who want to receive payments from a health organization or insurance company may be required to submit a report after 8, 24, 40, and 60 sessions. The report asks for information about the client's problem, the provider's goals and planned interventions, and an estimate of progress. The latter is related to the specific treatment goals and typically derived from assessment data.

Professional counselors have always had to justify their existence, but now the necessity of establishing indices of progress requires a scientific approach to being accountable.

Assessment Process

The process of assessment during counseling helps the professional counselor know *what* the target problem is, *who* defines it as a problem, *when* and *where* its occurrence is visible and perceived as a problem, and *how* well counseling is progressing.

A self-coaching model for assessment in empirical counseling is presented in Figure 5.1. The components of the model are discussed separately here.

Step 1: Determine the Focus of Counseling. At the beginning of the counseling process, the professional counselor needs to establish a cooperative and mutually respectful relationship with the client. First, the professional counselor verbally and behaviorally conveys that he/she wants to help the client and values the relationship with the client. Next, the professional counselor makes an inventory of the spectrum of concerns as seen by the client, and perhaps by others if the client is seeking help as a result of a referral. However, much of today's counseling will be through self-choice rather than the "medical model" of finding the problem and making a referral to a specialist.

Completion of this phase varies depending on the setting in which the professional counselor is working. For example, if the counselor is in private practice and a physician makes a referral (medical model), the referral will probably describe a specific concern the physician has about the client. The physician has most likely spent time with the client (e.g., perhaps a series of visits over several months), and the client has agreed that assistance is needed. However, the information conveyed by the physician to the professional counselor (i.e., the reason for referral) may not include the particular information necessary for the counselor to be of help to the client. Therefore, the professional counselor, by carefully interviewing and/or assessing the client, can acquire accurate information on the nature of the client's problem.

If the professional counselor is in a school setting, the referral may be a teacher's request for assistance. For example, the teacher might ask the counselor "to help Tammy adjust to the classroom because she's disrupting the other students." Of course, many reasons are possible for Tammy's behavior. The professional counselor's task, in this situation, is to help Tammy while at the same time assist Tammy's teacher. Again, the professional counselor must first identify the spectrum of issues.

STEP 1: DETERMINE THE FOCUS OF COUNSELING—establish a relationship with the client and identify issues and concerns to be addressed during counseling.

> Establish relationship
> Identify spectrum of issues and concerns

STEP 2: CLARIFY THE SITUATION—in cooperation with the client, the professional counselor clarifies the priority of issues and concerns for counseling and the target attributes or specific behaviors needing intervention. This step includes identifying the conditions and circumstances of the target issues and concerns occurrence.

> Narrow list of target issues and concerns
> Determine expected attainment from counseling (goals)
> Gather data on specific issue and concern behaviors

STEP 3: IDENTIFY COUNSELING ACTIVITIES—determine concrete, detailed information on what will be done, how and when it will be done, and duration. Within this step, plans are made for measuring the client's target behavior(s) several times during the counseling process.

> Determine procedures for counseling
> Determine procedures for assessment

STEP 4: INITIATE PLAN—implement Step 3 and derive meaning by analyzing and interpreting data from the assessment. Utilize the results from the data anlysis and, if necessary, make revisions in the counseling process.

Figure 5.1. Self-coaching model of preliminary assessment for empirical counseling.

In contrast to the example of the physician's referral, Tammy's teacher has more than likely spent considerable time with the class and is likely to know much about Tammy and the other students. The teacher.

however, may not be able to convey to the professional counselor the type of information necessary for helping Tammy. The counselor may need to obtain additional information by carefully interviewing the teacher, and exacting specific data concerning Tammy's behaviors.

Step 2: Clarify the Situation. Usually the professional counselor's second step in individual assessment is to focus upon the primary concern(s) of the client. For a professional counselor to be presented with a spectrum of issues and concerns (e.g., inadequate social skills, marital difficulties, and uncertain vocational goals) is not infrequent. At times, establishing multiple goals for counseling is feasible, and measurement of each is necessary. On other occasions, and when possible, several different issues can be rank ordered when they are not of comparable importance to the client. In most situations, the professional counselor is likely to have identified several, if not a host, of target behaviors. Therefore, the counselor may have difficulty determining the priority of help needed and the associated specific, operational goals. This requires determining the priority of target concerns for counseling. Sundel and Sundel (1975) suggested the following general principles as a guide for the professional counselor (and, if possible, the client) when selecting a priority concern.

1. Select the concern with which the client or significant other is immediately concerned.

2. Select the concern which if continued will have the most aversive consequences for the client, significant others, or society thus minimizing the amount of pain inflicted on the client or others.

3. Select the concern with which the client would have immediate success thus providing the client with increased motivation and trust in the professional counselor and the counseling process.

4. Select the concern that needs attention before any other problem can be resolved.

During the clarifying stage of the assessment model, the professional counselor, in cooperation with the client, determines goals and objectives for counseling by gathering information about specific behaviors that the client considers important to the counseling outcome. These behaviors might be to speak-up more frequently in class or to reach a decision about the behavior of one's spouse.

The professional counselor identifies the focus of counseling within the larger situational context of its occurrence. To return to Tammy, the professional counselor would specify other elements related to her target concern(s). This might involve, but not be limited to, spending a period of time in Tammy's classroom to observe her reactions to the academic material, the teacher, and other children; her behavior when assignments are made; and her responses and/or reactions when called upon. Also, the counselor wants to obtain detailed information on the methods that *have been* tried by the teacher to help Tammy adjust to the classroom. In addition, the counselor may decide that more information is necessary from other significant people in Tammy's life, such as the school nurse, personnel director, and parents. Again, the professional counselor, through careful interviewing, can provide information, in exact detail, concerning which of Tammy's behaviors are of concern and what has taken place. The professional counselor is interested in the *who* and *where* of the target concern.

Finally in Step 2, the professional counselor gathers data about specific behaviors. In all cases, specific and concrete information needs to be obtained.

Step 3: Identify Counseling Activities. In Step 3 of the self-coaching model, the professional counselor describes in some detail the procedures to be used when working with a client (i.e., develops a counseling plan). Needed is information on what is to be done, how it will be done, and when it will be done (i.e., timing and duration). Basically, the components of the counseling process that the counselor has reason to believe are important to the counseling outcome need to be determined. Only when counseling procedures are planned are they modified or adapted to a new situation. Identifying counseling activities is necessary and important if the counselor is to improve counseling procedures and to help others.

Step 4: Initiate Plan. The professional counselor next begins to implement the activities in Step 3. Through an analysis of data, meaning is derived for the purposes of evaluating the client's progress and, if necessary, making revisions in the counseling process.

By being able to collect data early in the counseling process, the professional counselor is able to develop a substantial baseline for viewing progress. Baseline refers to measures of the specific behavior prior to, or at the beginning of, counseling. An attempt should be made, initially, to collect data on as large a number of measures of a client's behavior(s) as possible. As counseling proceeds, non-important or unhelpful measures can be abandoned and helpful measures retained.

ASSESSMENT GUIDELINES WITHIN EMPIRICAL COUNSELING

The following guidelines assist the professional counselor in using assessment within empirical counseling.

State the Target Concern
Using Precise Wording

Target problems of each individual client should be defined operationally in ways that make them as concrete and as observable as possible. Ambiguity must be avoided by being certain that every word used means exactly what it is intended to mean, and reflects experience(s) or actual events. For example, clients will often conceptualize issues in global terms, including psychological constructs such as depression or improved self-concept, rather than actual events. However, concerns should be defined as a series of behavioral indicators. When a client is concerned about his/her being depressed, being depressed would be defined by behaviors such as seeing friends infrequently, not leaving home, rarely smiling, and crying frequently. Accordingly, the professional counselor helps the client conceptualize the presenting situation (i.e., depression) as observable and reportable events. Concreteness is directly related to observable events that are assessable. This type of specification also results in counseling goals that are more assessable.

The following activities to be used during intake sessions have been suggested by Barlow, Hayes, and Nelson (1984) to help define goals in concrete terms.

Acceptable Evidence. The professional counselor asks the client "what would be acceptable evidence of having attained the desired goal?'' For example, returning to the earlier global problem of depression, acceptable evidence of improvement might include being able to leave home, visiting friends more frequently, and crying less often.

Three wishes. A second question to help define a global concern in specific terms is to ask the client "if any three wishes could be granted, what would they be?" As an illustration, a client who complained of being depressed might wish that he/she could spend more time with friends, join a sports club, or cry less often.

Typical Day or Week. Asking clients what they view to be a typical day or week helps to specify current issues. The concerns can be further highlighted by asking the client to describe an ideal typical day or week. The contrast between current behavior and ideal situation helps the counselor to establish targets for counseling. With the client whose self description is one of feeling worthless, for example, an ideal typical week might include being able to speak to his/her supervisor without a faltering voice and to reduce the number of self-defacing statements about his/her work.

Use Observation

The virtue of observation is that the professional counselor is able to assess information *in vivo* and to obtain data on behaviors that may have been overlooked or overemphasized during an interview. In certain settings such as schools, correctional facilities, businesses, industries, or college and university residential life facilities, many kinds of observations can be made, ranging from the informal (i.e., mentally noting what is happening during a period of time) to the more formal use of scales in which behaviors are precisely categorized and described by a counting procedure. Not all observations necessarily need to be completed by the professional counselor. A short training period can enable persons such as teacher aides, supervisors, or residence-hall assistants to accurately observe and record behaviors.

The "power" of observation is the potential for objectivity when done by a trained observer. An untrained observer is likely to overlook certain behaviors and/or overemphasize others. This is especially true for people particularly close to or involved with the client, as would be the situation if parents or other untrained persons were recounting (from memory) their observations. Many parents view their childrens' behaviors as cute or as special family attributes rather than in the context of how well their child functions in a particular social situation.

Observer training and counselor-prepared checklists are valuable tools for precise identification of those behaviors important to counseling. Although several methods exist by which behaviors may be measured and recorded, the following are more frequently used.

Anecdotal Records. These are written descriptions of everything the observer sees. The advantage of this procedure is that the observer obtains an overview of the client's behavior. Unfortunately, to be done well, an anecdotal record requires continuous observation over an extended period of time.

Measurement of Prior Data. This works well in agency and institutional settings where keeping records is standard protocol. In school settings, grade books, attendance records, tardy notifications, and student's academic work grades can be used. Statements of rule violations and levels of production are sources for measurement in correctional facilities.

Event Recording or Frequency Counting. This is the calculation of the number of occurrences of one or more specific behaviors during a time interval (e.g., half-hour, day, or week.) This procedure works well for behaviors that have definable beginnings and endings. Counselors may have clients do event recordings of the client's target behaviors using wrist counters or other mechanical counters.

Measurement of duration, as a procedure, is helpful in recording behaviors that may occur infrequently but last a long time. In this method, the observer measures the length of time of a given event or behavior.

Checklist and Behavior Rating Scales. These are helpful because they provide descriptions of the behaviors to be observed. They can be either commercially developed instruments available from a variety of different companies, agencies, or institutions or they can be developed specifically for the client.

Interval Recording and Time Sampling. These are effective procedures for many behaviors. With interval recording, the observer decides upon a specific time period and divides it into equal units, such as three-minute segments. The observer then records whether or not the behavior(s) of interest occurred during a given unit. With time sampling, equal unit intervals are used, but observation is made at the end of each interval and the observer records whether the behavior(s) of interest is being exhibited at the moment of observation. Tabulation is done by counting the number of intervals during which (for interval recording) or at the end of which (for time sampling) the behavior occurred, and dividing that sum by the total number of observation units to obtain the percentage of time the behavior(s) occurred.

Obtain Several Measures for
Each Target Area and Goal

Obtaining multiple measures for each target area and, consequently, each counseling goal is helpful for counselors. Multiple measurement provides the counselor with a more accurate estimate of the true measure of a client's concern (Barlow, Hayes, & Nelson, 1984). Several factors contribute to the absence of a true measure. One affect can be attributed to method variance, or the production of different results because different methods of measurement were employed (e.g., observation, self-ratings, and questionnaires). Another factor is the variation in content measured by different instruments. For example, data derived from observations of a client's social skills in a public gathering are different from data gathered through a self-report method whereby the client rates personal feelings during the public gathering. Because of the inconsistency among different measures of the same target behavior or counseling goal, using multiple measurement makes more sense. The counselor who uses several measures will achieve a convergence of data and therefore a more accurate estimate of the client's true progress.

Choose Measures That are
Sensitive and Meaningful

Measures of client behavior can vary by the degree to which they are sensitive and meaningful. To assess therapeutic changes during weekly counseling sessions, sensitive, meaningful, and precise measures are needed. Consider Robert, a very shy person who has sought counseling to help reduce his retiring behavior. One means of assessing Robert's progress during the counseling process would be to record eye contact during role-playing sessions. However, while this would provide a precise measure, the counselor cannot be certain that eye contact is related to shyness. Robert might show weekly improvements in eye contact, but his overall shyness could remain unchanged. Therefore, relying on sensitive measures only for assessing improvement will not necessarily provide meaningful data. This phenomenon involves construct validity. To avoid the problem of weak construct validity, the counselor also would use other criterion measures of the client's improvement; measures that will be more meaningful but perhaps less precise.

Meaningful measures tend to be more global and as a consequence are not as sensitive to gradual change during counseling. A meaningful measure in Robert's situation might be to have his family or friends rate his shyness on a one-to-five rating scale each week. Although this form of assessment would have construct validity and would closely relate to the shyness, it would be insensitive to small increments of progress. The best course of action for the professional counselor would be to use both types of measures to assure precision or sensitivity and meaningfulness.

An example that illustrates the necessity for both meaningful and sensitive measures as well as the use of standardized tests to measure progress is Ruth, a child referred to the professional counselor for underachievement. (In most school settings, the professional counselor spends a substantial portion of time working with students like Ruth.) One possibility is for the professional counselor to use the *Wide Range Achievement Test* as a meaningful global measure, but the test is insensitive to small, gradual changes. An alternative would be to administer the test two or three times a year (e.g. at the beginning, middle, and end of the counseling program) and to more frequently use sensitive measures such as performance on homework and in-class assignments, class participation, and in-class quizzes.

The virtue of using both sensitive and meaningful measures can be further illustrated by considering a client who is not functioning well at a job because of emotional factors which interfere with cognitive functioning. Of concern are sensitive and meaningful measures that can be used by the professional counselor to assess affective factors. A number of techniques are available, thereby permitting professional counselors to assess personality in a variety of ways depending on their training and counseling orientation. A commonly used global measure would be the *Minnesota Multiphasic Personality Inventory* (MMPI). Although the *MMPI* has strong construct validity (i.e., if scores improve notably on the *MMPI* , the belief is that the client's affective state is improved), it may be insensitive to gradual changes. Also, because some reservations exist about the appropriateness of professional counselors assessing personality, many counselors have given little attention to using the *MMPI*. Other global measures that could be employed are the *California Personality Inventory (CPI)* or the *Myers-Briggs Type Indicator (MBTI)*, but again, these may be insensitive to gradual improvement during counseling. To compensate for this weakness, more sensitive measures could be used in conjunction with the above-mentioned global measures as indicators of gradual improvement. Included among these measures are a client's questionnaire responses, work completed on the job, and number of irritable responses made when working.

Both sensitive and standardized global measures have their advantages and disadvantages. In general, standardized global measures generally have good construct validity and normative reference points, while sensitive measures generally are more reflective of gradual changes during counseling, but have poor construct validity.

Collect Measures at the Beginning of Counseling

Professional counselors can frequently determine or develop a reasonable hypothesis about a client's behavior(s) during the intake interview or during Step 1 of the assessment process. If sufficient information is available, the professional counselor and the client can immediately begin to collect measures of behavior. However, additional information is needed before developing a hypothesis. Consider Norman, who is having trouble relating to a female friend for whom he cares. Situations arise when he is with her that tend to arouse old angers and resentments he has about distrusting women. When this happens, he automatically tries to "squash" the feeling, resulting sometimes in strong reactions of guilt and anxiety. He believes his behavior is wrong or inappropriate, but he is not sure why. Likewise, he is anxious about why he feels the way he does. The latter may be the basis for his inability to "sit still," to complete routine duties on his job, and to sleep at night. As an assessment measure, the professional counselor may arrange for Norman to maintain a weekly log for a week, recording sleeping and waking times, duties completed at work, and a daily rating of his ability to behave calmly (i.e., "sit still").

Repeat the Same Measures
During and After Counseling

Another counseling aid is the collection of the same data during and after counseling using the same measures that were employed early in the counseling process. The beginning counselor might believe that measures taken at the beginning and the conclusion of counseling are adequate for assessing improvement. The resulting pre-post measures of client change are better than no measures, but not as helpful as continuous or repeated assessments. Repeated measures have the added benefit of possible use as feedback during counseling. Thus, the professional counselor can acquire on-going information on behavior changes as well as data for determining whether the planned approach to counseling needs to be continued or altered. Also, as a result of continuous measurement, additional effects which might be contributing to the client's problem can be assessed.

As a means of illustration, the results of the record keeping undertaken by Norman (i.e., sleeping and waking times, duties completed at work, and daily ratings of his ability to remain calm), form a history of Norman's progress. What could become apparent is that Norman's condition appears worse on some days than it does on others. In this situation, the professional counselor could explore the factors that make these times more difficult for Norman. Identifying specific events would then provide suggestions for more helpful counseling.

Record Conditions When
Assessments are Made

Ideally, the professional counselor needs to obtain assessments under similar conditions if accurate comparisons are to be made across measurements. The underlying assumption is that behavior tends to be associated with or influenced by the situation in which it occurs (e.g., the number of people present and the location). The more situations vary when assessments are being made, the more unreliable will be the comparison of the behavior being examined.

An important matter is that the conditions under which a behavior is being measured be as similar as possible for each assessment. When variations occur, they should be noted so their influence on the behavior being measured can be defined. By minimizing the situational variation in the context for assessment, a more accurate and comparable measurement is obtained.

Record Convenient Measures

Assessment of any behavior is influenced by a number of factors, e.g., time, cost, and convenience of assessment, and appropriateness of the measure. Earlier in this chapter, a recommendation was made that a number of measures be taken of a client's behavior(s) in order to obtain a more valid appraisal of changes in behavior and to enable the merging of information about aspects of the client's situation. The professional counselor also needs to consider data derived from a variety of measures because no one "true" measure of a behavior exists. However, obtaining all measures with the same frequency is not necessary. Measures that are inconvenient to obtain because they are costly, obtrusive, or require an extensive amount of time (i.e., trained observers in naturalistic settings, video taping client behavior, selected psychological measures, and selected standardized tests) may be taken less frequently than more convenient measures which are unobtrusive, easily completed, or low in cost (e.g., self-rating forms, daily or weekly logs, and checklists). However, remember that taking inconvenient measures infrequently rather than not at all is advantageous since the measures will provide another informational dimension about a client's progress.

Derive Meaning

Data analysis is necessary in order to derive meaning from assessment. One means of analyzing data is to chart the measures of a client's behaviors (see Figure 5.2). Graphing data is convenient and provides the professional counselor as well as the client with a visual analysis of the client's progress. An analysis of the charted data not only aids in determing whether the counseling procedures being used are effective, but it also serves as a helpful counseling technique during the counseling process.

Figure 5.2 illustrates the charting of a client's behavior over a period of five weeks. Time, from baseline through treatment and follow-up, is usually entered on the abscissa (horizontal line). The measurement illustrated in Figure 5.2 was conducted on a daily basis, but it could have

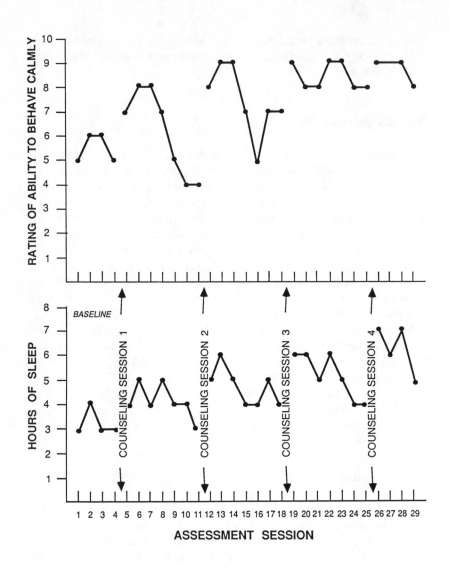

Figure 5.2. Chart of a client's behavior over a period of five weeks.

been undertaken on a weekly basis or any other meaningful unit of time. The measure is indexed on the ordinate (vertical line) and needs to be appropriate to the data being gathered. If a self-rating scale is being used, a simple counting of the numerical responses could serve as the score and therefore, the ordinate would be indexed by arithmetic numerals. If a rating scale is used, the number of positive responses could yield a score. To index the ordinate with positive rather than negative attributes is important (e.g., number of times a client avoided a problem rather than the number of times the client had a problem).

If, as suggested, several measures are obtained for a client, including them on the same graph is desirable. The same abscissa could be used, even if some entries are weekly measures and others are daily. However, if the scaling unit varies from measure to measure, different ordinates are necessary. Also helpful is including any significant events that might occur during counseling sessions. Recording all measures and events on the same graph enables the counselor to view whether the recordings relate or vary in any noticeable pattern.

SUMMARY

In this book, assessment is synonymous with standardized testing; the means of exposing a person to an established set of questions for the purpose of obtaining a score. Assessment also may be part of the larger process known as empirical counseling. However, the latter involves much more than just the administration of tests. When professional counselors assess clients during empirical counseling, they consider (1) the way their client performs in and reacts to a variety of tasks in a variety of settings or contexts, (2) the meaning of a client's performances in view of the total functioning of the client, and (3) possible explanations for the client's performances during counseling.

Although clients can be assessed *ad infinitum,* increased emphasis has been on the study of observable, operationally defined behavior and a decrease in emphasis on unobservable thoughts, motives, drives, traits, and general functioning as measured through assessment. Mental health practitioners, who have been required to defend their activities when working with individual clients, have had considerable difficulty defending the psychometric adequacy of using normative measures to assess some hypothetical norm, and the relevance of the information provided by the instruments. Professional counselors must work with clients using standardized and empirical assessment approaches concurrently. They must take into consideration assessment data designed to discover general laws or rules that apply to people in general (i.e., nomothetic data), and they must attempt to obtain information about particular event(s) and respective conditions (i.e., idiographic data).

Assessment is helpful because it enables the professional counselor to plan counseling and to assist the client. But an assessment procedure should be selected on the basis of its appropriateness for counseling with a particular client. Initially, the professional counselor's selection of assessment methods will be guided by the type and intensity of counseling to be provided. The underlying theme of this chapter is that better quality counseling is provided when assessment information is utilized than when no assessment information is employed. The professional counselor can use a wide variety of assessment approaches within both conventional and empirical counseling, as long as the selection is suitable for helping clients realize thier respective goals.

Chapter **6**

CAREER DEVELOPMENT AND COUNSELING

All animal species on earth engage in "work." In the so-called lower order animal species, work is almost exclusively associated with the gathering and/or cultivation of food and the development and maintenance of protective habitats. Work in those contexts is physiologically and biologically necessary for the continued existence of the respective species. The same is of course true for human beings; they must "work" to have the food and shelter necessary for continued life. However, with humans, an additional psychosocial dynamic is associated with work. Among people in most societies of the world, work has value and meaning beyond fulfillment of subsistence needs; it has potential to fulfill psychological and social needs as well. Concern about and attention to this uniquely human psychosocial aspect of work are the bases of large portions of human social, economic, political, educational, and legal systems. Particularly pertinent here is that these needs are also the basis for a large portion of mental health. That is, for most people in most societies, the nature of a person's "work" is integrally related to what the person *is*.

Attention to work as an important part of the human experience not only spurred the beginning of the counseling profession as discussed in Chapter 2, but also remains a major focus in counseling. The historical antecedents within the counseling profession, in combination with preeminent values attributed to work in contemporary society, have prompted counseling theorists, researchers, and practitioners to explore thoroughly the nature of work, its roles and functions in the human condition, and most importantly, ways for people to find and attain the work that is best-suited to and most satisfying for them. Moreover, these activities are likely to continue. For example, Gysbers (1984) has identified four major relevant trends. Summarized, they are as follows:

1. The meanings given to career and career development continue to evolve from simply new words for vocation (occupation) and vocational development (occupational development) to words that describe the human career in terms of life roles, life settings, and life events that develop over the life span.

2. Substantial changes have taken place and will continue to occur in the economic, occupational, industrial, and social environments and structures in which the human career develops and interacts, and in which career guidance and counseling takes place.

3. The number, diversity, and quality of career development programs, tools, and techniques continue to increase almost in geometric progression.

4. The populations served by career development programming, and the settings in which career development programs and services take place, have increased greatly and will continue to do so.

One of the by-products of the attention given to work and its place in the human condition has been the generation of a subset vocabulary within the counseling profession. Therefore, some of these terms must be clarified before the career development and counseling activities of professional counselors can be discussed further.

The world of work may be configured along a system of levels. For example, a *job* (used here as synonomous with *position* or *placement*) is a set of identifiable and specific functions which a person is paid to perform. Because essentially similar jobs are performed by different people in different settings, an *occupation* (used here as synonomous with *vocation*) has been defined as "a group of similar jobs found in different industries or organizations" (Herr & Cramer, 1984, p. 15). Relatedly, because individuals usually have more than one occupation in the course of their lives, the term *career* has been defined as "the sequence of occupations in which one engages" (Tolbert, 1974). Some, however, have viewed the definition of career as "a series of occupations" as too restrictive and therefore have broadened the definition. For example, Zunker (1981) stated that, "*Career* is not only used to indicate the activities and positions involved in vocations, occupations, and jobs, but also includes related activities associated with an individual's lifetime of work" (p. 3). Similarly, Super (1976) defined the concept of career as

> The course of events which constitutes a life; the sequence of occupations and other life roles which combine to express one's commitment to work in his or her total pattern of self-development; the series of remunerated and nonremunerated positions occupied by a person from adolescence through retirement, of which occupation is only one; includes work-related roles such as those of student, employee, and pensioner together with complementary avocational, familial, and civic roles. (p. 4)

Super's definition of career is noteworthy in several regards. For one, it suggests the centrality of work in people's lives and therefore reflects values typically held in society. For another, it conveys the diversity and complexity among the many life factors associated with work. One of the factors which has recently received more attention is leisure. Herr and Cramer (1984), citing Super (1976), used the term *avocational* (in place of leisure) to refer to "an activity pursued systematically and consecutively for its own sake with an objective other than monetary gain, although it may incidentally result in gain" (p. 15). The term "*a*vocational" also reflects the centrality of work in peoples' lives and therefore has been favored by some career development theorists. However, some authors more recently have proposed that leisure exists apart from work and, therefore, that the term leisure is preferable over avocational (Bloland & Edwards, 1981). This perspective is reflected in not-related-to-work definitions of *leisure,* such as one by Loesch and Wheeler (1982) who defined it as, "Any activity an individual knowingly (i.e., consciously) chooses to define as leisure" (p. 36) or one by Neulinger (1974) who stated that "any activity carried out freely, without constraint or compulsion, may be considered to be leisure" (p. 15). In any event, regardless of the term used, leisure is now viewed as an integral component of the term career (McDaniels, 1984).

In attempting to help people achieve the jobs, occupations, and careers for which they are best suited and which will be most meaningful for them, professional counselors are concerned with facilitating individuals' *career development* (used here as synonomous with *occupational* or *vocational* development). Herr and Cramer (1984) defined career development as "the total constellation of psychological, sociological, educational, physical, economic, and chance factors that combine to shape the career of any given individual..." (p. 14). Similarly, Tolbert (1974) defined career development as "the lifelong process of developing work values, crystallizing a vocational identity, learning about opportunities, and trying out plans in part time, recreational, and full time work situations" (p. 25). Professional counselors' career development facilitation activities primarily consist of fostering the development of one major characteristic or trait (i.e., career maturity), and two major skills (i.e., decision making and career management) in their clients. The characteristic, *career maturity,* may be viewed as a developmental, multidimensional construct. Super (1957) has presented a widely accepted set of components of career maturity which includes orientation toward work (attitudinal dimension), planning (competency dimension), consistency of vocational preferences (consistency dimension), and wisdom of vocational preferences (realistic dimension). The first skill area, *decision making,* has been defined as "a systematic process in which various data are utilized and analyzed according to explicit procedures and outcomes are evaluated in terms of desirability" (Tolbert, 1974, p. 27). The second skill area, *career management,* was defined by Herr and Cramer (1984) as, "The personal state of actively and consciously participating in shaping one's career and accepting responsibility for the activities and choices made toward those ends" (p. 15). Taken collectively, the greater the extent to which an individual develops this characteristic and these skills, the greater the likelihood will be that the individual will achieve an appropriate and satisfying career.

Several terms have been used to provide descriptions of professional counselors' career development facilititation activities. The broadest term used is *career guidance,* which was defined by Herr and Cramer (1984) as "A systematic program of counselor-coordinated information and experiences designed to facilitate individual career development and, more specifically, career management..." (p. 15). Similarly, Tolbert (1974) stated that career guidance, "encompasses all of the services that aim at helping [individuals] make occupational and educational plans and decisions" (p. 27). The general set of activities which fall under the rubric of career guidance is typically subdivided into the categories *career education* and *career counseling.* Career education involves integrating career development concepts and activities into educational curricula.

Typically, the primary purpose and focus of career education is the organized and systematic provision of information about various aspects of the world of work so that individuals can make "informed" and therefore, theoretically, "intelligent" job, occupation, and career choices. Career counseling also often includes the provision of information, but extends beyond career education in the attempt to help individuals use and act upon the information provided. For example, Healy (1982) stated that:

> Career counseling is specialized counseling focused on career implementation and planning. The career counselor helps a client to generate and use personal and career information, to obtain and to interpret experiences relevant to careers, to set goals and to solve problems, and to evaluate progress. (p. 173)

Both career education and career counseling will be discussed at greater length later in this chapter. However, before either of them can be fully understood, the major theoretical perspectives on career development used in the counseling profession must be addressed.

THEORIES OF CAREER DEVELOPMENT AND COUNSELING

Herr (1986) has aptly summarized the purposes of, and alluded to the diversities among, theories of career development:

> The theory and speculation encompassed by the term career development (used interchangeably with the earlier term vocational development) includes a variety of emphases and approaches. In general, these approaches attempt to describe why career behavior is different among individuals, how it comes to be that way, and the importance of such behavior in people's lives. (p. 175)

Other authors (e.g., Osipow, 1983; Whiteley & Resnikoff, 1978) generally agree with the purposes stated by Herr. However, perspectives on such theories vary considerably. For example, Herr (1986) described six different systems just for *classifying* theories of career development. All of these systems appear to have their respective merits and limitations and therefore, a selection is primarily a matter of preference. The one of choice here is the five-category system presented by Herr and Cramer (1984).

Trait-and-Factor or Matching Approach

Osipow (1983) presented a simplified and historical perspective on this approach to career counseling when he wrote that:

> The oldest theoretical approach has been known by a variety of names, most commonly by the name of the trait-and-factor approach. This system assumes that a straightforward matching of an individual's abilities and interests with the world's vocational opportunities can be accomplished and once accomplished, solves the problems of vocational choice for that individual. (p. 9)

Attributed initially to Williamson (1939), the basic purpose of the trait-and-factor approach to career counseling is to "match" the characteristics of a client to jobs which require those characteristics, and in so doing identify the jobs which are, theoretically, most appropriate for that client. The "trait" portion of the trait-and-factor approach refers to client characteristics; in order to use this approach effectively, counselors must have extensive and valid information about their clients' characteristics. The "factor" portion refers to characteristics of various jobs; in order to use this approach effectively counselors also must have extensive knowledge of the world of work and the requirements for specific jobs. Accordingly, trait-and-factor career counseling has been referred to colloquially as the "know the client, know the job" approach.

A significant question within this approach is what information about clients needs to be known by professional counselors? Herr and Cramer (1984) have identified ten major types of information usually sought by professional counselors, paraphrased here as follows:

1. *Abilities*—clients' general intelligence and specific aptitudes. Cognitive abilities are important to the types of work clients are able to perform, the education and/or training for which they are eligible and in which they are likely to succeed, and their potential levels of success and attainment in various occupations.

2. *Needs and Interests*—clients' psychological needs and vocational interests. Psychological needs are important in that appropriate work must fulfill some, and probably many, of clients' needs. Similarly, clients are not likely to find their work attractive, enjoyable, and satisfying if their jobs are not consistent with their vocational interests.

3. *Stereotypes and Expectations*—clients' perceptions of the natures of particular jobs and occupations. Clients often act upon stereotypic perceptions and expectations about jobs regardless of the accuracy of their perceptions and expectations (unless presented with information which "corrects" their perceptions and expectations).

4. *Significant Others*—people in clients' lives who are viewed as important and valued and/or who serve as role models. Clients' significant others potentially have strong influences on clients' training, occupational choices, and career aspirations.

5. *Values*—clients' internalized beliefs about the worth of various aspects of life in general, and work in particular. Clients' values also are potentially strong influences on their occupational choices and aspirations.

6. *Residence*—clients' living situations and lifestyles. The realm of clients' environments, lifestyles, and experiences in part determines their educational and occupational possibilities and their perceptions of the world of work.

7. *Family*—persons perceived as closely related to a client. Family members typically exert strong influences on clients' values, lifestyles, experiences, and personal characteristics, and therefore on the courses of their careers.

8. *Adjustment*—clients' levels of adaptation in the world. Clients who are not personally well-adjusted in the world are not able to make effective work-related decisions or to perform occupational activities effectively.

9. *Risk-taking*—clients' abilities and desires to engage in probabilistic decision-making. Clients' risk-taking abilities are influential in determining career opportunities potentially available to them.

10. *Aspirations*—clients' vocational and personal goals. Aspirations are viewed as primary determinants of clients' achievement and success motivations.

This list is extensive, but not exhaustive. However, it does illustrate the comprehensiveness of the information which is sought about clients within this approach.

In order to obtain efficiently and effectively the desired comprehensive information about clients, professional counselors using the trait-and-factor approach to career counseling use tests and inventories extensively. Historically, the relatively early development of trait-and-factor career counseling was a primary impetus for the development and use of tests throughout the counseling profession. The tests and inventories that have been developed are typically subdivided into five general categories: intelligence, aptitude, achievement, personality, and interest. "Purist" trait-and-factor career counselors use tests or inventories from each of these categories in their career counseling activities. More typically, however, professional counselors following this approach only use tests or inventories to obtain information which cannot be obtained expeditiously from other sources (e.g., the client, academic or employment records, or counselor observation).

A second significant question within this approach is what information about jobs needs to be known by counselors? Responses to this question have resulted in a plethora of job/occupation/career information systems and of activities related to the use of the systems, some of which will be discussed later in this chapter. In general, these systems at least provide information on the activities specific to a job, preparation and/or training necessary for entry to the job, the "nature" of the work involved (e.g., levels of involvement with data, people, or things), and future trends and possibilities in the career of which the job is a part. More sophisticated systems also provide information about characteristics and abilities of people who have been successful in and are satisfied with the job and suggest methods for determining suitablility for the job. Brayfield (1950) proposed that occupational information is used to fulfill three functions within the context of trait-and-factor career counseling: (1) *informational,* wherein the client has accurate information from which to make informed decisions, (2) *readjustive,* wherein the client's perceptions and understandings are aligned with the "realities" of the world of work, and (3) *motivational,* wherein the client seeks a job which has the greatest potential to be meaningful and satisfying. Thus, the provision of occupational information within the context of trait-and-factor career counseling is viewed as essential not only to the client's understanding of the world of work, but also to the counseling process itself.

The trait-and-factor approach to career counseling in the manner proposed by Williamson, Brayfield, and others, is not widely used today primarily because of increasing complexities in understanding both people and jobs, as well as the nature of society. When Williamson originally presented his propositions for trait-and-factor career counseling, considerably fewer jobs were available, the jobs themselves were less complex, and people's choices were limited. In general, "life was simpler" then. Today, the world of work is exceedingly complex, people's life-styles and vocational opportunities are vast, and understanding people is complicated by the many factors which need to be considered. Thus, the possibility of effectively "matching" a client to a job on the basis of knowledge of the person and knowledge of the job is now considerably more remote. None the less, the trait-and-factor approach to career counseling is significant because many of its basic tenents are evident in other approaches to career development and counseling.

Decision Approaches

In sharp contrast to the trait-and-factor approach, decision approaches to career development, and counseling toward that end, focus much more on the *process* of how work-related decisions are made. The major supposition in these approaches is that people will have effective career development if they are able to make decisions effectively. Two fundamental assumptions underly this supposition. The first is that people strive to *maximize gains* and *minimize losses* through the work-related decisions they make. In this context, "gains and losses" are not necessarily monetary; they may be in terms of life-style, success, prestige, happiness, security, or any of a variety of other psychosocial and environmental factors or conditions. The second assumption is that at any choice-point, people have several alternatives available to them. One alternative is, of course, to "do nothing." Another is to "do something," and this assumption holds that several "somethings" always can be done. In a broad sense, then, the purposes of decision approaches to career counseling are to help people to (1) identify choice-points and choice options and (2) enhance people's decision-making skills and abilities.

Herr (1986) noted that three major personal factors are relative to an individual's decision-making behaviors. The first is *risk-taking style;* the degree to which an individual is willing to live with ambiguity and uncertainty of outcomes. The second is *investment;* the monetary and/or psychosocial "capital" the person uses to either create a choice or enhance the probability of the success of a choice. The third is *personal values;* the things, ideas, and perspectives the individual identifies as having personal worth. Each of these factors need to be considered individually and collectively in order for individuals to make work-related decisions effectively (Herr & Cramer, 1984).

Two major theoretical perspsectives underly decision approaches. The first is *expectancy theory,* which has as its basic premise that "motivational force" is a product of "expectancy" multiplied by "value." Any specific decision-making event involves consideration of a combination of the individual's perception of personal capability to achieve the potential outcome and the value the individual attributes to the outcome. Thus, expectancy theory holds that a person makes a decision toward an outcome the person believes can be achieved and which the person values. Career counseling based on this theory therefore incorporates, in part, clarification of the client's (typically self-perceived) capabilities and values.

The second major perspective is *self-efficacy theory.* Bandura (1977) proposed that an individual makes decisions primarily on the basis of the belief that a specific behavior can be performed; that is, that the individual can be self-efficacious. The level and strength of the person's belief determine whether a specific behavior will be initiated as well as the amount and duration of effort that will be expended in the behavior. Expectations about behavioral self-efficacy are derived from four sources: personal accomplishments, vicarious experiences, emotional arousal, and verbal persuasion. Thus, career counseling using this theory incorporates examination of the client's previous experiences and feelings about various aspects of work.

A considerable number of "decision-making paradigms" presented for use in the context of career counseling have been developed from these two theoretical perspectives, and most of them approximate conceptualizations of "scientific analysis." For example, Bergland (1974) stated that career-related decision making involves (1) defining the problem, (2) generating alternatives, (3) gathering information, (4) processing information, (5) identifying goals and making plans, and (6) implementing and evaluating activities. Relatedly, Pitz and Harren (1980) stated that any decision problem can be examined in terms of four sets of elements: *objectives* sought, available *choices,* possible *outcomes,* and *attributes* of the outcomes.

Gelatt (1962) proposed a decision-making paradigm for career counseling which contains three major components: *prediction* system, *value* system, and *decision* system. Accurate and timely information is essential for Gelatt's approach (Osipow, 1983). For example, the prediction system requires information about choice alternatives, possible outcomes and their associated probabilities; the valuing system requires information about relative strengths of preferences; and the decision system requires information about rules used in decision-making processes. An interesting formulation within Gelatt's approach is that decisions made can be viewed (by the client) as either final (i.e., terminal) or investigatory (i.e., allowing for decisions to be made so that additional information can be obtained upon which to make subsequent and presumably final decisions). Used within career counseling, Gelatt's paradigm represents a highly cognitive approach because of the focus on cognitive information. However, the approach allows for, and in fact typically includes, the use of both objective and subjective information.

Kalder and Zytowski (1969) also have proposed a three component model for a decision-making approach to career counseling. The first component, *inputs,* consists of elements such as personal resources, intellectual and physical characteristics, time, and monetary and other types of "capital." The second component, *alternatives,* consists of possible actions at choice points. The third component, *outputs,* consists of probable consequences of actions taken. Decision making in this model necessitates "scaling," or assigning relative weights to the various possibilities. That is, the alternative which theoretically should be selected is the one in which input "costs" and output "gains" are reasonably balanced. Implicit in this model is the assumption that the person making the decision has sufficient and valid objective and subjective information with which to do scaling (Herr & Cramer, 1984).

Krumboltz, Mitchell, and Jones (1978) presented an approach to career counseling based on social learning theory. They suggested that four sets of factors are most influential in work-related decision-making: (1) *genetic endowment and special abilities,* including gender, ethnicity, physical limitations, intelligence, and specific aptitudes; (2) *environmental conditions and events,* including job and training opportunities, social policies, labor market conditions, and technological events; (3) *learning experiences,* including instrumental learning (e.g., experiential learning, participation in formal educational experiences) and associative learning (e.g., observational learning, vicarious learning); and (4) *task approach skills,* including work habits, mental sets, perceptual and cognitive processes, and personal performance standards and values.

They also suggested that three categories of outcomes are possible from the interaction(s) of the four types of influencing factors: (1) *self-observation generalizations,* including evaluation of similarities and differences between self and others; (2) *task approach skills,* including cognitive and performance abilities and predispositions for coping with future environments and conditions; and (3) *actions,* including overt and covert movements toward progression in a career. Career counseling under this theory is comprehensive because it encompasses wide-spread information gathering and extensive analysis of information obtained.

Sociological Approaches

Sociological, sometimes called situational, approaches to career development and counseling evolved from the belief that other approaches placed too little emphasis on the context in which career development takes place. Herr (1986) stated that

> Situational or sociological approaches to career development accentuate the reality that one's environment both provides the kinds of choices from which one can choose and also shapes the likelihood that persons holding membership in different groups are likely to make certain choices and not others. A sociological or situational view of career development suggests that the narrowness or the breadth of the individual's cultural or social class boundaries has much to do with the choices the person is likely to consider, make, or implement. (p. 182)

Relatedly, Osipow (1983) observed that

> The sociological approach is fundamentally based on the notion that elements beyond the individual's control exert a major influence on the course of life, including educational and vocational decisions. Supporters of this view suggest that the degree of freedom of occupational choice a person has is far less than might at first be assumed and that one's self-expectations are not independent of the society's expectations. (p. 225)

Given that sociological and/or situational factors influence individuals' career developments, the question becomes which factors are most important and therefore merit the most attention? Unfortunately, a simple answer to this question is unavailable, and in fact, a multitude of factors have been suggested as being important. However, only a few of them can be briefly discussed here.

Culture and social class boundaries have been identified as major, usually restricting, factors in career development (Fredrickson, 1982). In general, although career progression is generally viewed as a primary means to "rise above one's station in life," such progression is not easily achieved, particularly for those in the lower socioeconomic strata (Osipow, 1983). The extant conditions in those strata often inhibit and obstruct career upward mobility because of limited economic and other resources, deemphasis on education and training, conflicting values, and lack of role models.

Chance encounters also have been viewed as significant factors in career development. Bandura (1982) described two major classifications of chance encounters in this regard. The first includes an individual's chance encounters with people who directly or indirectly exert strong subsequent influence on the individual's career-related decisions. The second is chance encounters with events; those happenings to which an individual is "accidently" exposed which also subsequently influence the individual's career-related decisions. Chance encounters are viewed as significant components of career development because of the roles they may play in changing, either positively or negatively, an individual's career motivations and aspirations (Bandura, 1982).

Social structures are also an important factor in career development, primarily because of the influences they exert on individuals' personality development. Because humans tend to be adaptive, they are responsive to the social structures in which they are enmeshed. When their social structures change, their personalities attempt to adapt to the changes. Regardless of the outcome of the attempt at adaptation, the change itself affects the individual's personality, and therefore affects the individual's existing career development pattern.

Sociological or situational approaches to career development are significant because they identify many factors not usually considered in "narrower" approaches. However, because of the complexities and expansiveness of the concepts and factors involved in sociological or situational approaches, career counseling based on such approaches are much less defined or distinct. Typically, sociological and situational considerations are usually incorporated as part of other career counseling approaches.

Personality Approaches

Approaches to career counseling and development in this category are related to the trait-and-factor approach in that they focus on individual characteristics but acknowledge that sociological and situational factors are strong influences in the development of an individual's characteristics. However, they are distinctive in that they focus almost exclusively on an individual's personal characteristics, and give very little attention to external factors such as job characteristics or sociological conditions. Moreover, whereas the trait-and-factor approach tends to focus on relatively easily-identifiable traits and abilities, personality approaches often involve "inferred" characteristics. Thus, personality approaches to career development and counseling are closely aligned with (aspects of) theories of personality, and attempt to relate those theories to occupational behavior.

Freud's psychoanalytic theory has served as the basis for some approaches. Osipow (1983) stated that "The most ambitious scheme for defining the process of career development within the psychoanalytic framework and with the appropriate language was proposed by Bordin, Nachmann, and Segal (1963)" (p. 42). They constructed a theoretical framework for career development based on a set of eight propositions:

1. Human development is continuous; early (i.e., in infancy) psychological and physiological activities are associated with those in adult life.

2. Sources of gratification are the same for children and adults; only the form of gratification differs.

3. The individual's pattern of needs develops early in life, usually during the first six years.

4. The occupation sought is related to the individual's needs.

5. The theory applies to all types of people and work, except where external (e.g., cultural or financial) factors preclude its application.

6. Work may be conceived of as the sublimation of infantile impulses into socially acceptable forms.

7. Either emotional blocking or a severe lack of information can inhibit fulfillment of occupational expectations.

8. A number of psychic dimensions and/or body zones can be gratified in any job.

According to Bordin et al., the eighth proposition covers the following psychoanalytic dimensions: (1) *nuturant,* including feeling and fostering; (2) *oral aggressive,* including cutting, biting, and devouring; (3) *manipulative,* including physical and psychological control; (4) *sensual,* including sight, sound, and touch; (5) *anal,* including acquiring and time-ordering; (6) *genital,* including erection, penetration, impregnation, and producing; (7) *exploration;* (8) *flowing and quenching;* (9) *exhibiting;* and (10) *rhythmic movement.*

Bordin, Nachmann, and Segal, as well as others, have presented research to support the notion that these propositions can be used to explain career behavior. However, the psychoanalytic approach to career development has not been employed extensively for several reasons. First, psychoanalytic personality theory has not been widely used in the counseling profession, and it follows that a career counseling approach based on it also would not be widely used. Second, this approach implies use of psychoanalytic interviewing techniques which are typically too time consuming for effective use by most professional counselors. Finally, the measurement of important constructs and dynamics in the approach is at best difficult, and therefore also not suited to the circumstances of most counselors.

A more popular personality approach to career development is the one developed by Roe (1956). Her approach involves a synthesis of several perspectives on personality. One of the primary ones involved is Maslow's (1954) theory of prepotent needs. Maslow proposed that human needs may be arranged in a hierarchy of low-order to high-order needs:

1. Physiological	5. Information
2. Safety	6. Understanding
3. Belongingness and love	7. Beauty
4. Self-esteem, respect, and independence	8. Self-actualiztion

According to Maslow (1954), people must fulfill lower-order needs (e.g., physiological, safety) before they can strive to fulfill higher-order needs (e.g., self-actualization). Roe used Maslow's conceptualizations to suggest that, in general, vocational behavior is the individual's attempt to fulfill certain needs and that the particular level of needs for which gratification is sought in part determines the nature of the behaviors used.

Roe also emphasized the importance of using the child-rearing practices to which the individual had been exposed, to help explain the individual's vocational behaviors. She described three general types of child-rearing practices. The first, *emotional concentration on the child,* includes the extremes of overprotection and overdemand on the child. Children raised under these conditions tend to have their lower-order physiological and safety needs met relatively quickly, but not their higher-order needs such as those for belongingness, love, and self-esteem. Therefore, the prediction would be that they would seek fulfillment of these needs through their occupations. The second type is *avoidance of the child.* The supposition in this condition is that neither the physiological nor emotional needs of children raised under these conditions are fulfilled, and therefore individuals seek "things" and limited contact with other persons in their occupation. The third type, *acceptance of the child,* involves the child being accepted as an integral part of a "democratic" family unit, wherein many of the child's needs are met. Therefore, an individual raised in this condition would seek fulfillment of the highest needs in an occupation.

A third major component in Roe's approach is attention to genetic endowments. In general, Roe suggested that genetic endowments, such as intelligence or physical ability, are mitigating factors in the manifestations of previous child-rearing practices and need fulfillment behaviors. That is, the specific vocational behaviors exhibited by an individual are influenced by the individual's genetic endowments.

Herr and Cramer (1984) summarized Roe's approach in commenting that

> Roe suggests then that there are relationships between...genetic propensities, and childhood experiences that shape individual styles of behavior, and that the impulse to acquire opportunities to express these individual styles is inherent in the choices made.... Thus, the strength of a particular need, the delay between the arousal of the need and its gratification, and the value that the satisfaction has in the individual's environment are the conditions ... that influence career development. (p. 114)

Roe (1956) developed a "fields and levels" occupational classification scheme to facilitate understanding of her approach. In her schema, the "fields" are classified by interest and the primary focus of the occupations while the "levels" are classified by degrees of responsibility, capacity, and skill. The "fields" identified by Roe are (I) Service, (II) Business Contact, (III) Organizations, (IV) Technology, (V) Outdoor, (VI) Science, (VII) General Culture, and (VIII) Arts and Entertainment. The "levels" identified are (1) Professional and Managerial, higher; (2) Professional and Managerial, regular, (3) Semiprofessional, Small Business; (4) Skilled; (5) Semiskilled; and (6) Unskilled. When these fields and levels are configured as a eight-by-six matrix, any occupation (theoretically) can be placed in a cell representing the appropriate combination.

Osipow (1983), in reviewing Roe's approach, commented that "The theory attends to every important aspect of vocational selection" (p. 19). Yet while the theoretical base of her approach is well-developed, career counseling methods derived from it are not now widely used by counselors. This is perhaps because of the difficulties in gathering some of the needed information (e.g., that pertaining to early child-rearing practices and their effects), but more likely because Holland's approach has become so popular among counselors that all other personality approaches have been overshadowed.

The basic premise of Holland's (1966, 1973) approach to career development and counseling is that an individual is the product of heredity and environment. In general, early genetic endowments develop under the influences of various environmental factors such that an individual develops preferred modes and methods for coping and dealing with social and environmental tasks. The most typical way a person responds to his or her environment is known as the person's *modal personal orientation*. Holland proposed six general classifications of modal personal orientations: realistic, investigative, artistic, social, enterprising, and conventional. Holland further proposed that these same six classifications are appropriate for characterizing work environments. In Holland's view, people search for those work environments which allow them to use their skills and abilities and to express their attitudes and values, and which contain aggreeable tasks and problems. Accordingly, vocational behavior is a result of the interaction between the personality and environmental characteristics. Moreover, "effective" career development is the result of an effective matching of personality and environmental characteristics. Because Holland described personality characteristics and work environments in the same terms, he emphasized a perspective that has a long history in society in general and in the counseling profession in particular; specifically, that "work is a way of life."

Because of the centrality of the personal orientation/work environment classification system in Holland's theory, the categories are summarized here.

Realistic—activities that require explicit, ordered, or systematic manipulation of objects, tools, machines, or animals, and that reflect aversion to education or therapy.

Investigative—activities that involve observational, symbolic, systematic, and creative investigation of biological, physical, and cultural phenomena toward the goal of understanding and control, and that reflect an aversion to socializing, repetitiveness, or persuasion.

Artistic—activities that are ambiguous, imaginative, free, and unsystematic toward the manipulation of physical, verbal, or human material to create art forms and products and that reflect an aversion to explicit, systematic, and organized experiences.

Social—activities that involve manipulation of others to inform, train, develop, cure, or enlighten and that reflect an aversion to ordered and systematic use of machines, tools, or materials.

Enterprising—activities that require manipulation of others to achieve monetary gain or organizational goals and that reflect an aversion to observational, symbolic, or systematic experiences.

Conventional—activities that involve systematic, ordered, and explicit manipulation of data and that reflect an aversion to ambiguous, exploratory, or unsystematic experiences.

These personality/environment types are usually referred to by the first letter of each word; hence, the "RIASEC" model. This model is usually configured as a hexagon, as shown in Figure 6.1. Adjacent types are presumed to have more in common than opposite types. That is, the Realistic type is more similar to either the Investigative or Conventional types than it is to the Social, Enterprising, or Artistic types. Further, because people rarely fit within a single type, they are usually assigned a

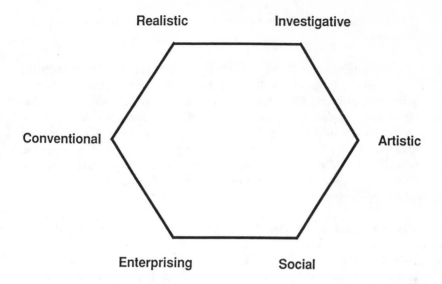

Figure 6.1. Holland's Hexagonal Model.

three-letter code. For example, a person assigned the code SEC would be presumed to be most like the Social type, next most like the Enterprising type, and next most like the Conventional type.

Holland's approach has found great favor among counseling researchers and practitioners. For example, literally hundreds of research studies have been completed on various aspects of Holland's theory. Relatedly, numerous assessment instruments and approaches have been developed in the context of Holland's theoretical propositions and more recently, other existing instruments have been modified so that their results can be interpreted within the context of those propositions. One reason for the extensiveness of these efforts is that, in the context of Holland's theory, a vocational *interest* inventory is also a *personality* inventory; a situation which expands the potential interpretations of any research effort. However, also acknowledged is that Holland and his associates have done much to spur interest. For example, Holland developed the *Vocational Preference Inventory* and the *Self-Directed Search,* two widely used vocational interest inventories, based on his theory. He and his associates also have developed a set of three-letter codes, based on the RIASEC model, for over four hundred occupations. This latter effort in particular has made his approach popular because of the ease with which the system can be used by both counselors and clients.

Although Holland's approach is popular, it is not without criticism. For example, Osipow (1983) stated that, "Holland's theory possesses some general utility for counselors in their conceptualization of occupational selection for their clientele, but it offers little specific advice in the way of suggestions about procedures and techniques that the counselors may use in their face-to-face work with their clients" (p. 110). None the less, Holland's approach remains commonly used, probably because people other than Holland have devised numerous counseling techniques based on the theory.

Developmental Approaches

These approaches differ from the previous ones in that they view occupational choice as a *process* instead of as an *act*. Occupational choice in this context also is not restricted to a certain period in life, but rather is a set of reoccurring events throughout the life cycle. Thus, career development may be viewed as an evolutionary process which is flexible, and in which individuals adapt their occupational choices to changing conditions in their lives.

Ginzberg and his associates (Ginzberg, Ginsburg, Axelrad, & Herma, 1951) stated that the developmental process of occupational decision-making "is not a single decision but a series of decisions made over a period of years" (p. 185). They proposed that this process is divided into a set of phases. The first, from birth to approximately age 11, is called the *Fantasy* stage. In it, individuals have "idealistic" and typically unrealistic conceptualizations of the jobs they would like to assume. The second phase, *Tentative,* lasts from approximately ages 11 to 17 and contains the subperiods of *interest, capacity, value,* and *transition.* Individuals gather information about various occupations and make extremely tentative occupational decisions during this phase. The last phase, *Realistic,* lasts from approximately ages 17 to 21 and contains the subperiods of *exploration* and *crystallization.* Individuals engage in initial work activities and make "final" occupational decisions during this phase.

In the early formulations, Ginzberg and his associates postulated that occupational choices are a series of "compromises" among various influencing factors and that choices are relatively final after individuals reach their early twenties. However, Ginzberg (1972) later revised these propositions, and then used the term *optimization,* rather than compromise, to imply that occupational choice is the result of the individual's attempt to maximize the benefits of any occupational decision. He also suggested that occupational decision-making continues throughout life rather than being finalized in young adulthood.

Ginzberg's efforts were significant; at that time they presented a very different view of career development. However, although Ginzberg spurred interest in developmental approaches to career development and counseling, his work was overshadowed by that of other developmental theorists.

Tiedeman and O'Hara (1963) presented a developmental approach that focuses upon the intersection of processes for the *anticipation* of occupational choices and *induction* into the occupation chosen. The *anticipation* process includes the *anticipation, crystallization, choice,* and *clarification* stages, wherein occupational alternatives are identified and explored. The *induction* process includes the *social induction, reformation,* and *integration* stages wherein the individual develops an understanding of the occupation chosen. Tiedeman and O'Hara proposed that career development is a continuing process of differentiating ego identity, and used Erikson's (1963) model of psychosocial crises at seven developmental stages as a means to explain differences in career development. They also stressed the interaction of the self-concept with the concept of career as both develop over time. More recently, Peatling and Tiedeman (1977) have also emphasized the individual's *competence, autonomy,* and *agency* as major factors in the career development process. In brief, this approach holds that career development is the "process of building a vocational identity through [personal] *differentiation* and *integration* as one confronts work" (Tolbert, 1974, p. 40). Thus, Tiedeman and his associates have espoused a holistic perspective on the nature of human career development.

Super's work on a theory of career development began shortly after Ginzberg's and, in part, was a reaction to what he perceived as deficiencies in Ginzberg's approach. Briefly, Super believed that Ginzberg failed to provide an effective definition of occupational "choice" and that the distinction between choice and "adjustment" was not as sharp as Ginzberg proposed (Herr & Cramer, 1984). Super's theory is multifaceted and borrows from a number of areas of psychology. He described it as a differential-developmental-social-phenomenological psychology (Super,

1969). Perhaps more appropriately, Osipow (1983) referred to Super's work as a developmental self-concept theory. Three components of Super's work have received the most attention; life stages and their associated developmental tasks, self-concept as related to occupational choice, and career maturity.

Life Stages. Super (1957, 1977) proposed five major life stages, each incorporating different developmental tasks that can be used to understand career development. The first stage, *Growth,* lasts from birth to approximately age 14. It includes the substages of *fantasy* (ages 4-10), *interest* (ages 11-12), and *capacity* (ages 13-14). The important developmental tasks in this stage are developing a *self-concept* and establishing an *orientation* toward the world of work. *Exploration,* the second stage, covers approximately ages 14 to 24, with the substage, *tentative,* existing approximately from ages 15 to 17. The primary developmental tasks in the *Exploration* stage are *crystallizing* a vocational preference, *specifying* the preference, and *implementing* the preference. The third stage, *Establishment,* lasts from approximately ages 24 to 44 and includes the substages of *stabilization* (ages 25-30) and *advancement* (ages 30-44). The major developmental tasks in this stage are *stabilizing* the vocational preference and *advancing* in occupations. *Maintenance,* the fourth stage, lasts from approximately ages 44 to 64. The major developmental task in this stage is *preserving* achieved status and gains. In the final stage, *Decline,* lasting from approximately age 64 on, there are two substages: *deceleration* (ages 64-70) and *retirement* (age 70-on). The major developmental tasks in this stage are *decelerating* occupational activities, and *disengaging* and *retiring* from occupational activities.

Vocational Self-Concept. *The second major component in Super's* approach is the development and implementation of the "vocational self-concept." A person's vocational self-concept is presumed to be a substantial and integral part of his/her total self-concept. Zunker (1981) stated that "the research has indicated that the vocational self-concept develops through physical and mental growth, observations of work, identification with working adults, general environment, and general experiences" (p. 9). The theory assumes that individuals choose occupations that are consistent with and allow expression of their vocational self-concepts. Thus, an individual's vocational self-concept is a major determinant of what work (i.e., occupations) will be appropriate for the individual. Commenting on the role of self-concept in career counseling, Herr (1986) noted that

Thus, career ... counseling must attend to the individual's need for in-depth and accurate information about vocational alternatives, but at least as importantly, the individual needs to be assisted to avoid unrealistic estimates of ability and vague understandings of personal values and preferences. (p. 190-191)

Career Maturity. The concept of *career maturity* (sometimes referred to as *vocational maturity*) plays an important role in Super's approach. The concept implies that specific behaviors are indicative of an individual's mastery of various developmental tasks. Different authors have proposed different components of career maturity, such as career exploration ability, decision-making ability, career planning ability, knowledge of the world of work and knowledge of preferred occupations. In addition, Super, Thompson, Lindeman, Jordaan, and Myers (1979) proposed career development skills while Crites (1973) proposed attitudes toward involvement in the choice process, orientation toward work, independence in decision making, preference for choice factors, and conceptions of the choice process. A basic assumption in Super's developmental stage approach is that the individual must master the tasks at one life stage before the individual can move to the next life stage. Therefore, measurement of career maturity is important because it allows inference about an individual's vocational development stage. Relatedly, conceptualizations of desired levels of career maturity at various life stages are frequently used as the bases for development of goals and objectives for various career guidance, education, and counseling activities.

The work of Super (1957, 1969, 1976), his associates, and others who have based their work on his, has been widely accepted within the counseling profession. In fact, Holland's (1966, 1973) and Super's approaches are preeminent to the extent that the vast majority of current career development and counseling activities can be traced directly to one of these two approaches.

CAREER GUIDANCE, EDUCATION, AND COUNSELING

Commenting on career education, Herr and Cramer (1984) stated that:

Sometimes it has been used virtually interchangeably with the term career guidance; in other instances, it has been used primarily to describe a process of infusing into instructional content and methods career development concepts by which the application of academic subject matter of any kind can be related to work or self-exploration. (p. 417)

In general, career education involves communication of information about jobs, the world of work, and career development concepts and approaches in the environments in which people exist. Two basic premises underly career education. The first is that left to their own devices, people will not have sufficient opportunities or resources to obtain comprehensive information about a variety of jobs and careers. The second is that such comprehensive information is essential for effective occupational and career decision-making. Traditionally, career-education activities have taken place primarily within educational systems and institutions. However, they have recently been extended into other situations such as business and industry, government, and the military.

Hoyt (1974) presented a summary of conditions formulated by the United States Office of Education (USOE) that serve as the basis of the need for career education. These include the following situation: (1) too many students leaving educational systems are deficient in basic academic skills necessary for effective adjustment in society and the world of work, (2) too few students are able to relate what they learn in school to the world of work, (3) the American educational system is considerably less pertinent to non-college-bound students than it is to college bound students, (4) the American educational system does not adequately serve the vocational needs of ethnic minorities, women, or the disadvantaged, and (5) too many students leaving educational systems are deficient in vocational skills, self-understanding and career decision-making skills, and work attitudes necessary for successful transition from school to work (Hoyt, 1974). In sum, educational systems were viewed as not doing as much as they should or could to prepare people for the world of work. This situation prompted a national impetus for career education.

The USOE's attention to career education resulted in the development of four national models for career education. The first is the *school-based* or *comprehensive* career-education model. This model was originally proposed as a method for revitalizing schools from within by infusing ideas, experiences, and skills (related to work and careers) not typically found in them. The primary goals for this model included students' developments of career awareness, self-awareness, positive appreciations and attitudes toward work, decision-making skills, economic awareness, skill awareness and begining competence, educational awareness, and educational identities. However, over 1000 other specific goals were developed in the construction of activities designed to implement these general goals (Herr & Cramer, 1984).

The second model, *employer-based* or *experienced-based,* was designed to meet the needs of students who did not do well in traditional learning environments. This model has goals similar to those for the first model, but the natures of the learning experiences involved are quite different. In this model, a significant portion of "education" occurs through direct involvement in on-going work activities. Thus, under this model, students "learn by doing" through placements at actual employer sites in the community.

The third model is called the *home/community-based* model. This model was developed to be useful to adults, and has goals such as the development of educational delivery systems in the home and community, new placement systems, new career education programs (specifically for adults), and more competent workers. The model makes extensive use of television and other mass media, referral sources, and community resources to facilitate learning among out-of-school adults.

Rural/residential, the fourth model, was developed to help entire disadvantaged, rural families improve their economic and social situations through intensive programs at residential centers. This model was implemented on a very limited basis, but the results of those efforts were generally favorable.

Because the conveyance of information is the primary (but certainly not the only) purpose of career education, a considerable number of resources about the world of work have been developed. Relatedly, a multitude of sources exists from which counselors can obtain such information for use in their respective settings and with their respective clients. Therefore, because of the large numbers involved, only a few representative examples can be presented here.

Until relatively recently, almost all occupational and career resources were in the form of printed material. These materials ranged from occupational briefs to the far more complete *Dictionary of Occupational Titles* and the *Occupational Outlook Handbook,* from biographies of workers to stories in magazine form, and from brochures to newspapers. In fact, so many printed materials are available that counselors may become mind-boggled by the choices confronting them! Relatedly, public, private, governmental, and religious agencies as well as companies, corporations, and not-for-profit organizations all offer many different types of materials which are potentially suitable for an equally diverse array of audiences. Thus, counselors have the wide-ranging flexibility to either purchase a "complete career information system" or to develop a "home grown" system. That's the "good news." The bad news is that such systems require considerable storage space, frequently require sophisticated filing systems, and rapidly go out-of-date in regard to the information presented.

More recently, a variety of visual media have become available. These resources include filmstrips, multimedia presentation packages, films, and videotapes. These media have the advantage of a presentation format that is "more interesting" than those of printed materials, but many of the disadvantages of printed materials are also applicable to visual media.

One form of information conveyance that has found favor with many counselors is the "direct contact" approach. Generally, four types of activities are subsumed under this heading. The first is *simulations,* typically in the form of role-playing, in which clients "interact" with persons who have particular types of work and/or career knowledge. The second is *interviews,* in which clients interact with persons actually occupying particular jobs and/or involved in careers in which clients are potentially interested. The third type is *field trips,* wherein clients visit a particular employment setting for a limited time period to observe the work being done and talk with various employees. The final type is *apprenticeships,* which involve clients working in particular jobs, usually for pay, for reasonable time periods so that they can gain an understanding of the work involved in the occupation. While these activities are "popular" with clients, they necessitate considerable time investments by counselors to arrange and coordinate them.

The most recent advancement in occupational and career information systems is the use of computers and computer technology. Among the most widely known systems are the *System of Interactive Guidance and Information* (SIGI), *Information System for Vocational Decisions* (IVSD), *Educational and Career Exploration System* (ECES), *Computerized Vocational Information System* (CVIS), *DISCOVER II, Guidance Information System* (GIS), *Colorado Career Information System* (COCIS), *CHOICES,* and *FUTURE I* (Zunker, 1981). Each of these systems, and others like them, allow the client to "interact" with the computer both to gain information and to explore occupational and career possibilities. The advent of microcomputer versions of some of these systems has made them particularly attractive for career education because of reduced costs and the opportunity for clients to use them without substantial investments of the professional counselors' time. However, Sampson and Pyle (1983) have noted that such systems should never be used to "replace" career education or counseling by a professional counselor because of the limitations of such systems as well as ethical considerations.

Career education is one of the major components under the broad rubric of career guidance; career counseling is the other. Career counseling quite obviously focuses on the facilitation of clients' decision-making and career development activities and is similar to other types of counseling in that it may be conducted individually or in groups. Brammer and Shostrom (1960) identified three types of goals for career counseling, including helping clients to (1) confirm choices already made, (2) clarify career objectives, or (3) discover facts about themselves and the world of work and then to use the information in decision-making. In both individual and group career counseling, the counseling process begins with the establishment of rapport between the professional counselor and the client(s). In the next step, the professional counselor, typically in collaboration with clients, determines if career counseling is merited or if the client(s) need(s) some other type of counseling. If career counseling is indicated, the professional counselor proceeds to implement strategies consistent with a theoretical orientation.

Herr and Cramer (1984) have identified eight assumptions underlying career counseling intervention strategies: (1) many factors beyond control of the client will influence the client's decision-making; (2) clients are not able to obtain or process all information relevant to decision-making; (3) during counseling, clients are only able to make decisions that will allow them to achieve some of their objectives; (4) clients' decisions are typically evaluated in terms of the process used to reach them rather than on the basis of outcomes; (5) clients can be taught how to make decisions; (6) sometimes factors unknown to either the counselor or the client defeat the purposes of career counseling; (7) the importance of various factors in clients' decision-making varies across clients and the reasons for the variations are often unknown; and (8) career counseling presumes client motivation, but appropriate client motivation is not always present in the career counseling process. Although these assumptions may seem negative, they are not intended to be. Rather, they describe some of the "obstacles" with which career counselors must contend and they therefore provide a "realistic" perspective on the conditions under which career counseling is usually conducted.

One of the ways to maintain positive perspectives within career counseling is to do it in the context of empirical counseling as presented here. The individual and group counseling approaches presented in Chapter 4 and the assessment approaches presented in Chapter 5 are particularly noteworthy in this regard because they are readily adapted to the purposes of career counseling. Used in conjunction with any of the variety of available occupational information systems, the techniques presented in those chapters enable professional counselors, in collaboration with their clients, to develop appropriate goals, use effective strategies, and achieve desirable and measurable outcomes.

SUMMARY

Today, career education and career counseling are infrequently conducted as distinct activities; more typically they are included as parts of comprehensive career guidance programs (Herr & Cramer, 1984). Historically, such programs usually have been conducted in educational systems such as elementary, middle/junior high, or secondary schools, and colleges and universities, primarily because they were initiated by professional counselors and/or educators affiliated with those systems. More recently, career guidance programs have been started in business, industry, and other non-educational settings. For example, many "Employee Assistance Programs" incorporate career guidance components, activities, and services. In general, career guidance programs are now available to a large majority of people in society, and the number of programs continues to increase.

The broad goal of career guidance programming is the facilitation of individuals' career development through the provision of services and activities that can be responsive to any of the variety of career development needs of the individuals for whom the programs were established. This is indeed a lofty goal. However, effectively planned and implemented comprehensive career guidance programs are able to achieve it.

Chapter 7

CONSULTATION

Jack Wooten, a social worker, recently returned from a site visit at a community mental health center located in a neighboring state. As a result of his visit, he wants to integrate new ideas into his employment setting, but he is unsure whether some of the activities will work. Jack believes he could clarify his concerns and plans by talking with another person who shares his interest.

Martha, an employee of the telephone company, is missing more and more days, and she frequently leaves work early complaining of back trouble and headaches. At work, she often becomes frustrated and "lashes" out at people. Jane Martin, Martha's supervisor, recognizes that a change has occurred in Martha's behavior, that Martha is unhappy, and that something needs to be done. However, she is unsure what to do. She would like to discuss the situation with someone else who is knowledgeable of human behavior.

In each of the above vignettes, the individual can benefit from a counselor serving as a consultant. For a more specific illustration, we present the example of Laura Gordon.

Laura needs help. She is a first-grade teacher in an elementary school that has a traditional orientation toward educating children. Currently, Laura is experiencing some problems in her classroom for which she is unprepared. The students like her and she feels comfortable in the school environment, but she is having frequent classroom disturbances which are affecting the children's learning process. Several of the students disrupt the class by constantly talking to themselves at a level that is barely audible, but still distracting. Two other children in Laura's class move around the room at times when all the children are to be seated. The children's disorderly conduct also occurs outside the classroom: in the hallways, the lunch room, and the playground area. The principal senses that Laura is losing control of the class and believes the children are not learning. Laura, who wants to be a successful teacher, recognizes that the principal is unhappy. She has tried "threats," sent children to the office, and contacted parents about their respective child's inappropriate behavior, all to no avail. As a result of the situation, Laura is having serious doubts about her choice of teaching as a career and whether she will be able to finish the academic year in her present assignment. Unhappy, fatigued, and disillusioned, she is unsure what to do. She views quitting as the only solution but is afraid that she may be unable to obtain another teaching job because of a low evaluation she will receive from the principal.

Laura's situation has reached an intolerable level for her, for the principal, and for the children. She is in need of assistance from someone regarding these professional matters; the person of choice is a professional counselor serving as a consultant. The professional counselor acting in a consulting role helps other professionals with possible solutions to professional problems by listening and reacting, and by providing assurance, relief, and help with stress reduction. In this consultation process, the professional counselor will help Laura with her problems with the children in her class. Thus, the focus of the process actually is on helping the children, as opposed to helping Laura as would be the case in a counseling process.

Consultation implies a process for helping other professionals (i.e., individuals, groups, or agencies) to cope with their problems, and therefore to function more effectively and with greater satisfaction. Consultation may be referred to as an "indirect" function for professional counselors because the counselor helps others (i.e., the consultees) in working with still others (i.e., the persons/clients, receiving the services provided by the consultees). The helping function of consultation is an important part of the professional counselor's role, primarily because of the growing belief that assisting other professionals to function more effectively is ultimately the most parsimonious and far-reaching use of the professional counselor's skills, efforts, and time. Through the provision of consultation services, professional counselor's are able to impact far more people than they could impact directly. Further, the consultation process is most comprehensively effective when it is used for preventive purposes; when the counselor helps consultees help others to avoid future difficulties.

The most efficient time for consultation is when professionals (i.e., consultees) are not under excessive stress and want to explore possible alternative behaviors or discuss their ideas with someone else before they try them. The provision of consultation in these situations creates more confident professionals. Laura's situation, however, has gone beyond a point where preventive efforts can be implemented. With problems similar to Laura's, the professional counselor as a consultant must provide an opportunity for the consultee to "think aloud" and to aid in reducing stress and providing relief so that the consultee can decide upon appropriate courses of action to undertake.

Consultation is not a specialty with a single professional identity; it is an activity practiced in almost every profession. Surprisingly, however, the literature on research in and the practice of consultation is almost non-existent. In particular, evidence of successful consultation as a preventive intervention, other than anecdotal or descriptive analysis, is hard to locate. A related and unfortunate problem is the numerous meanings and/or connotations attached to the term consultation. For example, as used by physicians, consultation means meeting with a patient to discuss the patient's medical condition, but in many businesses, the term means being engaged in work-related conversation with another person. Then too, attorneys use the term in reference to any meeting with a client. None of these examples, however, adequately reflects the use of the term consultation within the counseling profession.

The use of consultation in mental health activities (i.e., counseling) was pioneered by Caplan (1970), who wrote that consultation is a voluntary, non-supervisory relationship between professionals for the purpose of aiding the consultee(s) with improved professional functioning. He further indicated that this may involve helping a consultee with current work problems related to a specific client or program or with anticipated future concerns. Caplan (1970) also suggested that consultation reduces areas of misunderstanding so that consultees may be able to cope more effectively with the same type of problem in the future.

A somewhat more expansive view of consultation has been provided by Bindman (1964).

> ...[C]onsultation is an interaction process of interpersonal relationship that takes place between two professional workers, the consultant and the consultee, in which one worker, the consultant, assists the other worker, the consultee, to solve a problem of a client or clients, *within the framework of the consultee's usual professional functioning*...A secondary goal of the process is one of education, so that the consultee can learn to handle similar cases in the future in a more effective fashion, and thus enhance his [her] professional skills. (p. 367)

As specified by Caplan's and Bindman's definitions, the consultee-consultant relationship is voluntary and collegial or co-professional, and the focus of the consultation activity is professional as it relates to the consultee's client or problem. Blocher (1974) described consultation as a process of helping that occurs between a professional helper (consultant) and a help seeker (consultee) who has a professional responsibility for another person (client). It is a temporary collegial—cooperative relationship that is concerned with a current or potential work problem.

Indicating what consultation *is not* as performed by the professional counselor is sometimes helpful. Within the counseling profession, consultation is not therapy, advocacy, liaison with agencies, direct service, or administrative control over the consultee. Nor is it collaborating or working with (i.e., as in co-counseling) parents and colleagues jointly to provide a direct service to their child or client, respectively. These components violate the construct of consultation as used in this book and as viewed by many professional counselors. For example, assisting parents in resolving problems concerning their child is providing a direct service to the parents; the parents are the target of the service (and are not professional helpers or consultees).

Kirby (1985) defined consultation in terms of relationship conditions. She identified four conditions:

> consultant-consultee relationship is voluntary, the focus of consultation intervention is on a work situation or role of responsibility of the consultee, the consultant is functioning outside of the structural hierarchy, and the consultant is perceived as an expert in the area in which consultation is offerred. (p. 4-6)

She operationally conceived consultation as

a process whereby the consultant helps the consultees achieve their goals. Thus, the consultant facilitates the consultees' problem-solving process and, at times, guides, leads, or directs consultees as they use the consultant's expertise in their goal-seeking behavior. (p. 11).

Although consultation focuses on professional problems, an awareness of the consultee's coping skills and personality assets and liabilities is required. The integration of these characteristics is illustrated in Figure 7.1 which provides a conceptual view of the components and process of consultation.

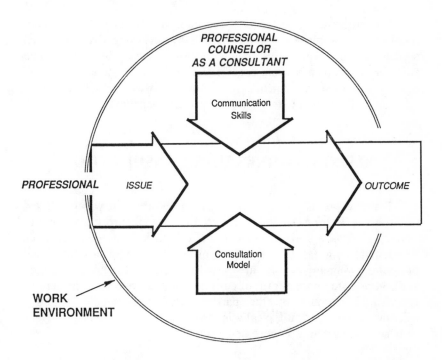

Figure 7.1. Conceptual view of the components and process of consultation.

Some of the communication skills associated with the counseling process are also part of the consultation process. Therefore, differences between counseling and consultation are dictated primarily by the theoretical framework of counseling and the model approach of consultation, as well as by their respective intentions. The term model is used to describe the structure of consultation because the area, unlike counseling, has not obtained a level of sufficient substance to warrant use of the term theory.

One major difference between counseling and consultation is that the consultant-consultee relationship is more objective and emotionally external than is the counselor-client relationship, which is more personal and involves disclosure of emotions. In addition, the target of consultation is problem-solving as it relates to professional functioning, whereas the target of counseling is primarily personal adjustment.

The professional counselor's consultation role in individual consultation can be more easily understood by reviewing five often-used models; training-workshops, mental-health, process, behavioral, and atheoretical problem-solving consultation. Of course these models will often be modified, combined, or varied in some way to more adequately meet the individual needs of the professional consultant.

TRAINING-WORKSHOPS CONSULTATION

Training-workshops are a type of consultation in which selected traditional educational methods are used to provide information and to develop skills as a basis of prevention. A distinction needs to be made between training and teaching. In contrast to teaching or educational programs wherein people are usually passive listeners, training-workshops encompass a form of consultation that involves considerable experiential learning by the participants. For example, training-workshops consultation typically involves putting participants in dyads or triads to learn and practice new skills.

To effect training-workshops consultation, mental health agencies, schools, or college and university offices of student affairs often have one or two day "retreats." More common, however, are designated periods of time (e.g., "office", "work", "in-service", or "conference" days), during which clients are not seen, classes are cancelled, and/or offices are closed, and instead a variety of professional activities take place in the context of a training workshop conducted by a consultant.

Approaches to training-workshops and staff participation vary by setting. For example, with clinical mental-health counselors, one-way mirrors can be used to permit observation of (usually simulated) counseling sessions. A professional counselor as a consultant conducts the sessions while other counselors observe through the one-way mirror, and consultant-led group discussions follow the sessions.

Professional counselors also often help other professional personnel (e.g., teachers, administrators, ministers, or social workers) to work with problems specific to their respective employment environments. The professional counselor's training and experience in communication skills, and knowledge of consulting models and mental health, are used to enable groups of professionals to function more effectively. For example, training-workshops may involve meeting with a group of concerned teachers to discuss ways of working with children with behavior problems, incidences of substance abuse, or adolescent suicide. Yet another example is the professional counselor as a consultant working with a group of vocational rehabilitation counselors or residence-life staff members to improve their communication skills.

Most training-workshops conducted by professional counselors have clearly defined purposes and are preventive in nature. They are usually held to enable other professionals to share "here-and-now" (i.e., current and immediate) problems and to get help with practical solutions. Also, these solutions may be used with problems that could be encountered in the future. If problem areas have not been determined before the counselor is called upon to run the training workshop, the professional counselor, as a consultant, typically surveys the group members to determine their concerns. The professional counselor who serves as a training-workshop consultant has an extremely potent role in helping other professionals and therefore needs to be particularly knowledgeable of their specific needs.

The following example provides a typical sequence of events during a training-workshop on substance abuse. A professional counselor was asked to conduct a training workshop concerning substance abuse interventions for college age students because a group of university residence-life directors believed they were insufficiently skilled to help people with problems in this area. Also, the group held ambivalent attitudes and values concerning the topic (i.e., whether they *should* have to do something about the problem). The professional counselor surveyed the group and found that the specific concern was how to handle certain aspects of drug prevention without causing unfavorable reactions from their students. Another concern was that the other student-development staff members and parents felt that the directors were, at a minimum, ambivalent about the problem, if not neglectful. The professional counselor's survey further revealed an unexpected amount of ignorance about drugs and physiological effects of substance abuse.

With this basic information, the counselor formulated and planned the training-workshop to contain two parts. For part one, a pharmacologist was engaged to give instruction on the most commonly abused drugs and their psychotropic effects. For part two of the training-workshop, which followed the more formal didactic presentation of the pharmacologist, the counselor-as-consultant divided the participants into small groups of five or six. Then, role playing was used, during which one participant assumed the "helper's" role and the others became the "helpees." The helpees were given directions to assume the role of "badgers," asking every conceivable question about drugs, such as "Is it harmful?" "What does snorting mean?" "Is 'crack' any worse than smoking pot?" or "How do you know that drug use relates to poor grades?" The helper assumed a supportive role as well as trying to be specifically helpful to the helpee asking the question. During the session, much anxiety was generated when the helper was not familiar with the terms used and had no well-formulated response to such questions. However, through role playing, helpers were able to practice making accurate responses to questions, without implying value judgments. Once the helpers had the opportunity to become more familiar with the often-asked questions and commonly used slang words and terms, their initial anxiety decreased and their abilities to provide effective responses increased.

MENTAL-HEALTH CONSULTATION

Caplan's (1970) mental-health consultation is the prototype of most consultation models used in the counseling profession. Caplan based his model on psychodynamic assumptions about human behavior and purported that predictable deficit areas of professional behaviors include the professional's lack of skills, self-confidence, knowledge, or objectivity. The model emphasizes the process of a triadic relationship in consultation; consultant, consultee, and client. In Caplan's approach, the focus of consultation can be client-centered case, consultee-centered, program-centered, or consultee-centered administrative.

Client-centered case consultation is the classical triadic approach which involves a consultee seeking assistance from a consultant about a client. The focus is on the client, although the consultant does not have direct contact with the client; any assistance afforded a client from the consultant is effected through the consultee.

Consultee-centered consultation concentrates on the consultee's professional problem. The process and focus is usually dyadic (i.e, the consultant and consultee), with the target being the consultee.

Program-centered consultation involves a consultant helping with an organization's problem. This approach is also dyadic, except that the focus is on the organization.

Consultee-centered administrative consultation has as its goal either improving administrators' problem-solving skills or helping them in the broad area of skill deficit and/or emotional entanglement with an issue(s).

An important component of, and typical impetus for, mental-health consultation is the consultee's loss of professional objectivity. Caplan suggested that the loss of objectivity is created when a consultee has identified with the problem (e.g., the client reminds the consultee of an event or person in their past) or it may be due to a much more severe problem (e.g., the consultee has a characterological disorder such as being paranoid, histrionic, or avoidant). Caplan described these situations as "theme interference," wherein the consultee fits the client into a previously determined unconscious category and links him/her to an inevitable outcome; e.g., a syllogism of A being linked to B. To illustrate, a consultee who perceives a client as "passively demanding" may see the client's success in working with co-workers as doomed to failure. The syllogism is unconsciously dynamic because, subconsciously, the consultee does not really believe that the counseling can be effective. To help the consultee with theme interference, Caplan suggested (1) "unlinking," or alleviating the consultee's subconscious perception, or (2) "theme-interference reduction," which involves the consultant trying to help the consultee construct other possible outcomes.

PROCESS CONSULTATION

The process consultation model emphasizes behavioral, group-dynamic dimensions within an organization by examining the effects of communication on each strata of the organization as it pertains to the attainment of its goals. The origin of the process consultation model, which is frequently identified with Schein (1969), rests in social psychology. It is primarily a group problem-solving approach that seeks to make people more aware of the interpersonal communications that are negatively affecting their work productivity and attitudes. Process consultation also is known as *organizational development* (OD) and is frequently used to improve organizational functioning by concentrating on and working with small groups of employees. The model attempts to strengthen the organizational system by optimally using existing personnel to produce and enhance a growth-oriented environment. A counselor-as-consultant using the process consultation model seeks to help members of the organization to understand the interactional patterns that may be interfering with the goals of the organization.

Schein (1969) suggested that interactional patterns which interfere with an organization's functioning include inconsistent decision-making styles, hidden personal agendas, poor leadership skills, inappropriate agenda setting, "scapegoating," or inappropriately high levels of competition. Consultants using this approach also are sensitive to problems with the structural system and/or managerial procedures within the organization.

Schein (1969) recommended the following seven interacting and overlapping steps for process consultation: (1) initial contact with the client organization, (2) definition of the consultation relationship, including both the formal and psychological contracts, (3) selection and setting of a method of work, (4) data gathering and diagnosis, (5) intervention, (6) involvement reduction, and (7) termination. Process consultants are seldom experts within the organizations or industries for which they are providing consultation. Instead, they are usually professionals whose focus or target of interest is the "how" of the interpersonal process within an organization. In summary, process consultation is oriented toward manifesting and facilitating the many levels and potentially effective modes of communication that exist in an organization. William Culp (1985) presented a case study of organizational consultation in a business corporation (pp. 235-287).

BEHAVIORAL CONSULTATION

The behavioral model of consultation is based heavily on the assumption that changes in an environment will necessarily change the behaviors of people in that environment. This approach is particularly well suited for consulting with professionals employed in settings such as schools, prisons, hospitals, and other controlled and regulated environments.

Like the mental-health consultation model, the behavioral consultation model is a problem-solving approach. It is based on social learning theory, with client and consultee problems conceptualized as having evolved from direct or vicarious previous learnings. The consultant's goal is to ascertain what the problem or target behavior is, determine and isolate environmental variables that foster or support the target behavior, and suggest environmental changes that will diminish the probability of the behavior continuing. Also, the consultant who employs this model utilizes the principles and traditional behavioral techniques of behavior modification (e.g., shaping, chaining, successive approximation, or modeling) to produce new behaviors. In addition, the behavioral consultation model may include other learning principles and models such as role playing, homework assignments, and feedback.

Although behavioral consultation may be applied in any setting, the usefulness of behavioral techniques in schools is particularly well-documented. Perhaps this is because teachers feel more comfortable with consultants who suggest techniques and interventions consistent with the learning principles with which the teachers are familiar.

ATHEORETICAL PROBLEM-SOLVING CONSULTATION

Myrick (1977) suggested an atheoretical approach to consultation which he believed is particularly well suited for professional counselors. The approach relies heavily upon communication skills described as "facilitative" (Wittmer & Myrick, 1974).

Myrick's (1977) consultation approach is a systematic set of procedures that follow seven steps. The first step focuses on identifying the consultee's problem. This is followed by the consultant clarifying both the emotional and behavioral aspects of the consultee's situation, primarily through encouraging the consultee to talk about feelings, specific behaviors that influenced the consultee's current ideas and situation, what the consultee expects to achieve, what has already been tried in attempting to correct the situation, and positive attitudes and behaviors already present in the situation. Step three involves identifying the goal(s) or desired outcome(s) for the situation. In step four, relevant behaviors applicable to the situation are observed and recorded by the consultee and possibly by the consultant. Next, the consultant and consultee develop a plan of action together, with the expectation that the consultee will play the major role in carrying out the plan. Step six is the initiation of the plan by the consultee under the "supervision" of the consultant. Step seven is follow-up; examining what has happened to determine whether the plan is working and/or changes, if any, need to be made in the plan. Myrick recommended this approach for both individuals and groups. This model, which is straightforward, progresses systematically, involves many already familiar skills and behaviors, and appeals to many professional counselors, particularly those working in school systems.

Myrick (1977) purported that the model is helpful with crisis, preventive, and developmental consultation. *Crisis consultation* is defined as assisting the consultee who is experiencing an urgent problem, such as an agency director who has a concerned board member coming in at the end of the day and is unsure how to approach the conference. *Preventive consultation,* the second type, is used when the consultee believes that an urgent problem is imminent. In this situation, the consultee has received signals that a problem will be developing if the situation is not handled correctly now. Finally, *developmental consultation* involves helping the consultee help others develop skills and behaviors that will either prevent problems in the future or enable them to cope effectively with problems should they arise. A current example of developmental consultation is the school counselor who helps teachers help students develop ways to avoid involvement with substance abuses.

AN EXAMPLE OF INDIVIDUAL CONSULTATION

Many times a professional counselor is approached for consultation in a rather informal manner. Other professionals, who want consultation but are uneasy about making a formal request for it, often seek out professional counselors, who have established themselves as consultants, in informal atmospheres such as a staff dining room or lounge area, or at a social event. The following illustrates such an exchange. "I hate to disturb you now with shop talk, but could I ask you about a case of mine—Marion? I don't think I am making as much progress with the case as I would like. She's immature, but I believe her behavior is a method to avoid taking responsibility for her actions. I have been seeing her weekly since October and during our sessions she has been timid, quiet, and generally non-responsive; the very behaviors that prompted her to see me. And, she is concerned about keeping up with her responsibilities at the insurance company where she works. She's a great person and I don't think there's anything seriously or pathologically wrong with her. Yet, I am worried that if I continue seeing her and she doesn't make any progress, she may think that she has a serious problem that can't be helped, and she may lose her job."

The professional counselor, in a consultant role, responded with "Yes, it's always a problem deciding if you are doing the right things with a client. What can you tell me about Marion?"

"She's young—just turned 18 in May. She graduated early from a small high school—just after she reached 16."

"What other people are closely involved in Marion's life? Others can sometimes play an important role in determining behavior. How about her parents or friends?"

"I'm not too sure. I have been focusing counseling pretty much as a job-related motivational problem."

"What approaches have you tried?"

"Primarily some time-management schemes; homework type assignments on time use. I've also been having her practice speaking to others at work. I thought that if I got Marion to interact with others she might come out a bit more and be less timid and quiet and do a better job at work."

By this time the professional counselor has helped the consultee to formulate the problem, and has learned what has been done. The consultant continued with "What other directions might you take?"

The consultee was relieved not to have been admonished by the counselor. "I could explore with Marion the influence that others in her life are having on her—specifically her parents. I recognize that she is young and, you know, maybe too much pressure is on her to keep up with those older employees."

The counselor-as-consultant replied "Specifically, how do you think you can approach Marion during your next session?" This question helps the consultee to think aloud about a plan of action.

"Well, I think I will tell Marion that I have been reviewing our sessions and believe that I would like to explore some new avenues which might be helpful. Also, if the parents are a dominant factor, as I now think they may be, I might suggest that we have a session or two which includes them."

"How do you think Marion will feel about that? Sometimes parents unwittingly can make it difficult for their child, even a young adult."

"Oh, I don't believe there would be a problem. I somehow sense the family is close."

"Try it and call me—let me know after your next session with her what's happening."

A week later, the professional counselor received a call from the consultee indicating that the last session went well and that indeed, Marion was feeling pressured into employment and marriage by her parents. In addition, a session had been established with the parents and Marion together.

The above example, in which the process of consultation has been considerably abridged, shows how the professional counselor and consultee interact as co-professionals, and not as an authority and subordinate. The consultee actually made the important decisions and the professional counselor, as consultant, primarily helped to clarify and provide support for the consultee's decisions. In effective consultative relationships, consultees perceive counselors-as-consultants as persons who respect and understand them, and are responsive to their needs.

The professional counselor, as a consultant, usually tries to respond to a consultee's request about a problem by helping the consultee to determine alternate solutions. However, although other professionals may ask a professional counselor for assistance with a problem in the work place, they are not always receptive to assistance. They want the situation to be different, but they prefer not to have to rely on others; a natural human tendency. Alternately, consultees sometimes want someone else to make the needed changes for them. This, of course, has to be resisted by consultants because they then leave the role of a consultant and become a provider of direct services. If this happens, the skills of consultees are not being further developed so they can respond more effectively with future cases, and efficiency is not being obtained within the agency; i.e., the "ripple effect" is non-existent.

Professionals within a given field may vary as much as professionals from different fields. Professional counselors, for example, differ in the amount and quality of training they have received, mainly because of variations in the college and university programs from which they graduated. They also may vary in intellectual functioning, personality characteristics, skills and abilities, and performance. In addition, even the most capable, enthusiastic and well-trained professional counselors will frequently find themselves incapable of handling all the problems with which they are confronted in their work setting. Situations may be encountered where a counselor lacks the skills, insight, or knowledge to work effectively with a given problem. At these times, boundaries for feelings of inadequacy are non-existent, and so it should be remembered that counselors, too, at times need consultation services.

Consultation is a dynamic process. It is a problem-solving activity, inherent in which are the elements of internal change, external demands, and the interface of both. Not only are the consultee and client affected, but the organization(s) for which they work also is(are) affected. Blake and Mouton (1983) noted that, "Education and consultation are probably two of the most important factors behind the forward movement of society" (p. iii). They also suggested that consultation may be the more meaningful factor because it has an even greater potential for widespread effect. When professional counselors-as-consultants help consultees, the consultees then can be successful with many, many people with whom they work and they can make far greater progress in the way they work. Thus, the potential of consultation as a professional-counselor function is unlimited. Its need is ever-present because of the constant concommitant need for new and better ways to solve a wide range of problems.

Chapter **8**

RESEARCH IN PROFESSIONAL COUNSELING

For new problems to develop as a professional field grows and matures is not an uncommon event. Of concern, however, are old problems that continue to exist. In professional counseling, the old problem of determining the role of research for professional counselors and trainees has become particularly acute during the past ten years. An influential factor has been the requirement of additional research resulting from forces outside as well as within the profession. These forces include the profession's increasing involvement with standards of practice, accountability, litigation, and the public's increasing use of counseling services.

The professional counselor is primarily a practitioner of applied behavioral sciences whose work is to help others solve problems. The need for a counselor's time to be devoted to the direct service of helping others is usually viewed as urgent by supervisors, administrators, managers, clients, colleagues, and sometimes by counselors themselves.

In contrast, conducting research is rarely viewed as urgent. Thus, professional counselors are often dismayed to find that many of their colleagues and clients fail to share the value they place on research. In fact, in some work settings research is viewed with suspicion and disdain. Such behavior can be attributed partially to the problem that many counseling service settings are beset by so many pressures and problems that they focus only on addressing the immediate *counseling* concerns with which they are confronted. In such settings, research is not viewed as an integral part of good practice, but rather as a luxury to be conducted only if time is available for it. The appropriate situation is somewhere between the extremes. Professional counselors *should* devote most of their time to counseling activities, but research is an appropriate, small proportion of their time *and* an important part of good professional counseling practice.

Of all the personnel employed in places where counselors work, the professional counselor in many situations will have had the most training in formal scientific inquiry. Therefore, counselors often spend time discussing the nature of research in counseling. What is perplexing is why the topic of research has generated such differences of opinion. Perhaps the term appears to be pretentious, implying that it "guarantees" new insights. Or perhaps it conjures images of the professional counselor using clients and other personnel as mere subjects in some type of laboratory experiment that is not "helping oriented." Neither of these points of view is correct. Scientific inquiry, or research, is required if professional counselors are to draw valid conclusions about, or to effectively evaluate, counseling.

Inherent in the viewpoint that research and scientific inquiry are synonymous with drawing valid conclusions and making decisions is the need to perceive research from a much broader perspective than has been true among other professional groups. The core of this view is that professional counselors must habitually inquire and maintain a critical attitude about their professional work. Respect for objectivity and unbiased conclusions is integral to the professional counselor's training. Thus, research is equated with inquiry and not just with traditional methods of data gathering and analyses.

Professional counselors are continually engaged in careful, scientific reviews of all their activities, although some of that research may not be structurally well-designed. In many work places, the procedures of rigorous, carefully controlled research studies admittedly are difficult, if not sometimes impossible, to carry out. Also, counselors do not ordinarily initiate studies which are removed from their work and clients. Most of their research is directed toward immediate concerns and not toward general problems in the field of counseling. The former can be described as research that addresses immediate concerns of a counseling situation (i.e., answering questions such as "What progress is being made during counseling?" and "What techniques are most effective with the client?"). The latter form of research addresses issues that are more theoretical and general such as the "why" and "how" of counseling. Although the distinction between these different forms of research is forced, it illustrates that research on what happens during counseling sessions focuses upon specific client situations where progress is of immediate concern to the counselor; it concentrates on information for helping the client. Research about the why and how of counseling, however, is more general and is concerned with inferences of basic issues about the process of counseling and other interventions; it is not necessarily specific to an individual client or group of clients. Researching the effect counseling is having on a client not only affects that client, but affects all other clients as well. For example, if a professional counselor answers questions about Kate's progress in counseling, the resulting information can be used to alter what happens with other clients. The likelihood of professional counselors systematically researching a client's progress is considerably greater than the likelihood of conducting research on "why" or "how" clients change because the former directly affects the agency, school, business, or practice.

Research as an aspect of professionalism in counseling is discussed further in Chapter 10. This discussion focuses on the nature of research practices by professional counselors. Research in counseling is often perceived as complex because of the terminology used. Therefore, the following discussion presents some of the important terms, concepts, and methods used with scientific inquiry.

Scientific inquiry or research is essentially a systematic and controlled extension of common sense (Kerlinger, 1986). Built into this extension is the development of theoretical structures and concepts that are continuously being tested and evaluated. Central to scientific inquiry is the research process with its basic components of reasoning and logic. The former can be delineated into deductive and inductive reasoning. In *deductive reasoning,* the logical progression is from the general to the specific; i.e., if a general idea or theory is true, then a specific behavior should be observable. *Inductive reasoning,* however, is inferential and progresses from the specific to the general; if a specific behavior is (consistently) observable, then a general idea or theory is true. In inductive reasoning, data are gathered and analyzed, and depending upon the outcomes of the research, generalizations or inferences are made that relate back to theoretical structures and concepts.

RESEARCH DESIGNS AND PLANS

Effective research involves structured and carefully developed methods referred to as *research designs or plans*. The type of design used by professional counselors may involve a *continuous-measurement time-series experiment* or a traditional *pre-post experiment*. Both forms of research are effective in measuring selected behaviors in counseling and both involve the element of experimental control. They differ by number of subjects, types of data generated, and types of questions studied.

Continuous-Measurement
Time-Series Designs

Continuous-measurement designs are particularly useful with single-subject (one client) research or studies involving small number of subjects (clients). This type of research is most often used to address questions of difference (e.g., is there a difference due to treatment?). Several sets of observations are undertaken through continuous (i.e., repeated) measurements during a given time period. Included in the data-gathering process are baseline (i.e., before counseling or intervention commences) information, continuous measurement during intervention, and post-intervention measurement. A client's behavioral characteristics are studied as well as the results of intervention.

With continuous measurement, the process is as important as the product or outcome, as is exemplified with the recording of baseline behavior and continuous performance data that are dependent upon intervention. Behavioral changes that occur as a result of intervention are attributed to the new condition since all other factors are (theoretically) held constant. Continuous measurement designs vary by treatment (i.e., intervention) format with the most common being the A-B, A-B-A-B, and multiple-baseline designs. A brief explanation of each follows.

A-B Design. Two phases constitutes this design; baseline (A) followed by intervention (B). The latter is initiated after the baseline behavior achieves a level of stability that provides a satisfactory estimate of pretreatment performance. The criterion for satisfactory stability is defined by the counselor.

With this design, the assumption is made that any change in behavior is a (direct) result of intervention. However, with only two phases, it is difficult to be certain that this assumption is accurate and/or valid. Extraneous factors occurring simultaneously with the commencement of intervention could also influence outcomes. A means of circumventing this possibility is to replicate the two phases as in an A-B-A-B design.

A-B-A-B Design. This design extends the A-B format to include a sequential replication of the two phases (i.e., A and B). If the pattern of behavior observed during the first two phases is replicated during the last two phases (i.e., the pretreatment baseline contingencies are reestablished during the third phase and the intervention contingencies of phase two are restablished during phase four), it can be assumed that the changes in behavior are accounted for by the intervention.

Although deliberately oversimplified, the following illustration demonstrates the use of a multiple-baseline design in counseling. The A-B-A-B format would be detrimental to the client. For example, if an intervention technique introduced during the second phase was found to be effective in helping a client with acting-out aggressions toward his/her peers, a reversal to the baseline to reestablish aggressive behaviors would not be desirable. In situations of this nature, a multiple-baseline design is an effective alternative.

Multiple-Baseline Design. In this design, multiple target behaviors are recorded simultaneously, and the respective baselines for the different behaviors are staggered. The assumption is made that subsequent behaviors serve as a means of control for the preceding behavior. Although deliberatley oversimplified, the following illustration demonstrates the use of a multiple-baseline design in counseling. The Jacksons, who worked for different accounting firms, had been married for seven years and sought the help of a professional counselor because of marital problems which focused primarily on communication with each other. They worked with the professional counselor over a period of five weeks for three communication problem areas: use of obscenities, shouting, and negative statements. Using a multiple-baseline design to examine counseling effectiveness, the professional counselor divided the measurement of effectiveness into five phases, each of which lasted one week. During each phase, data were collected by recording the frequency with which each of the communication problems occurred. The data gathered during phase one became the "baseline" data against which the frequency counts for the remaining phases were compared. During phase two (second week), the Jacksons went to separate rooms whenever either individual used an obscenity. During phase three (third week), the Jacksons continued with the procedure introduced during phase two but also went to different rooms whenever there was shouting. With phase four (fourth week), the Jacksons focused on negative statements, again going to separate rooms when this behavior occurred. They also continued largely on their own with the procedures introduced in phases two and three. The three procedures used in phase four were continued in phase five (fifth week) for purposes of follow-up data collection.

To recap the illustration using the Jacksons, after baseline conditions have been established for three behaviors, phase two is introduced; it consists of initiating intervention for the first behavior and continuing with the baseline conditions for the remaining two behaviors. In changing to the third phase, intervention is introduced for the second behavior and the baseline condition is continued for the third behavior only. Finally, during the fourth phase, the intervention is used with all behaviors. A change in performance for all behaviors upon initiation of the intervention confirms that the results are due to the treatment effect only. Thus, multiple-baseline designs are considered the most powerful of the time-series experiments. However, in many counseling situations, the most rigorous procedure that a professional counselor can reasonably use is the A-B design.

Traditional Experimental Designs

Characteristic of traditional experimental research is a focus upon the product; outcomes due to intervention. Questions studied in this form of research address relationships or correlations as well as differences. Unlike continuous-measurement designs, differences in traditional experimental designs essentially involve comparisons between groups of subjects or measurements within a group following intervention. Typically, fewer observations are made in traditional experimental research, with the outcomes often derived from a single performance measure on a group of subjects following intervention. Designs for this type of research vary, but are based upon three main formats: independent group comparisons, repeated-measures comparisons, and mixed-group comparisons. These three formats and correlational studies are briefly summarized below.

Independent Group Comparisons. Studies employing this format involve different groups, each of which is independent of the others (i.e., the performance of one group does not influence the performance of the other groups being studied). In addition to the criterion of independence, the assumption is (and must be) that the groups were "equivalent" before the administration of intervention.

Studies that investigate only one experimental variable are referred to as single-factor designs. Two-factor designs involve the investigation of two experimental variables in the same study. The number of levels in each factor may vary. A study with two factors, each of which contains two levels, is referred to as a two-by-two design which is denoted as 2 x 2, indicating that two factors are used and each has two levels. If the two factors vary in number of levels, the notation changes accordingly (e.g., 2 x 3, 3 x 2, or 3 x 4). For example, in a business or industrial setting. the counselor might assign a section of employees (group 1) to a wellness-workshop training program, while a second section (i.e., a control group) would not receive wellness training. The professional counselor then divides the participants in each group into level-A and level-B personality types. Thus, the counselor has formulated a 2 x 2 study that consists of two groups (group 1 and the control group) and two levels within each group (A and B personality types).

Repeated-Measures Comparisons. When the groups being studied are not independent of each other, or the same group of subjects are studied under two or more different conditions, a repeated-measures design can be employed. Studies of this nature may involve a pre-post design to compare differences due to treatment intervention (i.e., a pretest is administered, the intervention is employed, and a posttest is administered). As an example, repeated measures comparisons can be used by professional counselors to evaluate a group's progress. If a group of adult substance abusers is being studied for the purpose of examining their progress as a result of group counseling, Julie, their counselor, can gather data on the incidence of substance abuse, interpersonal relationship, and absenteeism at work prior to group counseling and again after counseling is completed. Of note, however, is that with this form of data gathering, Julie needs to use a number of pretest and posttest measurements to assure that she acquires an accurate indication of progress.

Mixed-Group Designs. Repeated measures can be employed with independent groups using a mixed-group design. This format is extremely flexible, allowing for variation in the number of repeated and independent variables. For example, the three conditions involved in a study may include one repeated and two independent, or two repeated and one independent, variables. Mixed-group designs can become rather complex and, therefore, their results are more difficult to interpret.

Correlational Studies. In addition to differences between or within groups, traditional-experimental research often involves studies of a sample of subjects to determine the degree to which two or more variables correlate, or vary together. Using a minimum of two measures on each subject, a correlation coefficient is computed to determine an estimate of the relationship between given variables, or to predict outcomes. For example, William, a professional counselor, is interested in answering the question, "How helpful are job-placement seminars for the future income of discharged employees?" To address this question, William could examine the relationship between income level and the frequency of the respective individual's attendance at the seminars.

FACTORS AFFECTING OUTCOMES

With the determination of an appropriate experimental design, consideration needs to be given to factors that can affect the outcome(s) of a research study; i.e., threats to internal and external validity.

Internal Validity

Internal validity is the basic minimum with which the results of an experiment are interpretable (Campbell & Stanley, 1963). Stated in a simplified manner, all systematic differences between the groups being studied are eliminated except the variable of concern; the research should be free of extraneous variables that may affect outcomes. When it is impossible to circumvent *all* threats to internal validity, those remaining need to be addressed in the interpretation of results. Drew (1976) reported eight threats to internal validity. They are briefly summarized in the paragraphs that follow.

One problem of internal validity that is difficult to control is *history;* specific incidents that can intervene during a study because the researcher may be unaware of them or unable to prevent their occurrence. An example is the effect an airplane crash (coincident with the research) had upon a client with a fear of flying. The counselor working with this client was pleased with the progress being made. However, when the client learned of the reported airline accident, the progressive trend suddenly reversed.

When studies involve a long period of time, *maturation* may become a threat to the internal validity of a study. For example, a subject's performance may be affected by his/her hunger or fatigue, or by aging if a longitudinal study is involved.

A third threat to internal validity is testing or *test practice.* Consideration needs to be given to whether change from pretest to posttest is due to treatment only or is due to test practice. Scores on a second, or post, test may be influenced simply by the experience of taking a pretest.

In addition to the subject's experience in test taking, consideration needs to be given to the affect that *instrumentation* may have upon the results of a study. Campbell and Stanley (1963) referred to this problem as "changes in the calibration of a measurement instrument or changes in the observers" (p. 175). Any changes made in the recording or scoring of a subject's responses during a study will subsequently affect the results of a study, and therefore threaten internal validity.

Assigning subjects to particular groups on the basis of typical (usually extreme) scores poses another threat to internal validity because of *statistical regression.* When typical scores are used, the risk is always present that during the study subjects may regress toward their average performance, resulting in groups that may be more equivalent than different.

Another factor that may affect study performance and threaten internal validity is the *Hawthorne effect.* It occurs when a subject's performance is affected merely as a function of being in a study and feeling "special" about it.

A seventh threat to internal validity is *bias in group composition.* This is of particular concern with "quasi-experimental" designs, which differ from experimental designs by the manner in which subject groups are formed. In experimental designs, groups are formed by sampling a single-subject pool in a systematic manner (e.g., random sampling). These groups are similar until treatment begins. However, in quasi-experimental designs, the groups may not be similar and are not necessarily derived from the same subject pool, because controlling for systematic differences that may exist between groups before the research begins is hard to do.

A final threat to internal validity is *experimental mortality,* or the loss of subjects. General loss of subjects is to be expected in research and often extra subjects are selected for the purpose of having a back-up or replacement pool. Experimental mortality, however, threatens internal validity when it results in significantly unequal numbers in comparison groups.

External Validity

External validity is concerned with generalizability; e.g., are the results representative of or applicable to the population studied? To facilitate external validity, a study uses subjects, settings, treatment variables, and measurement variables selected to be representative of another, usually larger, context to which the results are to be generalized. Threats to external validity that need to be circumvented (i.e., non-representative experimental setting, population-sample differences, pretest influence, and multiple treatment interference) are discussed in the following paragraphs.

The *experimental setting* needs to be arranged, as much as possible, like the setting to which the results will be generalized. Significant deviations from the nonexperimental setting may affect subjects' performances, resulting in a sample that is not representative of the intended original population.

Population-sample differences, or using a nonrepresentative sample from a given population, poses a great threat to external validity. The interpretation of experimental results must be generalizable to the population represented by the subjects, but this is not possible if significant characteristic differences exist between the subjects and members of the larger population. Therefore, care needs to be taken to use a correct procedure for selecting representative subjects.

Pretest procedures can sometimes create a *pretest influence.* In general, a researcher wants to be assured that performance will be due to subject-task interaction rather than the subject's ability to learn to perform a particular behavior. However, such procedures, if given to one set of subjects in the study and not another, can threaten external validity if the pretested subjects' sensitivity to the experimental variable being studied is decreased or increased.

When multiple treatments are administered to the same subjects, a cumulative effect referred to as *multiple-treatment interference* may influence their performance and the generalizability of results then becomes questionable. This will most often be true in counseling research when the effects of prior treatments have not dissipated before the next treatment is introduced, resulting in increased or depressed sensitivity to the experimental task.

SELECTING VARIABLES

An essential consideration in any research is selecting the variables to be measured; generally referred to as dependent and independent variables.

The dependent variable (i.e., that which is being measured) must logically relate to the behavior being studied. In addition, it needs to be observable, specific, and sensitive to performance differences. Because measurement of this variable provides an indication of a subject's actual level of performance, the most sensitive measure available should be used in order to assure precision of results.

The independent variable (i.e., the variable being manipulated and studied) is also referred to as the treatment. An independent variable can consist of more than one level. For example, if three methods of counseling were being compared, the dependent variable might be counseling effectiveness and the independent variable (i.e., counseling methods) would be divided into three levels, each representing one of the counseling methods.

SELECTING SUBJECTS

Three related factors need to be considered in the subject-selection process: appropriateness, representativeness and number of subjects.

Appropriateness

The subjects in a study need to fit the definition for the given population. As Kerlinger (1986) indicated, a population consists of all elements of any well-defined class of people, events, or objects being investigated. Consideration needs to be given to units or restrictions in the population as they relate to the topic being studied. This may result in selective inclusion or exclusion of particular potential subjects.

Representativeness

The subjects selected for a study need to be representative of the population if the research results are to be generalizeable to the given set of individuals, events, or objects. Several different sampling procedures exist: simple random, stratified random, proportional, systematic, and cluster sampling.

Simple Random Sampling. This process assures that each individual, event, or object in a given population has an equal chance of being selected for the study. The assumption is made that the characteristics of the population are presented in the subjects selected (i.e., sample) to the same degree that the characteristics exist in the population. However, the more heterogeneous a population is, the greater is the chance that the members' diverse characteristics will not be appropriately represented in the sample selected.

A variety of techniques can be used to randomly select subjects from a given population (e.g., drawing names from a hat). However, probably the most effective technique is using a table of random numbers. Each potential subject is assigned a number and then a table of random numbers is used to identify the appropriate subjects.

Stratified Random Sample. This process is used when two or more groups of individuals, events, or objects that are distinctly different on an important variable in the study are being studied. Each of these different sets or subpopulations, referred to as strata, must have representative subjects selected from it. Therefore, after the strata are clearly defined, a random sample is drawn from each of the respective strata.

Proportional Sampling. Occasionally, a particular subgroup represents only a proportion of the population. To avoid misrepresentation, the selection of subjects in this case needs to be proportionate to that of the larger population. In this sampling technique, the lists of sub-population individuals, events, or objects are developed using the same proportions that exist in the larger population, and subjects are then randomly drawn from each list in proportional representation..

Systematic Sampling. In this procedure subjects are systematically drawn from a population based on an appropriate arrangement of the list of individuals, events, or objects in the population. The names of individuals meeting the selection criteria are listed in a predetermined, unbiased manner, and the researcher randomly selects a starting point in the list and then selects every nth individual until the desired number of subjects is obtained. This technique is easily managed and therefore appealing to many researchers. However, caution is advised in that the list of potential subjects must be free of any influential trends in the ordering.

Cluster Sampling. Potential subjects for some studies may already be formed into predetermined groups or clusters. In these situations, clusters are initially selected and then the subjects are randomly selected from within the clusters. Consideration needs to be given to representative sampling of both the initially selected clusters and the actual subjects.

Sample Size

Because no set sample size is required under all conditions, the number of subjects "necessary" for a given study is unclear. One influential factor is the amount of variation in the population being studied. For example, smaller samples can be used with more homogeneous populations because less variation occurs. Likewise, populations containing a large amount of variation necessitate larger samples to better represent the variation. Because an adequate sample of behavior needs to be obtained, sample size must be judged according to the original population and its characteristics.

STATISTICAL ANALYSES

An important consideration in the process of developing a research study is the statistical procedures used to analyze the data collected. Decisions concerning data analyses are made when designing the study because the statistical tools used are dependent upon the purpose of the research undertaken and the type of data derived. Therefore, the selection of appropriate statistical analyses is important.

Type of Measurement Scale

The data to be analyzed vary by type of measurement scale used. The first type, *nominal* data, also referred to as classification or categorical data, consists of information in the form of mutually exclusive groups or categories. Each category is presumably distinct from the other categories, with the data serving only as labels of identification. Examples of nominal data include year in school, occupation, and yes or no responses to a question.

Ordinal data are characterized by rank-order measurements and an underlying continuum. The component of identity found with nominal data is extended to include the dimension of order and thus, a relative measure of "more than" or "less than." Measurements using Likert-type scales exemplify this data type; e.g., a five-step continuum from "none of the time" to "all of the time."

The properties of identity and degree of difference found in ordinal data are extended to include magnitude of difference (i.e., the property of additivity) for *interval data*. As its name implies, interval data address known and constant magnitudinal differences between scores; i.e., interval distances. Also characteristic of this type of data is an arbitary zero point. Examples of interval data include the Celsius and Fahrenheit temperature scales as well as calendar time.

The last type of data, *ratio* data, includes all the properties of interval data, except the zero point is not arbitrary. A score of zero represents total absence of the variable being measured. Examples of ratio data include response time, weight, and height.

Descriptive Statistics—Central Tendency

Descriptive statistics are used when the researcher only is interested in describing the group(s) being studied. This may be the only type of statistical analysis undertaken in a study or it can be followed with statistical analyses for inferential purposes, which will be discussed later.

Descriptive statistics can be divided into two general categories of measures; central tendency and dispersion or variance. The most common measures of central tendency are the mean, median, and mode.

Mean. Also referred to as the arithmetic average, the mean of a distribution of scores is derived by summing all the scores in a distribution and dividing the same by the number of scores in the set. Although this statistic is not used with nominal or ordinal data, it is the most frequently used measure of central tendency. It is more stable than the other measures of central tendency and is amenable to additional manipulation, making it useful in inferential statistics. However, the mean is affected by extreme, or outlying, scores. Therefore, if a distribution has a few extreme scores and accuracy of measurement is important, the median will be a more appropriate measure of central tendency.

Median. This measure of central tendency represents the middle point in a distribution of scores; the point above or below which half of the scores fall. The median is used with all types of data except nominal data.

Mode. The most frequently occurring score or interval in a distribution is referred to as the mode. This statistic is the only measure of central tendency to use with nominal data, but it also may be used with the other three types.

Descriptive Statistics—Dispersion Measures

The second category of descriptive statistic includes dispersion measures or the degree to which scores vary from a measure of central tendency. Statistics in this category are the range, semi-interquartile range, and standard deviation.

Range. The range, which provides a quick index of the amount of variability in a distribution, is determined by subtracting the lowest from the highest scores in the distribution, and adding 1. Therefore, the range, as a measure of dispersion, is limited in its usefulness because it is not representative of most of the data in the distribution.

Semi-Interquartile Range. A distribution is divided into four equal parts separated by points referred to as quartiles. Thus, 50% of the scores in a distribution fall between the first quartile (Q_1) and the third quartile (Q_3). The difference between Q_1 and Q_3 divided by 2 represents the semi-interquartile range. Because this statistic uses more of the scores in a distribution than does the simple range, it provides a more stable measure of dispersion, and a more representative picture of the distribution of scores.

Standard Division. Although this statistic is not as easy to calculate as the other measures of variability, it is used more often. The standard deviation, which provides a "standardized" measure of a score's deviation above or below the mean, is limited to interval and ratio data. The major advantages of this statistic are that it is used in many more complex statistics and it is considerably less affected by extreme scores.

Inferential Statistics

As implied, inferential statistics enable a counselor/researcher to make inferences that the treatment(s) in a study actually generated the observed performance(s). Implications also can be drawn from the resulting data to variables not directly involved in the study because inferential statistics provide an indication of the degree to which the results are due to treatment or to chance.

Studies involving this form of statistical analysis involve questions of difference or relationship. Also, a variety of statistical tests of significance can be employed. The acceptable probability level that the results are due to treatment rather than chance is usually $p < .05$ or $p < .01$. If $p < .05$ or $p < .01$, the results obtained in a study would be due to chance only 5 or 1, respectively, or less times out of 100.

Tests of significance are applied to either parametric or non-parametric statistics, depending upon reasonable and supportable assumptions made concerning the population being studied. Generally, nonparametric statistics require fewer and less rigorous assumptions about population parameters (i.e., values such as mean and standard deviation) than do parametric statistics. Also, nonparametric statistics can be applied to all types of data, but parametric statistical analyses may be used only with interval and ratio data. Larger sample sizes are also required for parametric statistical analyses, but this type of statistics can be applied to a greater variety of research questions.

Statistical Analyses
Addressing Relationships

The degree to which two or more phenomena are related or vary together are the focus of studies addressing relationship questions. The statistic that provides an estimate of the relationship between given variables is the *correlation coefficient*. This coefficient ranges from -1.00 to +1.00 with coefficients between zero and +1.00 indicating that the two variables tend to vary in the same direction; i.e., have a positive relationship. Negative correlations (i.e., coefficients falling between zero and -1.00) indicate an inverse relationship; the two variables vary in opposite directions. Correlation coefficients with higher numbers indicate stronger relationships while coefficients approaching zero are indicators of weak relationships. Likewise, a correlation coefficient of zero signifies a total lack of systematic variation between the two variables; they vary independently of one another.

The correlation technique employed depends on the type of data. When interval or ratio data are involved, the *Pearson product-moment correlation* is used (Miller, 1986). The *Spearman rank-order correlation* and *Kendall's tau* are typically used with ordinal data.

More than two variables can be compared using a multiple correlation analysis. This technique can be extended by a multiple regression analysis which provides a measure of the amount of variance in the dependent variable accounted for by each independent variable being studied. An alternative use of the multiple regression analysis is to predict the effectiveness of given treatments.

TRADITIONAL VERSUS SINGLE-SUBJECT RESEARCH

Although professional counselors apply scientific inquiry as the basis for helping others, they have done little to integrate science into counseling through traditional experimental research. Although this appears to be due to several reasons, the major problem, with few exceptions, is that traditional experimental designs have emphasized data collection using large groups of subjects, normative research, and analyses based on within-group or between-group treatments. Applying methodology of this nature to a counseling practitioner's problems poses immense practical difficulties (Gelso, 1985).

Traditional experimental designs also require, among other things, a large number of relatively homogeneous clients at a given period of time. Consider for example a professional counselor who is interested in studying the effectiveness of two treatment approaches for adolescents who are concerned with their sexual behavior. Using the traditional approach, the counselor would need approximately 30 clients matched on relevant background variables (e.g., age, gender, severity of problem, and history of previous treatment), who ideally would need to receive counseling within approximately the same timeframe. This in itself is a rather difficult task considering the type of clients and time allotment. Further, utilizing even a simple experimental design of a treatment group and no-treatment control group format to examine effects due to treatment would entail near-impossible demands for the professional counselor to meet. Of course, this illustration has deliberately been oversimplified. However, it does illustrate the problems encountered when conducting research using a traditional experimental design.

Another effect upon the professional counselor's use of traditional experimental research methodology is the ethical factors involved in selecting control groups by withholding treatment from clients. This, of course, should not be done without careful consideration of the risks involved for the untreated group. An interesting argument on this subject, advanced by Barlow, Hayes, and Nelson (1984), is that

> ...in most instances there is no evidence that the treatment works in the first place, which forms the basis for conducting research on its effectiveness. Therefore, one could argue that withholding an unproven treatment for a control group might be less of a risk than applying this treatment to the experimental group. (p. 26)

The traditional research methodology of working with large groups and determining average results, with associated disregard for individual differences, has limited relevance in contributing to improvements for specific clients. Therefore, traditional research methodology has had little influence in affecting the professional counselor's practice or self-evaluation because it has not been relevant to applied settings.

The question of what can be done remains. Goldman (1977), in recognizing the lack of influence of traditional research, advised professional counselors "...to return to the conception of research as imaginative searching by intelligent and informed people who are aware of the important questions that we as a profession and society in general need to have answered" (p.366). Goldman probably would agree that, while traditional comparison-group research designs remain indispensable tools for professional counselors, they have specific limitations that render them dysfunctional in situations and settings where counselors typically work.

An alternative would be to use single-subject designs for measuring and demonstrating the effect(s) of counseling. This type of design adapts the traditional experimental research approach to fit the practice of counseling. Single-subject methods can be generalized across all settings and situations because the techniques can vary depending on the particular circumstances and goals of each client. Also, the methods are not dependent upon any particular theoretical orientation, but rather reflect "a way of thinking." The basic elements of single-subject research consist of measuring change, relating this change to a particular aspect of counseling, and basing future professional actions on the observations.

Will debates about what should be the nature of research conducted by counselors ever be fully resolved? Probably not. Therefore, Gelso's (1985) statements provide a reasonable alternative:

> Attempts to solve the problem of low relevance create other problems (i.e., those caused by low rigor). If we attack these other problems by doing more rigorous research, for example, this makes for research that is less relevant to practice. Our solutions to problems create other problems. In effect, there are no ready solutions.
>
> My personal and partial solution to this apparent dilemma is to conduct a wide range of research along what may be labeled a rigor-relevance continuum. I also think that this is the most fruitful way for the field of counseling to proceed. If the pendulum of beliefs in counseling research swings too far to one side or the other (on the rigor-relevance continuum), the field and the amount and quality of knowledge that it generates will suffer. (p. 552)

AN OBSERVATION

Most professional counselors, in addition to applying scientific inquiry as the basis of helping others, also continue to read the research literature in counseling and attend professional meetings where research papers are presented. Also, professional counselors, who do research at their work places, are careful not to give their clients or others the impression that research is more important than the direct practice of helping. Clients and other personnel can easily perceive themselves as mere subjects in some type of laboratory experiment being directed by the counselor. Professional counselors avoid these problems by carefully explaining the value of the research activity and how it may help the client and other personnel in return.

Chapter 9

TRENDS IN PROFESSIONAL COUNSELING

Counseling is an emergent, evolving, and dynamic profession currently experiencing rapid growth and generally positive changes. Some of these changes have been discussed previously (e.g., counselor preparation; see Chapter 3) while others (e.g., professional credentialing) will be discussed in the next chapter. The remaining changes are difficult to categorize because they are occurring in literally every aspect of the counseling profession. However, for discussion purposes, these changes may be subdivided into those taking place in professional counselors' work settings, and those concerning the clientele with whom professional counselors work. Relatedly, changes in "where and with whom" are often associated with "how" counselors work. Therefore, some changes in methods and techniques also will be discussed.

TRENDS IN SETTINGS
WHERE PROFESSIONAL COUNSELORS WORK

Several places in this book have mentioned that the counseling profession has its heritage in school counseling. Today, a substantial number of professional counselors still work in public and private schools, and counselor employment in schools shows every indication of continuing to increase. This trend is evident not because of an increasing number of students in schools, but rather because the value and worth of having counselors in schools is becoming more widely recognized. This recognition, in turn, has evolved from school counselors assuming new, more appropriate, and more effective roles and responsibilities.

Secondary Schools

Historically, counselors have been working in secondary schools since the second decade of this century. Today almost every secondary school has at least one full-time school counselor. Traditionally, counselors in secondary schools focused most of their efforts on "college-bound" students, spent some of their time collecting "occupational information" for use by students, and spent the remainder of their time in more mundane activities (e.g., class scheduling and attendance monitoring). The current trend, however, is for counselors in secondary schools to be involved in activities deemed appropriate by professional associations (e.g., ASCA); those activities which benefit students most and which deemphasize clerical and administrative functions. Counseling in secondary schools also now emphasizes attention to the needs of all students, not just those who are academically talented. Counselors in secondary schools typically coordinate comprehensive career guidance programs suitable for students with widely varying circumstances, skills, abilities, and resources. Because such programs typically include use of computerized career development resources, most secondary school counselors also are using "modern technology" to be able to help more students. Relatedly, counselors in secondary schools are extending their effectiveness through greater use of group counseling, presentation of "classroom guidance" units, coordination of peer counseling programs, and involvement in "teacher-as-advisor" programs. Perhaps the most marked change in the role of counselors in secondary schools is in the area of consultation. Secondary school counselors now spend a considerable amount of time in consultation roles in helping teachers, administrators, and other school personnel to assist students with learning, personal, and other types of concerns. Thus, counselors in secondary schools are now much more involved in professionally appropriate roles and functions and considerably less involved in those activities which often fostered negative stereotypes of them.

Elementary Schools

The most recent significant advancement in school counseling was the advent of elementary school counseling. Substantial numbers of counselors first began working in elementary schools in the late 1960s and the early 1970s. Since then, the number of counselors in elementary schools has increased rapidly. This increase is attributable primarily to the realization that to do so is better for all concerned (e.g., students, parents, teachers) to attempt to prevent students' problems before they arise than to remediate problems after they have arisen. Thus, counselors in elementary schools spend most of their time and efforts focusing on preventive and/or *developmental* counseling activities. Classroom guidance units, small group counseling, and parent and teacher consultation are the primary methodologies used in developmental elementary school counseling. However, counselors in elementary schools also are involved in remediative counseling for students experiencing problems such as abuse, neglect, poor peer relationships, parental divorce, or learning difficulties.

Colleges and Universities

Counselors also have a long history of working in colleges and universities in counseling centers for students, as Deans of students, and in a variety of positions involving student affair activities, admissions, and residence hall life. However, at this time the roles and responsibilities of professional counselors vary and reflect requirements of the institution's size. Large colleges and universities tend to divide functions into highly specialized tasks and have staff in each area, while smaller institutions have a few people responsible for several programs.

Many professional counselors work primarily in counseling centers helping college students with vocational or social relationship/adjustment problems. However, computerized vocational development resources have done much to facilitate their career counseling work. Thus, more recently, they have been able to devote more of their attentions to students' "personal" concerns and problems. The growing recognition that "college students are also people" has greatly increased the types of problems to which counseling center counselors attend. For example, increasing numbers of college students experiencing problems such as parental divorce, anorexia, bulimia, marital difficulties, excessive stress, depression, or anxiety are seeking the services of counseling center counselors. Moreover, the increasing numbers of "non-traditional" students in colleges and universities (i.e., those who have returned to college after some lapse in their educational sequence) have necessitated that these counselors be able to help people with developmental and adjustment concerns. Perhaps the most dramatic change is the large numbers of college students seeking help for substance-abuse problems. Thus, counselors in colleges and universities today are providing counseling services for the full range of problems evident in society, but their work is generally restricted to students.

Community Agencies

Nowhere in the counseling profession has change been more dramatic than in the relatively recent increase in counselors working in community (mental health) agencies. This increase has greatly enhanced the "identity" of the counseling profession because it has brought about the recognition that professional counselors can provide valuable services to all people in society, not just students in educational institutions. Thus, the increase in counselors working in community agencies has allowed professional counselors to enjoy full membership status among the professions previously recognized as primary providers of mental health services.

Counselors working in community agencies are employed in many different types of agencies and involved with the provision of a wide variety of counseling services. Professional counselors work in community agencies such as community mental health centers, abused and/or victimized person facilities, geriatric centers, substance abuse (i.e., drugs, alcohol) program residential facilities, crisis and hot-line centers, half-way houses, runaway shelters, vocational rehabilitation centers, nursing homes, residential facilities for the elderly, and shelters for the homeless. Within these types of settings counselors provide services such as personal adjustment, marriage and family, sex, career, grieving and loss, educational, wellness, and personal development counseling. They work with people of all ages, from very young children to very elderly people.

Counselors working in community agencies traditionally have provided remediative counseling services. That is, people have typically sought services from the agencies after problems have arisen. This is still a major emphasis in counseling in community agencies. More recently, however, counselors in community agencies also have become involved in preventive counseling. Further, many activities are now being provided in many situations not previously encountered by counselors. For example, some counselors are now providing services in the context of Health Maintenance Organizations (HMOs). In commenting on the roles of counselors in HMOs, Forrest and Affeman (1986) stated

> The educational model as well as the medical model provides an important vehicle for the delivery of primary prevention. Most MHCs [mental health counselors] are generally well prepared in this area. They are trained in group facilitation, and much primary and secondary prevention can be delivered in group settings....The MHCs are aware that the patient's social support systems are a means of preventing physical illness, and MHCs commonly use processes for aiding in improving these systems.... (p. 69)

Thus, various counselors working in community agencies are also involved in literally all types of professional activities in the counseling profession.

A relatively small, but increasing, proportion of professional counselors are working in hospitals and other medical care facilities (e.g., renal care facilities and trauma centers). The counseling services provided by counselors in these settings are almost exclusively remediative in nature, primarily because clients enter the facilities to seek services for medical problems. Bereavement, or grieving and loss, counseling is one of the major services provided by counselors in these settings, although they also sometimes provide other types of services such as family, stress reduction, or sexuality counseling.

Business and Industry

A recent trend, and one that appears to have substantial potential, is the employment of professional counselors in business and industry (Lewis & Hayes, 1984). Smith, Piercy, and Lutz (1982) stated that

> A greater employee "entitlement" attitude is one reason for the growth of Human Resource Development (HRD) activities, programs, and practices within organizations....There are a number of other reasons for the expansion of HRD activities in the corporate setting. Governmental regulations...are external forces

causing an increase in counseling and HRD personnel positions. Technological changes and competition are other reasons that companies have begun to provide more counseling and HRD services to employees. Corporations have therefore become more involved in developing systematic career development programs for employees in addition to a variety of training and development activities. (pp. 107-109)

The employment of counselors in business and industry is based primarily on the adage that "a happy employee is a good employee;" an employee who is free from major personal problems is likely to be productive, punctual, have a low rate of absenteeism, and show allegiance to the employer. Counseling services in business and industry therefore are intended primarily to keep employees "happy" (i.e., functioning effectively in their work and personal lives). Counselors within business and industry are usually employed within the context of human resource development (HRD) or employee assistance programs (EAPs). Both of these types of programs typically involve provision of services such as interpersonal and/or employee relations training, career and life-style development (including leisure counseling), stress and/or time management training, and consultation about a variety of mental health concerns. EAPs also typically include provision of "personal" counseling services for employees (Lewis & Hayes, 1984).

Religious Congregations

An interesting mixture of professions is evident in the growing number of clerics (e.g., ministers, priests, sisters, or rabbis) who have completed counselor-preparation programs. Members of religious congregations often turn to their respective clerics for spiritual guidance and "counseling" about problems in their lives. Many clerics have realized that some of these people need assistance that is not readily amenable by religious/spiritual guidance alone; thus, they have need to provide counseling services in accord with the interpretations used throughout this book. The types of counseling services provided by clerics are many, but three seem to be most prevelant. One is bereavement or grieving and loss counseling. In the difficult times following deaths of loved ones, members of congregations typically seek solace from clerics. Facilitation of the bereavement process is therefore a common counseling activity for clerics. A second one is marriage and family counseling. Again, in times of marital and/or family problems or "crises," clerics are among the first to whom members of congregations turn for assistance. A third primary counseling activity for clerics is referral. That is, when people have problems, they often approach their respective clerics first, probably because they are aware that their clerics will maintain confidentiality about the problems. In these situations, clerics are instrumental in deciding whether the problems can be resolved through religious/spiritual guidance, counseling provided by the clerics themselves, or counseling services from (other) professional counselors. If the latter option is selected, these clerics also have to decide to whom to refer the people and to facilitate the referral process. Given the large numbers of people with whom clerics typically work, these latter activities are quite common for them.

Legal Systems

Another small, but growing, segment of professional counselors is working in the criminal justice and other parts of legal systems. For example, counselors working in correctional institutions primarily provide personal adjustment and career and life-style counseling for inmates, particularly those for whom release is imminent. Counselors working in other offender rehabilitation programs, such as those for sex-offenders or spouse (or other family member) abusers, focus primarily on remediation of the dynamics and/or situations underlying the offenses, as well as other types of counseling for problems related to the offenses. More recently, some professional counselors have become involved in providing counseling services within another part of the legal system: divorce litigation. These counselors are employed by the legal system (i.e., employed by a court as opposed to being employed by either of the litigants) to provide "divorce mediation" services prior to trial. The goal of counseling in this situation is to enable the litigants to achieve a mutually accepted marriage dissolution agreement instead of having it decreed by a judge. In essence, divorce mediation counseling is a very specialized form of marriage and family counseling.

Private Practice

The establishment of "private practices" is the dominant employment trend in the counseling profession today. The number of self-employed, and usually self-incorporated, professional counselors has increased significantly within the last few years, and the increase is likely to continue. This increase is primarily due to the fact that a substantial number of professional counselors are able to be financially solvent, and in a few cases financially affluent, from the proceeds of their private practices. This financial solvency is in part linked to professional credentialing (see Chapter 10). That is, more and more professional credentials (e.g., licensures, certifications) of counselors are being recognized as indicators of professional competence. In turn, as the status of their credentials increases, so do the costs of their services *and* the willingness of people and/or agencies to pay those costs. For example, a rapidly increasing number of insurance company policies now cover the services of professional counselors, who are usually licensed and/or certified. Insurance company reimbursements are known as "third-party payments." Similarly, a growing number of companies are providing reimbursements to counselors in private practice for services rendered to company employees; it is often less expensive for companies to pay private practitioners than to provide "in-house" counseling services.

The counseling services provided by various counselors in private practice run the gamut of the various services found in the counseling profession. Private practitioner counseling services can be found for any imaginable human mental health need. However, the vast majority of counselors in private practice have focused their activities on marriage and/or family counseling or counseling adolescents, and more recently on substance-abuse counseling. In addition, most counselors in private practice are heavily involved in consultation activities, particularly those relating to facilitation of human and interpersonal relations development and the provision of training workshops. Thus, most counselors in private practice are involved in multiple, but few, major professional activities in order to generate income.

These then are the major trends in the settings where professional counselors work. Collectively, they reflect the general trend in the counseling profession of counselors working in almost all types of settings. Indeed, identifying settings where counselors do not work is difficult.

TRENDS IN CLIENTELE
WITH WHOM COUNSELORS WORK

Just as the number of settings in which counselors work has expanded greatly in the last two decades, so too has the number of different types of people with whom counselors work. This general trend is of course partially a function of the increase in the number of settings. However, it is also a function of professional counselors actively having involved themselves in a greater variety of counseling services so that they could effectively serve more and different types of people. Thus, professional counselors have been and continue to be proactive in their efforts to serve increasing numbers of people. The people served can be categorized in several different ways, one of which is by stage in the life-span.

Preschool Children

One of the newest client groups for professional counselors is preschool children. The counseling profession's emphasis on developmental counseling in elementary schools has prompted some counselors to extend the emphasis to children before they enter school. Accordingly, some counselors are now providing services such as learning skills training, interpersonal-relationships facilitation, and social skills enhancement to very young children. Relatedly, because some young children have problems which need remediation, some professional counselors are also using techniques such as "play" counseling and "art" therapy to help these children. Counselors working with young children also often work with the children's parents to help the parents develop better parenting, behavior management, and child motivational skills. In general, counselors efforts with very young children often are intended to help the children "get a good start" in life, and sometimes to help them overcome the problems (e.g, abuse, neglect) they have already encountered.

Elementary-School Children

The vast majority of elementary-school children receive needed and/or desirable counseling services from counselors working in schools. However, counselors working in community agencies and private practice increasingly also are providing services to elementary-school children. Several reasons exist for this trend.

One is that school counselors simply have too many children with whom to work to provide effective services for all who need them. As a result, some parents are seeking other sources for assistance for their children.

A second reason is that some parents (inappropriately) fear that a stigma will be attached to their child(ren) if counseled in the school setting, and so they seek "less public" counseling services for their child(ren).

A third reason is that because school counselors must be able to provide many different types of counseling services, it is difficult for them to "specialize" in particular types of counseling; counselors in community agencies or private practice typically "specialize," and therefore (in some cases) are able to provide better services.

A fourth reason is that "court-ordered" counseling for children is increasing as more and more judges come to understand the nature and benefits of counseling services for children. An example of this is the increasing number of children who are being required by courts to receive counseling for problems resulting in delinquency. Typically, judges order such counseling services to be provided by counselors in community agencies or by counselors in private practice who have contractual arrangements with the judicial system.

Secondary-School Students

For reasons similar to those for elementary-school children, increasing numbers of secondary school age children (i.e., adolescents) also are being counseled by professional counselors in community agencies or private practice. Adolescence is a difficult period in any person's life because of "normal" problems such as emerging sexuality, changing peer relationships, academic pressures and strains, identity development, career exploration, disengagement from family and parents, and value conflicts. However, today, adolescents are also increasingly confronted with problems related to drug and alcohol abuse, delinquency, depression, parental divorce and (often) step-family acclamation, abuse, and a host of societal problems such as unemployment, discrimination, or threat of nuclear holocaust.

Many, many parents are unable to help their children through the difficulties of adolescence and so seek professional counseling services for their children. In addition, many, many youth themselves also are seeking counseling assistance with problems. In extreme cases, youth with severe problems receive counseling services from "crisis centers" or residential treatment (e.g., substance abuse) facilities. However, more typically, they receive counseling services from counselors in community agencies or private practice who specialize in working with youth.

Persons in Mid-Life

Among the newer groups for whom counseling services are being more frequently provided are persons in "mid-life." This time period is difficult, if not impossible, to define in terms of an age range because of changes in human longevity as well as conflicting interpretations about to which "life" it applies; is it the "middle" of actual life, marital and family life, or career life? More appropriately, the term mid-life applies to a person's situation in life. That is, the term mid-life is usually applied to people who have established and relatively stable life-styles, careers, familial situations, and behavior patterns, and who are not yet preparing for "retirement." Some people in this situation are so stable that "stability" becomes a problem for them. Colloquially, these people are asking themselves the question, "Is this all there is?" The problems manifested by people in mid-life who are experiencing generalized disenchantment are many and include such things as identity confusion, depression, marital and/or familial strife, career dissatisfaction, or substance abuse. Accordingly, these people seek counseling for a variety of purposes, and generally want to find "new" directions for themselves and their lives.

Older Adults

The "graying of America" is a colloquial phrase used to reflect the rapidly increasing average age of people in society, an increase that is attributable to increasing human longevity and the associated increase in the numbers of "older people" in society. The larger number of older people in society has in turn brought (overdue) greater attention to their life situations, needs, and problems. Riker (1981) stated

> [T]he need for help is great among older citizens in this country. Even a cursory look at statistical information regarding alcoholism and suicide among older persons highlights some of the extremes of mental health problems. Less extreme, but certainly suggestive of a general mental health problem of older persons, are the results of a 1980 nationwide study of 514 randomly selected Americans, 60 years of age and older. This study places those interviewed in three descriptive categories, as enjoyers (27%), survivors (53%), and casualties (20%)....The designation for each category seems to be self-explanatory, with casualties referring to those experiencing major difficulties in areas such as health, finances, or living conditions. For whatever reasons, the majority of this older population sample are survivors, while an additional 20% are facing major problems. The

range of the problems is considerable, the intensity varies, but the extensiveness among older persons seems inescapable. (pp. xvii-xviii)

Part of the response to this situation has been a rapid increase in counseling services specifically suited to older persons, often referred to as gerontological counseling. Older persons experience the myriad problems experienced by younger persons, but their life situations often add at least one major confounding factor: the perception of not having enough time left in their lives to resolve the problems. Moreover, the counseling needs of individual older persons tend to be generalized within their respective lives; if they have needs for counseling, they tend to have the needs in many aspects of their lives as opposed to in specific parts of their lives (Myers & Loesch, 1981). Thus, counseling services for older persons need to be comprehensive in scope, and professional counselors who work with older persons must be able to provide a variety of types of counseling services.

Intellectually Gifted and Talented People

In addition to life-span divisions, the clientele for professional counselors are also categorized by other human characteristics. Some of these are groups of people who would not ordinarily be expected to be in need of counseling services. For example, Myers and Pace (1986) summarized the professional literature and found the following problems to be evident among various intellectually gifted and talented people: depression, underachievement, perfectionism and overachievement, suicide, delinquency, peer relationship problems, career development problems related to potential for multiple careers, problems in making long-range plans, difficulties in dealing with deferred gratification, early career closure, and value conflicts with peer groups, family, and society. Myers and Pace (1986) also noted that, "Significant information is starting to accumulate on the needs of gifted persons, but there is very little experimental documentation of effective counseling and guidance strategies" (p. 550). Thus, gifted and talented persons are a group for whom counseling services are often appropriate, but also a group to whom professional counselors have only recently turned their attentions.

Ethnic Minority Groups

Recognition of the unique characteristics of various ethnic minority groups has prompted the counseling profession to attempt to be responsive to their needs through the provision of counseling services specifically suited for them. Ethnic minority persons of course may experience any of the problems for which counseling services are appropriate. However, they also may experience problems associated with social acclamation resulting from their unique characteristics and life situations. Moreover, counseling service delivery modes appropriate for persons in society's "majority" may not always be appropriate for members of ethnic minority groups. Therefore, professional counselors who provide counseling services to ethnic minority persons must be thoroughly knowledgeable of both the characteristics of various ethnic minorities and counseling approaches and techniques effective for working with them. Vacc and Wittmer (1980) stated

> Our belief is that helping professionals may hold the key to the process of reducing, if not eliminating, the social and emotional barriers which prevent many of America's subgroup members from becoming secure American citizens. To do this, helping professionals must make a concerted effort to understand cognitively the different subgroup members found among their clientele; an understanding that is over and above affectual understanding....[I]f helping professionals are inexperienced in the values and ways of a particular special population, these professionals will be ineffective when encountering members of that special population as...clients. (p. 6)

Genders

Provision of gender specific counseling services is another major trend in the counseling profession. The need for such specialized counseling services first became evident with recognition of the changing roles and status for women in society. As women entered the labor force in increasing numbers and as they pursued redefined (i.e., "nontraditional") roles in familial and interpersonal situations, they encountered problems which often made the transitions difficult. Westervelt (1978) stated

> Counselors know that [women's] changed or changing perceptions of self and society generate new sources of conflict and ambivalence and of guilt and shame, as well as new sources of motivation and new patterns of aspiration. (p. 2)

Thus, counseling services and techniques specifically for women evolved from their unique needs and situations, particularly the need to help women achieve their potentials and adjust effectively to new behavior patterns. Counseling services and techniques specifically for men evolved for similar reasons (i.e, changing roles and life situations), but at a slower rate. Scher (1981) stated that

> Most men are hidden from themselves and from others. Pressures from intimates and society, however, as well as self-engendered possibilities, are creating a slow

push toward greater openness to new potentials. The conflicts and problems that this push creates will and have brought men to counseling. (p. 202)

In general then, gender specific counseling helps males or females to contend with their respective problems and difficulties associated with their sex-role developments.

Abused Persons

A third clientele receiving increased attention and greater services from professional counselors is those having particular types of problems. One of the most striking subgroups in this category is abused persons. Abuse is usually used to refer to physical abuse (i.e., battering), but it also may include verbal abuse or neglect (i.e., necessary attention not provided). Abused persons include those from the very young to the elderly, all ethnicities, and both genders. The incidence of abuse is staggering; "every five years, the number of deaths of persons killed by friends and acquaintances equals that of the entire Viet Nam War" (Wetzel & Ross, 1983). Although abuse occurs among all types of people, women are by far the most frequently abused persons. Abuse against women most frequently occurs in two forms: physical abuse (e.g., by a spouse) and sexual assault (i.e., rape).

Any type of abuse results in at least a psychological trauma, and often an associated physical trauma, for the victim. Thus, counseling for abused persons is almost always remediative in nature and urgent in terms of immediacy. Counseling abused persons also typically necessitates that professional counselors work collaboratively with other professionals such as physicians, law enforcement officers, and attorneys. Counseling abused persons is among the most difficult types of counseling, yet it is also one in which more and more professional counselors are becoming involved.

Substance Abusers

Substance, usually alcohol and/or drug, abuse is another major problem for which increasing numbers of people are seeking counseling. Humans at literally any age after conception may encounter substance abuse problems. Indeed, substance abuse problems are so pervasive that almost everyone in society will be touched, either directly or by close association, by the problems. Professional counselors are increasing and intensifying their counseling services for substance abusers. Both remediative and preventive counseling services and strategies are being used in the effort to combat the substance abuse problems.

Traditionally, substance abuse counseling was most prevalent in community (mental health) agencies, schools, and residential treatment facilties. However, substance abuse counseling is increasingly being provided by counselors in private practice or as a part of employee assistance programs (EAPs) in business and industry. A wide variety of counseling approaches and strategies have been used to attempt to alleviate substance abuse problems. Unfortunately, no clear patterns of effectiveness have appeared. Thus, although professional counselors are making concerted efforts with regard to the provision of substance abuse counseling, proven tactics have not yet been established and counselors must continue to explore and use a wide variety of counseling methodologies to help people with substance abuse problems.

Holistic-Health Proponents

One group of people for whom counseling services are being provided more frequently are those interested in holistic health. Gross (1980) stated that

> Holistic health is an approach to well-being of people that includes the prevention of illness, alternative ways of treating illness, and the means by which good health and the full enjoyment of life can be achieved. The term *holistic* ...means whole in the sense that a living entity is more than the sum of its parts. It also connotes an interdependent system in which a change in one part of the system makes for changes in all other parts of the system. The application of holism to health is an attempt to overcome the mind/body dualism that has long characterized Western science and medicine. (p. 96)

A number of different terms have been used to refer to counseling aimed at facilitating holistic health, including wellness counseling, health counseling, and holistic counseling. Regardless of the term used however, the goal is to help people achieve better mental and physical health through greater reliance on their own innate physiological and psychological maintenance systems. To achieve this end, professional counselors typically use some remediative activities (e.g., help people stop smoking) and some preventive activities (e.g., stress management training). Such counseling is provided by counselors in a variety of settings, and is especially common in employee assistance programs.

Individuals With Sexual Problems

People with problems related to human sexuality are another major clientele for professional counselors. Unfortunately, however, the number of professional counselors who are able to provide effective sexuality counseling is limited. Schepp (1986) commented that only a few counselor preparation programs offer a specialization in sexuality counseling and that "to enter the field, one must usually obtain general professional preparation first and then take additional sexuality courses and [sexuality counseling] supervision" (p. 183).

In general, clients with problems related to sexuality may be divided into two subgroups: those who have sexual problems in the context of heterosexual relationships and those who have problems by virtue of sexual preference (i.e., homosexuality or lesbianism). In regard to the first group, the major problems for which counseling is sought usually relate to sexual functioning, such as problems of inability to achieve orgasm, premature ejaculation, or painful intercourse. In regard to the second group, the major problems for which counseling is sought sometimes relate to sexual functioning, but more often relate to problems such as sexual identity confusion, guilt, or generalized anxiety from generally unexpressed sexual preferences. Accordingly, professional counselors providing human sexuality counseling must be competent to counsel with regard to both the physical and psychological aspects of human sexuality.

Individuals With Marital
and/or Familial Problems

Finally, the fastest growing clientele for professional counselors is persons experiencing marital and/or familial difficulties. Relatedly, Hollis and Wantz (1986, p. 106), based on their longitudinal study of counselor preparation, indicated that specialization in marriage and family counseling is one of the most prominent trends among professional counselors and among students in counselor preparation programs. Most marriage and family counseling today is conceptualized and conducted within the perspective of "systems theory," which views the family as a system of interactive interpersonal relationships among family members. Steinglass (1979) has identified five concepts that characterize the nature of systems theory as applied to family counseling.

1. *The family is the system.* Because the actions of any family member necessarily impact other family members, the family, as opposed to individuals, is the unit of focus for treatment.

2. *Homeostasis.* Family systems seek stability and predictability by developing behaviors that foster internal stability, even if those behaviors are deemed inappropriate or "abnormal" by others.

3. *Identified Patient (IP).* Symptomology is viewed as a family process as opposed to an individual problem; however, one family member (the IP) usually exhibits the manifestation of the symptomology.

4. *Communication Patterns.* The family system functions through structural and interactional patterns that govern family (members') behavior.

5. *Transformation.* Because systems are dynamic, they have the capability to change (i.e., to develop more effective structural and interaction patterns).

Using this generalized framework, professional counselors conduct counseling with entire families to attempt to resolve problems of one or more family members. However, as Grunwald and McAbee (1985) reported,

> Counselors are finding that an increasing proportion of families coming for help can be classified into special categories, i.e., different from the usual father, mother, and children family unit. One in five children are living with a single parent. The divorce rate is well over forty percent and even greater for some ethnic groups. Live-in [unmarried] mates ... are common. All of these situations present some special problems for the family counselor as these special families seek assistance. (p. 245)

The problems addressed are myriad, and include those such as marital disharmony, drug abuse, children's delinquency, alcoholism, step-family adjustments, sexuality, and abuse. Although many counselors in many different settings provide marriage and family counseling, it is primarily provided by those in community agencies and in private practice.

SUMMARY

The preceding discussion has highlighted some of the trends in the major settings in which counselors work and in the clients with whom they work, and has alluded to some of the methods used by professional counselors. Of course other settings exist in which professional counselors work. Also many other types of people receive counselors' services and they provide many more specialized counseling activities than identified within this chapter. Primary description of the counseling profession today are an expansion and extension in positive directions over just a decade ago. Because of these trends the counseling profession's benefits to society are increasing.

Chapter **10**

PROFESSIONALISM IN COUNSELING

Wittmer and Loesch (1986) stated that, "A *profession* is typically defined as a vocational activity having (1) an underlying body of theoretical and research knowledge, (2) an identifiable set of effective skills and activities, and (3) a publicly professed, voluntarily self-imposed set of behavioral guidelines" (p. 301). The preceding chapters have discussed the theoretical, research, skill, and activity aspects of counseling and alluded to the guidelines for the conduct of counseling and for the people who provide it. These presentations support the concept, based on Wittmer's and Loesch's definition, that counseling *is* a profession. However, in order to give full credence to this conclusion, the guidelines for the conduct of counseling and for the people who are *professional* counselors need further elaboration. Therefore, this chapter will focus upon these necessary guidelines.

A set of attitudes, behaviors, and activities characterize professional counselors and differentiate them from others (e.g., lay-person "listeners," faith healers, palmists, advisors, or spiritualists) who purport to provide "counseling" services. Individuals, other than professional counselors, who counsel, do so on the basis of "intuition" or "natural ability" as opposed to providing counsel within the context of the definition of a profession. Professionalism in counseling encompasses the counselor's professional preparation and development as well as guidelines and parameters for the conduct of counseling and professional orientation. The professional preparation of counselors was covered at length in Chapter 3 and therefore will not be readdressed here.

Professional orientation describes the attitudes and perspectives that professional counselors hold about their work and their careers. Counselors manifest a professional orientation in many ways, including being members of professional organizations and associations, obtaining professional credentials, participating in professional self-development activities, and making contributions to the theoretical and knowledge bases of the counseling profession.

PROFESSIONAL ORGANIZATIONS FOR COUNSELORS

Counselors with a good professional orientation are members of professional organizations (used here as synonomous with professional associations) for three primary reasons. First, professional organizations provide the major information and activity resources by which counselors improve their counseling knowledge, skills, and performance. Second, professional organizations are a primary means for counselors to associate and interact with one another. Third, professional organizations provide the most effective means for counselors to facilitate improvement of the counseling profession. Therefore, reciprocal benefits are present for counselors and the counseling profession from counselors' memberships in professional organizations; professional organizations are the media through which the counseling profession benefits individual counselors, and vice versa.

A number of professional organizations exists to which professionally oriented counselors may belong. Many counselors are members of the American Psychological Association (APA), particulary Division 17, Counseling Psychology; Association for Marriage and Family Therapy (AAMFT); American Educational Research Association (AERA), particularly Division H: Counseling and Human Development; American Association for Counseling and Development (AACD) is the primary professional organization with which counselors affiliate. AACD has an organizational and functional structure typical of many professional organizations and therefore it is described here as an illustrative example.

The AACD headquarters building is located just outside Washington, D.C. in Alexandria, Virginia. The headquarters house the professional staff who are paid employees of the association, the AACD library, and resource and meeting rooms for association activities. The headquarters staff members are divided among several functional areas such as association administration and management, budget and finance, convention coordination, membership services, and professional media and publications. In general, the headquarters staff is responsible for AACD's on-going activities. Thus, the headquarters staff is a primary contributor to continuity within the association and the counseling profession.

As of December, 1986, the AACD membership exceeded 56,000 people located in the United States and approximately 50 foreign countries. Four types of membership are possible: (1) *regular,* for practitioners who have graduated from counselor preparation programs, (2) *student,* for trainees currently enrolled in counselor education programs, (3) *associate,* for professionals who are indirectly associated with the counseling profession such as test and book company representatives, program administrators, and supervisors, and (4) *life,* for practitioners who want a lifelong, regular membership. Regular members comprise the largest group, followed by student members, and then relatively small groups of associate and life members. Regardless of category, memberships and associated dues are annual for all except life members, with unlimited renewals except in rare cases where membership is denied on the basis of ethical and/or legal misconduct. AACD has an open enrollment system which allows new members to join at any time during the year.

In order to be responsive to the many different interests, needs, and circumstances of members, the AACD membership is partitioned in two different ways. One is a divisional structure, including the following 13 divisions:

American College Personnel Association (ACPA)
Association for Counselor Education and
Supervision (ACES)
National Career Development Association (NCDA)
Association for Humanistic Education and
Development (AHEAD)
American School Counselor Association (ASCA)
American Rehabilitation Counseling Association (ARCA)
Association for Measurement and Evaluation in
Counseling and Development (AMECD)
National Employment Counselors Association (NECA)
Association for Multicultural Counseling and
Development (AMCD)
Association for Religious and Value Issues in
Counseling (ARVIC)
Association for Specialists in Group Work (ASGW)
American Mental Health Counselors Association (AMHCA)
Public Offender Counselor Association (POCA)

The following two organizations currently hold "organizational affiliate" status which means that they are expected soon to become full-fledged divisions of AACD:

Military Educators and Counselors Association (MECA)
Association for Adult Development and Aging (AADA)

The general purposes and histories of these divisions were covered in Chapter 2 and so will not be discussed again here.

The second partitioning is by geographic regions. The four *Regional Branch Assemblies* are Southern, North Atlantic, Midwestern, and Western. AACD's regional components are referred to as "branch assemblies" because they are composed of the state-level branches (or counterparts) of AACD.

Professional counselors who join AACD may join as many divisions as they wish. In fact, the vast majority of AACD members belong to more than one division. Membership in a division requires payment of the respective division's dues in addition to those for AACD. Unlike the divisional structure, membership in a region is automatic by residential address, and does not require payment of additional dues.

The AACD governance structure is unicameral. The AACD Governing Council includes the AACD President, Past-President, President-Elect, Treasurer, Parlimentarian, Executive Director (from the headquarters permanent staff), and one representative from each of the divisions and regions. The AACD Governing Council meets at least bi-annually to conduct the association's business.

The benefits of AACD membership to professional counselors are too numerous to be listed here. However, some of the major benefits can be identified. First, in regard to professional publications, each AACD member receives the association's newsletter, the *Guidepost,* which is published 18 times per year, and the *Journal of Counseling and Development,* which is published 10 times per year. Members of divisions also receive divisional newsletters and journals that are typically published quarterly. Members of organizational affiliates receive quarterly newsletters. Next, AACD provides access to a wide variety of professional resources (e.g., films, videotapes, books, monographs, bibliographic search services) to its members. Third, AACD provides a variety of insurance programs for its members, including professional liability, life, and health insurance. Fourth, AACD maintains an active political involvement system (including lobbyists) for interaction with the Federal government, and therefore provides a means for members to interact with the Federal government. Relatedly, AACD has assisted with political involvement at state levels, particularly in regard to professional counselor licensure legislations. Fifth, AACD maintains a "legal defense fund" to which members can apply for funds if they become involved in work-related litigation.

Perhaps AACD's most visible benefit to its members is its annual national/international convention, held in the Spring of each year at a different site each year. The AACD convention is a primary means for professional counselors to interact with one another, participate in professional development activities, and keep abreast of new professional activities, issues, and trends. A placement service for professional counselors also is provided at each AACD convention.

AACD also has five corporate affiliates, each of which is a technically and legally separate organization, but one which has strong philosophical and theoretical ties to AACD. One of these corporate affiliates is the Council for the Accreditation of Counseling and Related Educational Programs (CACREP) which was discussed at length in Chapter 3. Two others are the National Board for Certified Counselors

(NBCC) and the National Academy of Certified Clinical Mental Health Counselors (NACCMHC), both of which will be discussed later in this chapter. The fourth is the International Association of Counseling Services (IACS). The primary purpose of IACS is to provide a means for accreditation of agencies (e.g., college or university counseling centers and community mental health counseling agencies) that provide counseling services. Toward that end, IACS conducts counseling agency program evaluations and publishes a directory of IACS accredited agencies. The fifth AACD corporate affiliate is the AACD Foundation (AACDF). It is a not-for-profit agency which helps the counseling profession and AACD through the management of property and financial holdings and the provision of funds for activities with special significance to the counseling profession (e.g., research).

AACD has 56 state and international branches. Each branch is a separate organization, has its own membership requirements, dues, and structure, and is defined geographically by state or regional boundaries (e.g., Ohio Association for Counseling and Development and the European Association for Counseling and Development). However, membership is usually open to any professional who wishes to join. Typically, a primary organization (e.g., North Carolina Association for Counseling and Development and Florida Association for Counseling and Development) as well as divisions parallel those in AACD, although most branches have fewer divisions than does AACD. The activities of the AACD branches typically reflect those of AACD. For example, most hold an annual convention, are involved in legislative activities (particularly those relating to counselor licensure), publish newsletters, and provide a variety of professional resources. The primary difference between AACD and its branches is of course the "scope" of their respective efforts; the AACD branches focus their activities on matters particularly pertinent to the professionals in the specific geographic area represented.

Active membership in professional organizations is a primary way for professional counselors to exhibit professionalism. It allows them to acknowledge to themselves and others that they are concerned about people in the world, vis-à-vis counseling services provided, and about their own competence and improvement as professional counselors. However, professional counselors can also demonstrate that they are concerned about professionalism in counseling, specifically, by seeking pertinent professional credentials.

PROFESSIONAL CREDENTIALS FOR COUNSELORS

Professional credentialing is usually viewed as encompassing three major professional activities: (1) counselor (academic) preparation program accreditation, (2) certification (and the closely associated practice registry), and (3) licensure (Loesch, 1984). In general, professional counselors seek these types of credentials in order to demonstrate that they have specific knowledge and skills for, and/or to be permitted to provide, certain types of counseling services. Thus, counselors who have certain professional credentials are presumed to be better able to provide certain types of counseling services in certain ways. The particular types and/or ways of counseling for which competence is presumed to be greater for credentialed than for non-credentialed counselors are reflected in the respective credentials.

Graduate of an Accredited Preparation Program

One "credential" a professional counselor can have is to be a graduate of an accredited preparation program. Because counselor preparation programs exist almost exclusively within institutions of higher education, almost all of them are accredited by some accrediting agency. The question then becomes, which accreditations are most pertinent to counseling? Many institutions of higher education are accredited by NCATE and many are accredited by regional accrediting agencies (see Chapter 3). However, both of these types of accreditations are very general in nature and have very little specific application to preparation for professional counseling. Thus, graduation from programs having only these types of accreditations is not a particularly strong credential for professional counselors. Comparatively, CACREP accreditation is specifically applicable to programs for the professional preparation of counselors. Therefore, graduation from a CACREP-accredited program is a much stronger professional credential for counselors. Moreover, this particular credential is increasingly being related to other professional credentials (e.g., certifications or licensures) that are especially appropriate for professional counselors.

Certification (and Registry)

Certification is the second type of credential important for professional counselors. It is a process whereby an agency, which may be either governmental or private, attests or affirms that an individual counselor has met the minimum qualifications established by the agency. The assumption underlying any certification process is that a "certified" counselor is able to do effectively the type(s) of counseling reflected in a particular certification (Loesch, 1984). Certification is usually referred to as a "title control" process because it only restricts the use of the title "certified;" it does not restrict who may engage in counseling activities or what types of counseling can be provided. Therefore, the primary advantage of any certification lies in the prestige associated with it. Such prestige has significant implications for professional counselors in several regards. For example, many employers give hiring preference to certified counselors. In addition, clients' initial perceptions of counselors are related to the *potential* for counseling effectiveness; the more favorable clients' initial impressions of counselors in terms of perceived competence, the more likely that counseling will be effective. Certification is one credential that usually increases clients' (initial) favorableness toward counselors (Wittmer & Loesch, 1986).

Professional certification activities for counselors have a very short history and it is only within the last decade or so that certification has been viewed as an important professional credential. Although the exact reasons for this newly developed emphasis are unknown, one probable reason is that only recently has a need arisen to be able to compare or "equate" counselors in a "mobile society."

The most prominent certification processes are national and in some cases international in scope. That is, because the minimum qualifications for such certifications are set by national agencies, they are independent of local (e.g., state-level) counselor preparation program idiosyncracies. Therefore, all counselors certified by a particular agency are presumed to have the same *minimum* competence level regardless of the respective preparation programs from which they graduated. Accordingly, certification is one indication of minimal "equivalence" across counselors. A note may be made that this perspective is similar to the *philosophy* underlying CACREP's program accreditation thrust. The primary difference of course is that accreditation focuses on the program and certification focuses on the individual.

Although the counselor certification process implemented by the NBCC is not the oldest, it is rapidly becoming the widest known among those specific to counselors. Therefore, a point will be made to exemplify counselor certification processes.

In the late 1970s, the Commission on Rehabilitation Counselor Certification (CRCC) and the National Academy of Certified Clinical Mental Health Counselors (NACCMHC) had been certifying rehabilitation counselors and mental health counselors, respectively; CACREP had accredited several counselor preparation programs, and several states had passed counselor licensure laws. These emphases on credentialing and the activities associated with them spawned within AACD interest in a counselor certification process. Thus, AACD mobilized its resources to evaluate existing counselor certification processes and to develop a plan for a broad-based counselor certification process. In 1981, AACD sponsored several meetings to develop specific plans, which eventually led to the first NBCC meeting in April of 1982, attended by representatives from AACD, other counselor certifying agencies, a state having a counselor licensure law, and a public representative. The group initiated plans for incorporation, established the initial criteria for certification, adopted an initial operating budget, developed a Code of Ethics, and established a schedule for subsequent activities. In addition, using information from a previous evaluative report that had identified deficiencies in existing assessment instruments for counselor certification processes, the group decided to initiate the development of a counselor certification examination specifically suited to NBCC's purposes (Loesch & Vacc, 1986).

Although both NBCC and CACREP are AACD corporate affiliates, they are constituted much differently. Whereas CACREP membership is open to representatives from various divisions within AACD, membership on the NBCC Board of Directors is not. Instead, the NBCC Board currently is composed of a Chairperson, Vice-Chairperson, Treasurer/Secretary, representative from a state having a counselor licensure law, public representative lay-person, and representatives from the NAACMHC, CRCC, and National Council for Certified Career Counselors (NCCCC). The NBCC is housed at the AACD headquarters in Alexandria, Virginia. The permanent staff consists of the NBCC Director of Administration, an Administrative Assistant, and seven other staff members. In addition, NBCC employs three consultants for technical assistance with the development and uses of its counselor certification examinations.

Counselors certified by the NBCC are presumed to have fulfilled the minimum, basic knowledge and skill requirements applicable to all professional counselors. Holding a certificate from NBCC is a *generic* certification because it does not imply that NBCC certified counselors can do any particular type of counseling, but rather that they have the minimum competence level necessary for any type of counseling specialization. The generic-level competence inherent in the NBCC certification process is based on the belief that, colloquially stated, all professional counselors must both "know some things and be able to do some things" (Loesch & Vacc, 1986).

The "know some things" component of the NBCC certification is evaluated in two ways, the first of which is an applicant's prior academic preparation. The *general* minimum academic requirement of NBCC certification is a master's degree in counseling. However, specific preparatory experiences, usually courses, also are required. In order to be certified by NBCC, applicants must have successfully completed academic experiences in "theories of counseling" plus six of the following areas: (1) human growth and development, (2) social and cultural foundations, (3) the helping relationship, (4) group dynamics, processes, and counseling, (5) life-style and career development, (6) appraisal, (7) research and evaluation, and (8) professional orientation. In essence, applicants must have had coursework in counseling theories plus six of the eight "core curriculum areas" of the CACREP accreditation standards.

The second part of the knowledge evaluation component is the NBCC counselor certification examination. The different forms of the NBCC examination also cover the eight "core curriculum areas" of the CACREP standards. Twenty-five questions are in each area, with 20 per area being scored for certification purposes, resulting in a possible score of 160. The remaining 40 questions on the examination are used to test possible new test items. Although subsection scores are reported, only the applicant's total score (i.e., the sum of the eight subsection scores) is used for performance evaluation purposes. The NBCC uses a modified Anghoff procedure to establish the minimum criterion score for the examination (Loesch & Vacc, 1986). One minimum criterion score for each form of the examination is compared to the examinee's total score. For example, the minimum criterion score for the April, 1986 form of the NBCC counselor certification examination was 87 while for the September, 1986 form it was 97; examinees who scored above 87 and 97, respectively, "passed" the examination (Loesch & Vacc, 1986). One should remember that the minimum criterion scores for each form of the NBCC examination are "statistically equated" so that the minimum criterion score is equivalent or comparable across forms of the examination relative to the different groups taking each form.

The "be able to do some things" component of the NBCC certification process involves consideration of an applicant's previous professional experiences. All applicants must provide documentation of successful completion of a *supervised* practicum or internship. Applicants who have not completed a CACREP-accredited preparation program must also provide documentation of successful completion of a minimum of two years, post-master's degree, professional-counseling experience of at least 20 hours per week. This requirement is waived for graduates of CACREP-accredited programs because of the extensive requirements for supervised counseling experience in the CACREP accreditation standards. In addition, all applicants must provide letters of reference attesting to their minimum professional competence as a counselor.

NBCC certification applicants who successfully fulfill the criteria are awarded the designation of *National Certified Counselor* (NCC). The initial NBCC certification period is five years, with renewal contingent upon successful completion of professional development activities. By the end of 1986, approximately 17,000 counselors had been designated as an NCC, and the NBCC application rate was approximately 1,000 per year.

In 1985, the NBCC incorporated the certification process previously administered by the NCCCC. The NCCCC had been created by AACD's National Career Development Association to implement a certification process specifically applicable to counselors specializing in career counseling (Sampson, 1986). The NBCC-NCCCC merger created a "two-tier" certification structure for the NBCC. Thus, the NBCC generic certification leading to the designation NCC is the basic tier and the NBCC specialized certification leading to the designation *National Certified Career Counselor* (NCCC) is the second tier. Professional counselors seeking the NCCC status must first attain NCC status. Additional academic, experiential and reference requirements, plus an additional examination also are used for this specialized certification. By the end of 1986, approximately 1200 professional counselors had been designated as an NCCC and the application rate was approximately 200 per year.

Another certification appropriate for many professional counselors is that provided by the National Academy for Certified Clinical Mental Health Counselors (NACCMHC). The NACCMHC was started primarily by members of AACD's AMHCA division in the 1970s to provide a means to certify mental health counselors. The NACCMHC certification process is similar to the NBCC's, but the eligibility criteria are more stringent because it is a specialized certification. The basic NACCMHC criteria include graduation from an accredited counselor preparation program that requires a minimum of sixty semester hours, at least two years of post-graduate degree relevant work experience, a minimum of 1500 clock hours of pre-application experience as a mental health counselor supervised by a person with NACCMHC certification or equivalent credentials, and successful completion of the NACCMHC examination. The certification status awarded is *Certified Clinical Mental Health Counselor* (CCMHC).

The Commission on Rehabilitation Counselor Certification (CRCC) provides another certification appropriate for many professional counselors. The CRCC was created through the joint efforts of AACD's ARCA division and the National Rehabilitation Association. As distinct from either NBCC or NACCMHC, CRCC has eight different eligibility categories, primarily because of the variations in rehabilitation counselor preparation programs, including some undergraduate-level programs. In general, the CRCC eligibility criteria include various combinations of academic preparation, relevant professional work experience, supervised rehabilitation counseling experience, and successful completion of the CRCC examination. The CRCC awards the designation *Certified Rehabilitation Counselor* (CRC).

The American Association for Marriage and Family Therapy (AAMFT) provides a professional credential which is similar to, but not synonomous with, a certification appropriate to many professional counselors. This credential is AAMFT *Clinical Member* status. The eligibility criteria include successful completion of specific academic experiences as specified by AAMFT, graduation from an accredited program, at least 200 hours of supervised work as a marriage and family therapist, and at least 1500 clock-hours of pre-application and two years of post graduate-degree professional work experience in marriage and family counseling.

Registry is closely related to certification. However, the term itself may be a misnomer because "registry, as used in the counseling and human development professions, is a publicly distributed list of professionals who have met some identified set of minimum qualifications" (Loesch, 1984, p. 4). A point of clarification needs to be interjected at this point because often confusion is found between certification and registry processes. This is because many certifying agencies, such as NBCC, NACCMHC, and CRCC, publish "registries" of the professional counselors they have certified. The distinguishing feature between certification and registry processes is the primary intent of the activity. With *certification,* the intent is to be certified and being listed on a registry is an artifact of the certification process. With *registry,* the intent is to get on the list. However, in actuality, this distinction is picayune because both processes are intended to identify those professional counselors who have some specified, usually minimal, level of competence.

Similar to certification processes, registering processes for counselors necessitate that applicants fulfill specified minimum criteria in order to be listed on the registry. In general, the eligibility criteria typically include graduation from an accredited graduate-level counselor preparation program, specified components of preparation, appropriate professional work experience, and successful completion of an examination. Currently, North Carolina is the only major entity or agency implementing a registering process for professional counselors.

Licensure

Being licensed is the third type of credential important for professional counselors. As distinct from certification, licensure processes are stipulated in law, implemented at the state level, legally constituted as stipulated by law, and geographically restricted in authority. Licensure is a legal process whereby a state agency regulates some of the practice of counseling within the state. The common exception is the school counselor who is not typically licensed by states but is legally permitted to do counseling. Thus, licensure is typically referred to as a "practice control" process because it usually controls who may do counseling. However, licensure is also a "title control" process because it also controls who may use the term "licensed counselor" (Loesch, 1984). The primary advantage of licensure then, as opposed to certification, is that licensure *permits* counselors to do certain types of counseling and restricts the use of the title "licensed." Of course, the prestige aspect of licensure has the same implications as it does for certification.

Licensure laws pertinent to the counseling profession have both commonalities and wide variations within the United States. For example, all states have licensure laws for counseling activities under the aegis of the title "psychologist." Typically, psychologist licensure laws require a doctoral degree from an accredited program, supervised professional work experience, an in-state residency period, letters of reference, and successful completion of an examination. Approximately ten states also license marriage and family counselors with requirements that are categorically similar but specifically different to those for psychologists (e.g., typically a master's degree is required instead of a doctoral degree). Approximately twenty states have counselor licensure laws. In the vast majority of cases, the title awarded is *Licensed Professional Counselor* (LPC). Again, the eligibility criteria are categorically similar, but specifically different, to those for psychologists.

A comparison of counselor certification and licensure processes reveals that many similarities and a few distinct differences exist. Primary among the similarities is that both certification and licensure are voluntary in nature. "Counseling" can be done by many people who are neither certified nor licensed and so these credentials are not "needed" in order to do "counseling." Rather, they are voluntarily sought by those who want to be truly "professional" counselors. Other similarities include requirements for payment of application and annual renewal fees, specific types of prior academic preparation, prior supervised counseling experience, prior work experience as a counselor, lack of "negative" personal characteristics (e.g., certain types of criminal convictions), and successful completion of an appropriate examination. In addition, certification and licensure are usually given for a specific time period, with renewal contingent upon successful completion of continuing professional development activities.

The primary difference between certification and licensure processes is the geographic region encompassed by the respective credential. Certifications are usually national in scope while licensure is granted for a specific state. However, reciprocity agreements among states often exist whereby one state agrees to honor the licensure criteria of another state Conversely, infrequently complete "reciprocity" exists between a certification and a state's licensure law even though many states use a certification examination, such as the NBCC counselor certification examination, as (or in lieu of) a state licensure examination.

Graduation from an accredited program, being certified, and being licensed then are the primary credentials of professional counselors. Those professional counselors who hold such credentials do so to signify that they are interested in and actively striving toward providing the best possible counseling services. Moreover, they are in accord with the basic philosophical premise of all professional credentialing, which is to protect the public welfare through the provision of services only by competent practitioners (Shimberg, 1982).

COUNSELORS' PROFESSIONAL DEVELOPMENT

Professional development is a general term used in the counseling profession to describe the activities in which professional counselors engage for the purpose of continuing to increase and improve their counseling knowledge and skills, primarily after they have become practitioners (i.e., after they have completed their counselor preparation programs). For several reasons, an abundance of "professional development" activities is available to professional counselors. First, many counselors simply want to improve themselves, and so participate upon their own initiatives. Also, as counselors progress through their careers, their functions and responsibilities evolve, and so they need "new" knowledge and skills to perform effectively. And another reason is that almost all counseling certification and licensure processes have "continuing education" (i.e., professional development) requirements for certification or licensure renewal. What is a surprise is the dearth of professional literature on professional development in counseling in general, what types of professional development activities are most appropriate, and which types are most effective. Indeed, although counselors' professional development "makes sense" *conceptually,* scant empirical support exists for the notion that it improves the ways counselors counsel. Why then are so many professional development activities being conducted?

The answer to the previous question most likely lies in the changing nature of society. As society and the world in which it exists evolve, so too do their impacts on people. People also evolve over the courses of their lives, and their needs, which can be addressed by counseling services, change and perhaps increase, concommitantly. These on-going states of change necessitate that the counseling profession and its members be ever improving in order to maintain competence and be effective. Therefore, even though little evidence is available to support the impact or effectiveness of professional development activities in counseling, the need for them is only too obvious; professional counselors must be constantly improving if they are to continue helping people effectively.

Perusal of the professional literature reveals that professional development activities for counselors have been suggested, developed, and implemented for literally every aspect of the counseling profession and/or for work with every type of person in society. Accordingly, to address all the types of activities here is not possible, but a few of the major categories of activities are included.

Counseling Skill Development or Refinement

This is by far the most common type of professional development activity in which counselors engage. Because of knowledge and skill advances derived from theory development, research, and practical experience, existing counseling techniques as well as related ones such as consultation techniques are continually being improved, and new techniques are being developed. Therefore, the modern professional counselor always has access to new, and presumably better, ways of doing things. Counselors extend their knowledge and improve their techniques primarily through participation in professional development activities such as training workshops, in-service seminars, convention programs, and self-instruction modules, or through consultation activities (see Chapter 7). Among these alternatives, the most common type is convention programs. Typically, over 800 different programs are presented at the annual AACD convention and innumerable others are presented at regional and state ACD conventions. Generally, these programs are open to anyone registered for the convention, with the exceptions being those few programs for which special fees are charged. The next most common professional development activity is training workshops. These, too, are innumerable because of the large number of organizations, agencies, and individuals presenting them. An example of this type of activity is the more than fifty different "Professional Development Institutes" (PDIs) presented by AACD at various times throughout the year and at various locations. The primary differences between convention programs and training workshops are that the latter are usually longer (e.g., one to three days versus one to three hours for convention programs) and they have larger fees (e.g., $100.00 to $500.00).

Supervision Skill Development

Another major area of professional development for counselors is supervision skill development. Supervision may be defined as a very specific type of consultation activity in which one person reviews and evaluates a counselor's work with clients toward the goal of maximizing the counselor's skills and effectiveness. Because more and more counselors as well as program administrators and managers, are becoming involved in supervision activities, an increase in professional development activities focusing on supervision recently has occurred. Hollis and Wantz (1986) noted that

> [T]he shift from [counselor preparation] department operated practicum and clinics to existing counseling settings similar to those that might hire graduates has shifted responsibilities for a major portion of the experiential training to community settings or in some cases service areas operated generally by an administrative area other than academic within higher education. (p. 115)

Another part of the impetus for this increase is licensure laws and certification policies that require supervised experience for licensure or certification eligibility and/or renewal. More than ever the counseling profession is acknowledging that supervision, like counseling, requires a strong knowledge base and proven skills in order to be effective. Thus, the counseling profession is emphasizing supervision skill development as an important professional activity for counselors.

Use of Technology

The third major area of professional development currently being emphasized in the counseling profession is use of technology. So-called "modern technology" in general, and microcomputers in particular, have the potential to dramatically impact the counseling profession; indeed, at least one "computer therapist" already exists (Wagman & Kerber, 1984). In discussing "high technology" in relation to the counseling profession, Harris-Bowlsbey (1984) presented three valid assumptions

> First, high technology will never replace high touch in the human resource development field. Although robots may make automobiles better and faster...human beings will never be better counseled or guided by robots, computers, or interactive videodisks. A second assumption is that high technology and high touch should be viewed not as opponents, but as potential partners. ... Third, presumably the profession's thinking about the merger of high technology and high touch is new and tentative; therefore the counselors whom we educate and supervise will need preservice and in-service training.... (p. 7)

Harris-Bowlsbey's third assumption is apparently true in that a multitude of professional development activities concerning the uses of computers in counseling have been offered, and they are extremely well-attended. Moreover, given the rapid advances in technology, this trend shows no sign of decreasing.

Burnout Prevention or Amelioration

The fourth major area of professional development for counselors is burnout prevention or amelioration. A classic question in the counseling profession is, who counsels the counselors? Counseling is an emotionally taxing activity that extracts an extremely heavy toll from counselors. Thus counselors, perhaps as much or more than people in any other profession, are susceptable to "burnout;" a state of emotional lethargy wherein motivation to perform is low and skills and talents are used inefficiently and ineffectively. Because of the increasing incidence of burnout among counselors, many professional development activities have been and are presented to help counselors avoid it. These activities are intended to enable counselors to monitor and moderate their professional (and sometimes personal) activities so that they are able to continually "regenerate their professional energies" and in so doing maintain and increase their level of effectiveness.

Participation in professional development activities is an important part of a counselor's professional orientation. It is the means by which professional counselors "keep current," improve, and remain professionally motivated. As with participation in professional organizations and attainment of professional credentials, participation in professional development activities benefits both counselors and the clients to whom they provide services.

PROFESSIONAL CONTRIBUTIONS BY COUNSELORS

The fourth aspect of professional orientation, making contributions to the theoretical and knowledge bases of the counseling profession, is much smaller in scope than the first three because only a small proportion of counselors are actively involved in it. That is, the primary means by which counselors make contributions to the profession in general is through research and publication activities, and only a small proportion of counselors conduct research and/or write for publication in professional journals. Two primary reasons have been offered for this unfortunate circumstance: counselors lack substantive research skills and therefore counselors are not comfortable, capable, or confident in conducting or publishing research, and counseling research results have not been readily applicable to counseling activities and therefore counselors see little value in it.

Goldman (1976, 1978) suggested that counselors are "turned off" to research because, among other reasons, during their training programs they were exposed to unreasonable expectations for research activities. He stated that the counseling profession has "sanctified precision, measurement, statistical methodology, and the controlled laboratory experiment" (Goldman, 1976, p. 545), and in so doing has set the standards for research and publication so high that most counselors or trainees feel incapable of achieving it and therefore don't try. Empirical evidence to support Golman's position is scarce, but results of counselors' performance on the NBCC counselor certification examination seem to suggest that research is among counselors' lesser areas of competence. Scores on the Research and Evaluation subsection of the NBCC examination have been consistently lower than those for other subsections (Loesch & Vacc, 1986). Thus, possibly counselors, in general, do not have great degrees of proficiency in research. However, Goldman (1977) also has argued that extensive research skill proficiency is not really necessary for counselors to conduct meaningful research. Rather, he posited that counselors should strive to conduct research that is within their realm of competence.

The debate over counselor's levels of proficiency in research is unlikely to be resolved, and in fact little reason remains to continue the debate. Even if counselors' research proficiency levels are low, forces within the counseling profession are present which will more than likely result in their elevation. Specifically, moderately high research proficiency levels are evident in all counselor preparation program standards (such as CACREP's), in counselor certification (such as NBCC's), and in licensure requirements. Therefore, counselors will have to have at least minimal levels of research competence in order to achieve those credentials.

The lack of relevance-of-research results to counseling practice has been suggested by many authors, but perhaps most notably by Goldman and his collaborating authors (1978). They suggested that counselors should not strive to investigate problems that fit "rigorous" research standards, but rather should adopt presumably less rigorous research approaches that fit the the problems with which counselors are confronted. Thus they advocate making research activities more relevant to counseling practice by focusing on the actualities of counseling situations rather than on adherence to traditional and presumably higher research methodology standards. Mehrens (1978) has taken an alternative position.

> Those who wish to relax rigor often seem to hope that sloppy research will increase relevance. I posit that it is seldom, if ever, the case that relevance and rigor are purely ipsative. Increasing rigor need not always demand the examination of a less relevant problem; examining a more relevant problem need not always mean that we must relax the rigor. (Mehrens, 1978, pp. 10-11)

In essence, Mehrens is arguing that the way for counselors to gain relevant information from counseling research is to use the most rigorous methods; that in fact the best information comes from the most rigorous research methodology.

Again, further argument in this regard is unlikely to be productive. The major point that should be understood is that regardless of the individual approaches or perspectives posited, consensus seems to be present among authors that counselors should engage in research activities. Engels and Muro (1986) commented that

> Vacc and Loesch (1983) offered excellent general and specific suggestions and questions regarding the necessity for research as a means of self-regulation and self-evaluation, leading to a fruitful progressing and maturing in all aspects of the profession. We join in advocating inquiry as an integral, ongoing part of preparation programs and professional practice, with dedication to scientific and human inquiry and a healthy skepticism to generate a dialectic for ongoing improvements in effectiveness and data to document those improvements. (pp. 301-302)

Thus, research and the subsequent publication of its results by professional counselors not only is consistent with the empirical counseling approach advocated in this book, but is also the primary means by which counselors improve the counseling profession.

The four components of professional orientation described comprise much of professionalism in counseling. However, they are not the totality of professionalism in counseling because they are activities specific to professional counselors. Those aspects of the professionalism in counseling which involve both counselors and clients also must be considered to complete the discussion.

ETHICAL AND LEGAL ASPECTS OF COUNSELING

Two sets of "behavioral guidelines" exist to which all professional counselors adhere: ethical standards and laws. Ethical standards are guidelines created by a group of professionals (e.g., AACD members) to govern the professional behaviors of the members of the group. Laws, in the present context, are the state statutes that govern the behaviors of counselors practicing in the state where the statutes apply. No Federal statutes exist pertaining directly to professional counselors' *counseling* activities. Ethical standards and laws pertaining to counseling practice are often theoretically and sometimes practically intertwined, primarily because both are intended to protect clients' welfare. However, they are separated here to facilitate their discussion.

Ethical Standards

Ethical standards applicable to professional counselors have been created by a number of professional associations, such as AACD, APA, and AAMFT, as well as by counselor certification agencies, such as NBCC or NACCMHC. However, because the AACD ethical standards are the ones most commonly espoused by professional counselors and because they are typical of sets of ethical standards, they are discussed here.

Part of the *Preamble* of the AACD Ethical Standards (1986; see Appendix A) explains why they were created:

> The specification of ethical standards enables the Association to clarify to present and future members and to those served by members, the nature of ethical responsibilities held in common by its members.

By definition, ethical standards reflect value, moral, and social judgements. Thus, they are intended to communicate to both counselors and clients the value judgements, reflected in behavioral statements, made by professional counselors about how counselors should behave and how counseling should be practiced.

Eight major sections can be found in the AACD Ethical Standards. The first section, Section A: *General,* covers facets of counselors' responsibilities to clients, colleagues, and employing institutions; communication of professional qualifications; and provision of professional services. Section B: *Counseling Relationship* delineates specific guidelines for the conduct of individual and group counseling processes, including topics such as confidentiality, record-keeping, and client selection. Because "testing" is often a component in counseling processes, guidelines relating to it are covered in Section C: *Measurement and Evaluation.* Section D: *Research and Publication* presents guidelines for the conduct of research and publication by professional counselors. The importance of consultation as a professional activity is reflected in the ethical guidelines given for it in Section E: *Consulting.* Because of the increasing incidence of counselors with "private practices" (i.e., self-employments), Section F: *Private Practice,* provides guidelines specifically applicable to this type of counseling service provision. Section G: *Personnel Administration* covers guidelines for administration and/or management of counseling program activities. The importance of effective preparation for professional counselors is reflected in the Section H: *Preparation Standards.*

All ethical standards are important for professional counselors. However, the ones receiving the greatest attention are those related to the concept of *confidentiality.* Hopkins and Anderson (1986) succinctly summarized the basis for this attention.

> The effectiveness of the relationship between counselor and client hinges precipitously on a fulcrum of trust. Unless the client has complete trust in the counselor, it is unlikely that information can be freely exchanged between the two; when that exchange cannot occur, the purpose of the relationship is frustrated. Complete trust can be established only if the counselee believes that his or her communications with the counselor will remain confidential. (p. 5)

In accord with this perspective, ethical standards admonish that an unethical procedure occurs when counselors disclose information about and/or received from clients without the clients' expressed *and* explicit permission. However, the ethical standards do identify two exceptions to this general principle. First, counselors are ethically permitted to discuss a client's concerns and/or behaviors with another counselor in a consultative capacity, *provided identifying information about the client is not disclosed and the counselor-consultant is not placed in a "conflict of interest" situation.* This exception is allowed so that consultative assistance may be obtained if it is necessary to the counselor to provide effective services for the client. Second, counselors are ethically permitted, and in fact *required,* to disclose the client's situation to others when, in the counselor's best professional judgement, the situation indicates that a clear and imminent danger is possible to the client and/or others. This exception is allowed because clients are sometimes self-injurious (e.g., suicidal) or pose a serious threat to the physical and/or psychological well-being of others.

Adherence to ethical standards by professional counselors is voluntary and self-imposed; ethical standards have no basis in law. Therefore, professional counselors follow ethical standards because they "want to" (i.e., believe such behaviors are in the best interests of their clients and the counseling profession), and not because they "have to." However, note that agencies providing ethical standards for professional counselors have policies and procedures for acting upon allegations of ethical misconduct. For example, AACD's standing Ethics Committee is charged with the responsibility for investigating and evaluating allegations of ethical misconduct by AACD members. AACD can not take direct legal action against a member found guilty of ethical misconduct, but it can invoke professional sanctions (e.g., revocation of membership), which in turn could have significant professional implications for the counselor found guilty. Similarly, counselor certification agencies, such as the NBCC, can revoke the certification of an NCC or NCCC found guilty of ethical impropriety.

Legal Aspects

The concept of confidentiality so prominent in ethical standards for counselors has a parallel in law. *Privileged communication* is the term for confidentiality established in and based upon law. That is, some professionals (e.g., physicians; attorneys; religious officials including priests, ministers, and rabbis) may have statuatory exclusion from disclosure of information obtained from clients during professional interactions with those individuals. Laws regarding the application of privileged communication to various professionals are created at the state level and vary widely among states in terms of scope and applicability. For example, almost all states grant privileged communication to physicians and attorneys for interactions with their clients, about two-thirds of the states grant it to religious officials for interactions with their penitents, and only a few states grant it to professional counselors for their counseling interactions with clients.

Because most professional counselors do not have the right of privileged communication for their interactions with their clients, adherence to ethical standards in general, and to those standards relating to confidentiality in particular, is significantly important. Hopkins and Anderson (1986) provided the rationale for this importance:

> [I]n the absence of any clear statuatory authority or case law precedent to guide a court of law in judging a case involving the conduct of a counselor, courts generally apply the standard of care given by similarly situated professionals, in this case counselors. Courts may also look to the self-imposed standards of the profession to determine liability. Although no appellate court has yet turned to the ethical standards promulgated by the American Association for Counseling and Development for guidance in resolving a case involving a counselor's conduct, it is possible this will occur in the near future. Thus, counselors would be well advised to act in accordance with the standards of counselors in their local community and to study thoroughly and follow the Association's ethical standards where they apply as a means of avoiding potential liability. (p. 3)

Thus, a professional counselor's ethical behavior has good *potential* to be interpreted as synonomous with legally defensible behavior for most counseling activities.

Although professional credentialing has done much to enhance the status of counselors and the counseling profession, it has had one deleterious effect. Specifically, it has brought attention to counselors and what they do, and in so doing apparently has identified them as yet another group "ripe" for malpractice suits. Indeed, the number of malpractice suits brought against professional counselors has increased dramatically since the beginning of this decade, and at present the indication is that the rate will continue to increase.

Most malpractice actions against counselors fall under the *law of tort,* the central concept of which is negligence. Counselors may be negligent in their professional activities in several ways. For example, Hopkins and Anderson (1986) suggested that professional counselors may be held negligent if they (1) use procedures not in the realm of accepted practice, (2) use techniques for which they are not trained or competent, (3) fail to follow procedures known to be more helpful, (4) fail to explain potential consequences of treatment, (5) defame clients' character, or (6) invade clients' privacy.

A more specific aspect of negligence is the counselor's *duty to warn.* In the case *Tarasoff vs. Regents of the University of California,* a California court ruled that a counselor not only had the right, but also an *affirmative obligation,* to inform potential victims of threatened harm learned from client's statements during a counseling process. This ruling is of course consistent with the AACD Ethical Standards. Together, they emphasize that counselors have responsibilities that extend beyond individual clients, and that counselors are liable if they do not assume those responsibilities.

A concept closely related to *duty to warn* is *informed consent*. In the counseling profession, *informed consent* is usually associated with the conduct of research. Thus, when counselors conduct research involving human subjects and/or information stored in their records, they must (a) inform the research subjects of the nature of the research and (b) obtain attested permission (i.e., a signature on an informed consent form) from the subjects (or in the cases of minors, from their parents or legal guardians).

Record-keeping is another area where legalities exist regarding counselors' activities. For example, the *Family Educational Rights and Privacy Act of 1974* stipulates that adults, or the parents or legal guardians of minors, have legal access to all information in *official* records maintained by any institution or agency that receives any amount of Federal funds. This legislation apparently does not apply to *unofficial* (or personal) records (e.g., case notes) maintained by counselors. However, whether such unofficial records are susceptible to subpoena from a court of law has not been clearly defined. Thus, counselors must exercise caution in placing materials in clients' records. Moreover, counselors must exercise caution in the release of information contained in clients' records. In general, counselors should not release or distribute information from clients' files without expressed and explicit written permission from the clients.

In summary, the multifaceted nature of a professional orientation requires that professional counselors attend carefully to what they do and how they do it. Moreover, to have a professional orientation, counselors must be proactive; that is, they must consciously determine and evaluate how to behave and then consciously behave in appropriate ways. Fortunately, most professional counselors have an effective professional orientation.

CONCLUSION

Becoming a professional counselor is not easy. Much has to be learned, many skills have to be developed, and an appropriate orientation has to be adopted. Further, learning and skill development must continue across the lifespan and therefore *being* a professional counselor also is not easy. However, professional counselors enjoy many, many intrinsic and extrinsic rewards, and so the benefits far outweigh the efforts expended. More importantly, society gains significantly from professional counselors' activities. Indeed, professional counselors do much to make the world a better place in which to live. What greater good can exist than that?

CODE

OF

ETHICS

CODE OF ETHICS

(Adapted from the Ethical Standards of the
American Personnel and Guidance Association)

Approved on July 1, 1982

PREAMBLE

The NBCC is an educational, scientific, and professional organization dedicated to the enhancement of the worth, dignity, potential, and uniqueness of each individual and thus to the service of society.

The specification of a code of ethics enables the NBCC to clarify to present and future certified counselors, the nature of ethical responsibilities held in common by the certified counselors.

Section A:
General

1. The certified counselor influences the development of the profession by continuous efforts to improve professional practices, services, and research. Professional growth is continuous throughout the certified counselor's career and is exemplified by the development of a philosophy that explains why and how a certified counselor functions in the helping relationship. Certified counselors must gather data on their effectiveness and be guided by their findings.

2. The certified counselor has a responsibility both to the individual who is served and to the institution within which the service is performed to maintain high standards of professional conduct. The certified counselor strives to maintain the highest levels of professional services offered to the individuals to be served. The certified counselor also strives to assist the agency, organization, or institution in providing the highest caliber of professional services. The acceptance of employment in an institution implies that the certified counselor is in agreement with the general policies and principles of the institution. Therefore, the professional activities of the certified counselor are also in accord with the objectives of the institution. If, despite concerned efforts, the certified counselor cannot reach agreement with the employer as to acceptable standards of conduct that allow for changes in institutional policy, conducive to the positive growth and development of clients, then terminating the affiliation should be seriously considered.

3. Ethical behavior among professional associates, both certified counselors and non-certified counselors, must be expected at all times. When information is possessed that raises doubt as to the ethical behavior of professional colleagues, whether certified counselors or not, the certified counselor must take action to attempt to rectify such a condition. Such action shall use the institution's channels first and then use procedures established by the NBCC.

4. The certified counselor neither claims nor implies professional qualifications exceeding those possessed and is responsible for correcting any misrepresentations of these qualifications by others.

5. In establishing fees for professional counseling services, certified counselors must consider the financial status of clients and locality. In the event that the established fee structure is inappropriate for a client, assistance must be provided in finding comparable services of acceptable cost.

6. When certified counselors provide information to the public or to subordinates, peers or supervisors, they have a responsibility to ensure that the content is general; unidentified client information should be accurate, unbiased, and consist of objective, factual data.

7. With regard to the delivery of professional services, certified counselors should accept only those positions for which they are professionally qualified.

8. In the counseling relationship the counselor is aware of the intimacy of the relationship and maintains respect for the client and avoids engaging in activities that seek to meet the counselor's personal needs at the expense of that client. Through awareness of the negative impact of both racial and sexual stereotyping and discrimination, the certified counselor guards the individual rights and personal dignity of the client in the counseling relationship.

Section B:
Counseling Relationship

This section refers to practices and procedures of individual and/or group counseling relationships.

The certified counselor must recognize the need for client freedom of choice. Under those circumstances where this is not possible, the certified counselor must apprise clients of restrictions that may limit their freedom of choice.

1. The certified counselor's primary obligation is to respect the integrity and promote the welfare of the client(s), whether the client(s) is (are) assisted individually or in a group relationship. In a group setting, the certified counselor is also responsible for taking reasonable precautions to protect individuals from physical and/or psychological trauma resulting from interaction within the group.

2. The counseling relationship and information resulting therefrom be kept confidential, consistent with the obligations of the certified counselor as a professional person. In a group counseling setting, the certified counselor must set a norm of confidentiality regarding all group participants' disclosures.

3. If an individual is already in a counseling relationship with another professional person, the certified counselor does not enter into a counseling relationship without first contacting and receiving the approval of that other professional. If the certified counselor discovers that the client is in another counseling relationship after the counseling relationship begins,

the certified counselor must gain the consent of the other professional or terminate the relationship, unless the client elects to terminate the other relationship.

4. When the client's condition indicates that there is clear and imminent danger to the client or others, the certified counselor must take reasonable personal action or inform responsible authorities. Consultation with other professionals must be used where possible. The assumption of responsibility for the client(s) behavior must be taken only after careful deliberation. The client must be involved in the resumption of responsibility as quickly as possible.

5. Records of the counseling relationship, including interview notes, test data, correspondence, tape recordings, and other documents, are to be considered professional information for use in counseling and they should not be considered a part of the records of the institution or agency in which the counselor is employed unless specified by state statute or regulation. Revelation to others of counseling material must occur only upon the expressed consent of the client.

6. Use of data derived from a counseling relationship for purposes of counselor training or research shall be confined to content that can be disguised to ensure full protection of the identity of the subject client.

7. The certified counselor must inform the client of the purposes, goals, techniques, rules of procedure and limitations that may affect the relationship at or before the time that the counseling relationship is entered.

8. The certified counselor must screen prospective group participants, especially when the emphasis is on self understanding and growth through self disclosure. The certified counselor must maintain an awareness of the group participants' compatibility throughout the life of the group.

9. The certified counselor may choose to consult with any other professionally competent person about a client. In choosing a consultant, the certified counselor must avoid placing the consultant in a conflict of interest situation that would preclude the consultant's being a proper party to the certified counselor's efforts to help the client.

10. If the certified counselor determines an inability to be of professional assistance to the client, the certified counselor must either avoid initiating the counseling relationship or immediately terminate that relationship. In either event, the certified counselor must suggest appropriate alternatives. (The certified counselor must be knowledgeable about referral resources so that a satisfactory referral can be initiated). In the event that the client declines the suggested referral, the certified counselor is not obligated to continue the relationship.

11. When the certified counselor has other relationships, particularly of an administrative, supervisory and/or evaluative nature with an individual seeking counseling services, the certified counselor must not serve as the counselor but should refer the individual to another professional. Only in instances where the individual's situation warrants counseling intervention and another alternative is unavailable should the certified counselor enter into and/or maintain a counseling relationship. Dual relationships with clients that might impair the certified counselor's objectivity and professional judgment (e.g., as with close friends and relatives, sexual intimacies with any client) must be avoided and/or the counseling relationship terminated through referral to another competent professional.

12. All experimental methods of treatment must be clearly indicated to prospective recipients and safety precautions are to be adhered to by the certified counselor.

13. When the certified counselor is engaged in short-term group treatment/training programs (e.g., marathons and other encounter-type or growth groups), the certified counselor ensures that there is professional assistance available during and following the group experience.

14. Should the certified counselor be engaged in a work setting that calls for any variation from the above statements, the certified counselor is obligated to consult with other professionals whenever possible to consider justifiable alternatives.

Section C:
Measurement and Evaluation

The primary purpose of educational and psychological testing is to provide descriptive measures that are objective and interpretable in either comparative or absolute terms. The certified counselor must recognize the need to interpret the statements that follow as applying to the whole range of appraisal techniques including test and nontest data. Test results constitute only one of a variety of pertinent sources of information for personnel, guidance, and counseling decisions.

1. The certified counselor must provide specific orientation or information to the examinee(s) prior to and following the test administration so that the results of testing may be placed in proper perspective with other relevant factors. In so doing, the certified counselor must recognize the effects of socioeconomic, ethnic and cultural factors on test scores. It is the certified counselor's professional responsibility to use additional unvalidated information carefully in modifying interpretation of the test results.

2. In selecting tests for use in a given situation or with a particular client, the certified counselor must consider carefully the specific validity, reliability, and appropriateness of the test(s). General validity, reliability and the like may be questioned legally as well as ethically when tests are used for vocational and educational selection, placement, or counseling.

3. When making any statements to the public about tests and testing, the certified counselor must give accurate information and avoid false claims or misconceptions. Special efforts are often required to avoid unwarranted connotations of such terms as IQ and grade equivalent scores.

4. Different tests demand different levels of competence for administration, scoring, and interpretation. Certified counselors must recognize the limits of their competence and perform only those functions for which they are prepared.

5. Tests must be administered under the same conditions that were established in their standardization. When tests are not administered under standard conditions or when unusual behavior or irregularities occur during the testing session, those conditions must be noted and the results designated as invalid or of questionable validity. Unsupervised or inadequately supervised test-taking, such as the use of tests through the mails, is considered

unethical. On the other hand, the use of instruments that are so designated or standardized to be self-administered and self-scored, such as interest inventories, is to be encouraged.

6. The meaningfulness of test results used in counseling functions generally depends on the examinee's unfamiliarity with the specific items on the test. Any prior coaching or dissemination of the test materials can invalidate test results. Therefore, test security is one of the professional obligations of the certified counselor. Conditions that produce most favorable test results must be made known to the examinee.

7. The purpose of testing and the explicit use of the results must be made known to the examinee prior to testing. The certified counselor must ensure that instrument limitations are not exceeded and that periodic review and/or retesting are made to prevent client stereotyping.

8. The examinee's welfare and explicit prior understanding must be the criteria for determining the recipients of the test results. The member must see that specific interpretation accompanies any release of individual or group test data. The interpretation of test data must be related to the examinee's particular concerns.

9. The certified counselor must be cautious when interpreting the results of research instruments possessing insufficient technical data. The specific purposes for the use of such instruments must be stated explicitly to examinees.

10. The certified counselor must proceed with caution when attempting to evaluate and interpret the performance of minority group members or other persons who are not represented in the norm group on which the instrument was standardized.

11. The certified counselor must guard against the appropriation, reproduction, or modification of published tests or parts thereof without acknowledgement and permission from the previous publisher.

Section D:
Research and Publication

1. Guidelines on research with human subjects shall be adhered to, such as:
    a. *Ethical Principles in the Conduct of Research with Human Participants,* Washington, D.C.: American Psychological Association, Inc., 1973.
    b. Code of Federal Regulations, Title 45, Subtitle A, Part 46, as currently issued.

2. In planning any research activity dealing with human subjects, the certified counselor must be aware of and responsive to all pertinent ethical principles and ensure that the research problem, design, and execution are in full compliance with them.

3. Responsibility for ethical research practice lies with the principal researcher, while others involved in the research activities share ethical obligation and full responsibility for their own actions.

4. In research with human subjects, researchers are responsible for the subjects' welfare throughout the experiment and they must take all reasonable precautions to avoid causing injurious psychological, physical, or social effects on their subjects.

5. All research subjects must be informed of the purpose of the study except when withholding information or providing misinformation to them is essential to the investigation. In such research the member must be responsible for corrective action as soon as possible following completion of the research.

6. Participation in research must be voluntary. Involuntary participation is appropriate only when it can be demonstrated that participation will have no harmful effects on subjects and is essential to the investigation.

7. When reporting research results, explicit mention must be made of all variables and conditions known to the investigator that might affect the outcome of the investigation or the interpretation of the data.

8. The certified counselor must be responsible for conducting and reporting investigations in a manner that minimizes the possibility that results will be misleading.

9. The certified counselor has an obligation to make available sufficient original research data to qualified others who may wish to replicate the study.

10. When supplying data, aiding in the research of another person, reporting research results, or in making original data available, due care must be taken to disguise the identity of the subjects in the absence of specific authorization from such subjects to do otherwise.

11. When conducting and reporting research, the certified counselor must be familiar with, and give recognition to, previous work on the topic, as well as to observe all copyright laws and follow the principles of giving full credit to all to whom credit is due.

12. The certified counselor must give due credit through joint authorship, acknowledgement, footnote statements, or other appropriate means to those who have contributed significantly to the research and/or publication, in accordance with such contributions.

13. The certified counselor must communicate to other counselors the results of any research judged to be of professional value. Results reflecting unfavorably on institutions, programs, services, or vested interests must not be withheld for such reasons.

14. If certified counselors agree to cooperate with another individual in research and/or publication, they incur an obligation to cooperate as promised in terms of punctuality of performance and with full regard to the completeness and accuracy of the information required.

15. Ethical practice requires that authors not submit the same manuscript or one essentially similar in content, for simultaneous publication consideration by two or more journals In addition, manuscripts published in whole or in substantial part, in another journal or published work should not be submitted for publication without acknowledgement and permission from the previous publication.

Section E:
Consulting

Consultation refers to a voluntary relationship between a professional helper and help-needing individual group or social unit in which the consultant is providing help to the client(s) in defining and solving a work-related problem or potential problem with a client or client system.

1. The certified counselor, acting as consultant, must have a high degree of self awareness of his/her own values, knowledge, skills, limitations, and needs in entering a helping relationship that involves human and/or organizational change and that the focus of the relationship be on the issues to be resolved and not on the person(s) presenting the problem.

2. There must be understanding and agreement between certified counselor and client for the problem definition, change goals, and predicted consequences of interventions selected.

3. The certified counselor must be reasonably certain that he/she or the organization represented has the necessary competencies and resources for giving the kind of help that is needed now or may develop later and that appropriate referral resources are available to the consultant.

4. The consulting relationship must be one in which client adaptability and growth toward self-direction are encouraged and cultivated. The certified counselor must maintain this role consistently and not become a decision maker for the client or create a future dependency on the consultant.

5. When announcing consultant availability for services, the certified counselor conscientiously adheres to the *NBCC Code of Ethics*.

6. The certified counselor must refuse a private fee or other remuneration for consultation with persons who are entitled to these services through the certified counselor's employing institution or agency. The policies of a particular agency may make explicit provisions for private practice with agency clients by members of its staff. In such instances, the clients must be apprised of other options open to them should they seek private counseling services.

Section F:
Private Practice

1. The certified counselor should assist the profession by facilitating the availability of counseling services in private as well as public settings.

2. In advertising services as a private practitioner, the certified counselor must advertise the services in such a manner so as to accurately inform the public as to services, expertise, profession, and techniques of counseling in a professional manner. A certified counselor who assumes an executive leadership role in the organization shall not permit his/her name to be used in professional notices during periods when not actively engaged in the private practice of counseling.

The certified counselor may list the following: highest relevant degree, type and level of certification or license, type and/or description of services, and other relevant information. Such information must not contain false, inaccurate, misleading, partial, out-of-context, or deceptive material or statements.

3. Certified counselors may join in partnership/corporation with other certified counselors and/or other professionals provided that each member of the partnership or corporation makes clear the separate specialties by name in compliance with the regulations of the locality.

4. A certified counselor has an obligation to withdraw from a counseling relationship if it is believed that employment will result in violation of the *Code of Ethics*. If the mental or physical condition of the certified counselor renders it difficult to carry out an effective professional relationship or if the certified counselor is discharged by the client because the counseling relationship is no longer productive for the client, then the certified counselor is obligated to terminate the counseling relationship.

5. A certified counselor must adhere to the regulations for private practice of the locality where the services are offered.

6. It is unethical to use one's institutional affiliation to recruit clients for one's private practice.

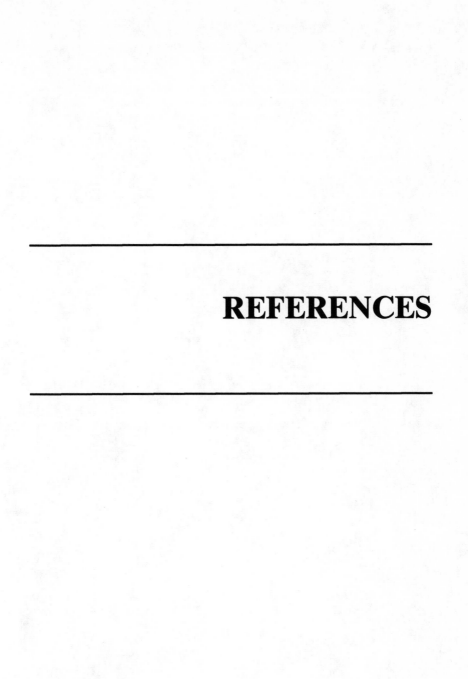

REFERENCES

REFERENCES

Adler, A. (1958). *What life should mean to you.* New York: Capricorn Books.

Adler, A. (1964). *Problems of neurosis.* New York: Harper & Row.

Adler, A. (1972). *The neurotic constitution.* Freeport, NY: Books for Libraries Press. (Originally published in 1926).

American Association for Counseling and Development. (1986). *Ethical standards of the American Association for Counseling and Development.* Washington, DC: Author.

Bandura, A. (1977). Self-efficacy: Toward a unifying theory of behavior change. *Psychological Review, 84,* 191-215.

Bandura, A. (1982). The psychology of chance encounters and life paths. *The American Psychologist, 37*(7), 747-755.

Bardon, J.I., & Bennett, V.C. (1974). *School psychology.* Englewood Cliffs, NJ: Prentice-Hall.

Bartlett, W.E., Lee, J.E., & Doyle, R.E. (1985). Historical development of the Association for Religious and Values Issues in Counseling. *Journal of Counseling and Development, 63*(7), 448-451.

Barlow, D.H., Hayes, S.C., & Nelson, R.O. (1984). *The scientist practitioner.* New York: Pergamon.

Belkin, G.S. (1984). *Introduction to counseling.* DuBuque, IA: W.C. Brown.

Bergland, B.W. (1974). Career planning: The use of sequential evaluated experience. In E.L. Herr (Ed.), *Vocational guidance and human development* (pp. 350-380). Boston: Houghton Mifflin.

Bindman, A.J. (1964). The psychologist as a mental health consultant. *Journal of Psychiatric Nursing, 2,* 367-380.

Blake, R.R., & Mouton, S.S. (1983). *Consultation.* Reading, MA: Addison-Wesley.

Blocher, D. (1974). *Developmental Counseling* (2nd. ed.) New York: Ronald Press.

Bloland, P.A., & Edwards, P.B. (1981). Work & leisure: A counseling synthesis. *Vocational Guidance Quarterly, 30,* 101-108.

Bordin, E.S., Nachmann, B., & Segal, S.J. (1963). An articulated framework for vocational development. *Journal of Counseling Psychology, 10,* 107-116.

Brammer, L.M., & Shostrom, E.L. (1960). *Therapeutic psychology.* Englewood Cliffs, NJ: Prentice Hall.

Brayfield, A.H. (1950). Putting occupational information across. In A.H. Brayfield (Ed.), *Readings in modern methods of counseling* (pp. 212-220). New York: Appleton-Century-Crofts.

Campbell, D.T., & Stanley, J.C. (1963). *Experimental and quasi-experimental designs for research.* Chicago: Rand McNally.

Caplan, G. (1970). *The theory and practice of mental health consultation.* New York: Basic Books.

Carkhuff, R.R. (1974). *The art of helping.* Amherst, MA: Human Resource Development Press.

Carroll, M.R., & Levo, L. (1985). The Association for Specialists in Group Work. *Journal of Counseling and Development, 63*(7), 452-454.

Corey, G. (1981). *Theory and practice of group counseling.* Monterey, CA: Brooks/Cole.

Council for the Accreditation of Counseling and Related Educational Programs. (1986). *Accreditation procedures manual and application for counseling and related educational programs.* Washington, DC: Author.

Cox, W.E. (1985). Military Educators and Counselors Association. *Journal of Counseling and Development, 63*(7), 461-463.

Crites, J.O. (1973). *Career Maturity Inventory.* Monterey, CA: California Test Bureau/McGraw-Hill.

Cronbach, L.J. (1970). *Essentials of psychological testing* (3rd ed). New York: Harper & Row.

Culp. W.H. (1985). Organizational consultation: A case study. In J. Kirby (Ed.), *Consultation: Practice and practitioner* (pp. 235-287). Muncie, IN: Accelerated Development.

DiMichael, S.G., & Thomas, K.R. (1985). ARCA's journey in professionalism: A commemorative review on the 25th anniversary. *Journal of Counseling and Development, 63*(7), 428-435.

Drew, C.J. (1976). *Designing research and evaluation.* St. Louis, MO: Mosby.

Egan, G. (1986). *The skilled helper.* Monterey, CA: Brooks/Cole.

Ekstrom, R., & Johnson, C. (1984). Introduction and overview. *Journal of Counseling and Development, 63*(3), 63.

Engels, D.W., & Muro, J J. (1986). Silver to gold: The alchemy, potential, and maturing of ACES and CES. *Counselor Education and Supervision, 25*(4), 289-305.

Erickson, E.H. (1963). *Childhood and society* (2nd ed.). New York: Norton.

Forrest, D.V., & Affeman, M. (1986). The future of mental health counselors in health maintenance organizations. *American Mental Health Counselors Association Journal, 8*(2), 65-72.

Fredrickson, R.H. (1982). *Career information.* Englewood Cliffs, NJ: Prentice-Hall.

Freud, S. (1911). Formulation regarding the two principles of mental functioning. *Standard Edition, 12,* 218-228.

Gelatt, H.B. (1962). Decision-making: A conceptual frame of of reference for counseling. *Journal of Counseling Psychology, 9,* 240-245.

Gelso, C.J. (1985). Rigor, relevance, and counseling research: On the need to maintain our course between Sycila and Charybdis. *Journal of Counseling and Development, 63*(9), 551-553.

Ginzberg, E. (1972). Restatement of the theory of occupational choice. *Vocational Guidance Quarterly, 20*(3), 169-176.

Ginzberg, E., Ginsburg, S.W., Axelrad, S., & Herma, J. (1951). *Occupational choice: An approach to general theory.* New York: Columbia University Press.

Goldman, L. (1976). A revolution in counseling research. *Journal of Counseling Psychology, 23,* 543-552.

Goldman, L. (1977). Toward more meaningful research. *Personnel and Guidance Journal, 55,* 363-368.

Goldman, L. (Ed.). (1978). *Research methods for counselors.* New York: Wiley.

Gross, S.J. (1980). The holistic health movement. *Personnel and Guidance Journal, 59*(2), 96-102.

Grunwald, B.B., & McAbee, H.V. (1985). *Guiding the family: Practical counseling techniques.* Muncie, IN: Accelerated Development.

Gysbers, N.C. (1984). Major trends in career development theory and practice. *Vocational Guidance Quarterly, 33*(1), 15-25.

Harris-Bowlsbey, J. (1984). High touch and high technology: The marriage that must succeed. *Counselor Education and Supervision, 24*(1), 6-16.

Healy, C.C. (1982). *Career development: Counseling through the life stages.* Boston: Allyn and Bacon.

Herr, E.L. (1985). AACD: An association committed to unity through diversity. *Journal of Counseling and Development, 63*(7), 395-404.

Herr, E.L. (1986). Life-style and career development. In M.D. Lewis, R.L. Hayes, & J.A. Lewis (Eds.), *An introduction to the counseling profession* (pp. 167-214). Itasca, IL: F.E. Peacock.

Herr, E.L., & Cramer, S.H. (1984). *Career guidance and counseling through the life span* (2nd ed.). Boston: Little, Brown & Company

Hock, E.L., Ross, A.O., & Winder, C.L. (Eds.). (1966). *Professional preparation of clinical psychologists: Proceedings of the Conference on the Professional Preparation of Clinical Psychologists meeting at the Center for Continuing Education, Chicago, Illinois August 17 - September 1, 1965.* Washington, DC: American Psychological Association.

Holland, J.L. (1966). *The psychology of vocational choice.* Waltham, MA: Blaisdell.

Holland, J.L. (1973). *Making vocational choices: A theory of careers.* Englewood Cliffs, NJ: Prentice-Hall.

Hollis, J.W., & Wantz, R.A. (1986). *Counselor preparation 1986-89: Programs, personnel, and trends, sixth edition.* Muncie, IN: Accelerated Development.

Hopkins, B.R., & Anderson, B.S. (1986). *The counselor and the law* (2nd ed.). Washington, DC: AACD Press.

Hopson, B. (1982). Counseling and helping. In R. Holdsworth (Ed.), *Psychology for career counseling* (pp 61-79). Great Britain: Macmillan Press.

Hoyt, K.E. (1974). *An introduction to career education.* U.S. Office of Education Policy Paper. Washington, DC: Author.

Ivey, A. (1971). *Microcounseling: Innovations in interviewing training.* Springfield, IL: Thomas.

Johnson, C.S. (1985). The American College Personnel Association. *Journal of Counseling and Development, 63*(7), 405-410.

Kagan, N., & Krathwohl, D.R. (1967). *Studies in human interaction: Interpersonal process recall stimulated by videotape.* East Lansing, MI: Educational Publication Services, College of Education, Michigan State University.

Kalder, D.R., & Zytowski, D.G. (1969). A maximizing model of occupational decision-making. *Personnel and Guidance Journal, 47,* 781-788.

Kemp, C.A. (1970). *Foundations of group counseling.* New York: McGraw-Hill.

Kerlinger, F.N. (1986). *Foundations of behavioral research* (3rd ed). New York: Holt, Rinehart and Winston.

Kirby, J. (1985). *Consultation: Practice and practitioner.* Muncie, IN: Accelerated Development.

Krumboltz, J.D., Mitchell, A.M., & Jones, B.G. (1978). A social learning theory of career selection. In J.M. Whitely and A. Resnikoff (Eds.), *Career counseling* (pp. 100-127). Monterey, CA: Brooks/Cole.

Lewis, J.A., & Hayes, B.A. (1984). Options for counselors in business and industry. *Counseling and Human Development, 17*(4), 1-8.

Loesch, L.C. (1984). Professional credentialing in counseling-1984. *Counseling and Human Development, 17*(2), 1-11.

Loesch, L.C., & Vacc, N.A. (1986). *Technical manual for the NBCC counselor certification examination.* Washington, DC: National Board for Certified Counselors.

Loesch, L.C., & Wheeler, P.T. (1982). *Principles of leisure counseling.* Minneapolis, MN: Educational Media Corporation.

Maslow, A.H. (1954). *Motivation and personality.* New York: Harper & Row.

McDaniels, C. (1984). The work/leisure connection. *Vocational Guidance Quaterly, 33*(1), 35-44.

McFadden, J., & Lispcomb, W.D. (1985). History of the Association for Non-White Concerns in Personnel and Guidance. *Journal of Counseling and Development, 63*(7), 444-447.

Mehrens, W. A. (1978). Rigor and reality in counseling research. *Measurement and Evaluation in Guidance, 11(1), 8-13.*

Mehrens, W.A., & Lehmann, I.J. (1984). *Measurement and evaluation in education and psychology* (3rd ed.). New York: Holt, Rinehart and Winston.

Meyer, D., Helwig, A., Gjernes, O., & Chickering, J. (1985). The National Employment Counselors Association. *Journal of Counseling and Development, 63*(7), 440-443.

Miller, E. (1986). *Basic statistics: A conceptual approach for beginners.* Muncie, IN: Accelerated Development.

Milliken, R.L., & Kirchner, R. (1971). Counselor's understanding of student's communication as a function of the counselor's perceptual defense. *Journal of Counseling Psychology, 18,* 4-18.

Minkoff, H.B., & Terres, C.K. (1985). ASCA perspectives: Past, present, and future. *Journal of Counseling and Development, 63*(7), 424-427.

Myers, J.E., & Loesch, L.C. (1981). The counseling needs of older persons. *The Humanist Educator, 20*(1), 21-35.

Myers, R.S., & Pace, T.S. (1986). Counseling gifted and talented students: Historical perspectives and contemporary issues. *Journal of Counseling and Development, 64*(9), 548-551.

Myrick, R.D. (1977). *Consultation as a counselor intervention.* Ann Arbor, MI: ERIC Counseling and Personnel Services Information Center.

Neulinger, J. (1974). *The psychology of leisure.* Springfield, IL: Thomas.

Ohlsen, M.M. (1970). *Group counseling.* New York: McGraw-Hill.

Osipow, S.H. (1983). *Theories of career development* (3rd ed.). Englewood Cliffs, NJ: Prentice-Hall.

Page, R.C. (1985). The unique role of the Public Offender Counselor Association. *Journal of Counseling and Development, 63*(7), 455-456.

Peatling, J.H., & Tiedeman, D.V. (1977). *Career development: Designing self.* Muncie, IN: Accelerated Development.

Pitz, G.F., & Harren, V.A. (1980). An analysis of career decision-making from the point of view of information-processing and decision theory. *Journal of Vocational Behavior, 16,* 320-346.

Riker, H.C. (1981). Preface. In J.E. Myers (Ed.), *Counseling older persons Volume III Trainer's manual for basic helping skills* (pp. xvii-xx). Washington, DC: American Personnel and Guidance Association.

Roe, A. (1956). *The psychology of occupations.* New York: Wiley.

Rowe, W., Murphy, H.B., & De Csipkes, R.A. (1975). The relationship of counselor characteristics and counseling effectiveness. *Review of Educational Research, 45,* 231-246.

Sampson, J.P., Jr. (1986). *Preliminary technical manual for the NBCC career counselor certification examination.* Washington, DC: National Board for Certified Counselors.

Sampson, J.P., Jr., & Pyle, K.R. (1983). Ethical issues involved with the use of computer-assisted counseling, testing, and guidance systems. *Personnel and Guidance Journal, 61*(5), 283-287.

Schein, E. (1969). *Process consultation.* Reading, MA: Addison-Wesley.

Schepp, K.F. (1986). *Sexuality counseling: A training program.* Muncie, IN: Accelerated Development.

Scher, M. (1981). Men in hiding: A challenge for the counselor. *Personnel and Guidance Journal, 60*(4), 199-202.

Schwab, R., & Harris, T.L. (1981). Personal growth of counselor trainees. *Counselor Education and Supervision, 20*(3), 219-224.

Sheeley, V.S., & Eberly, C.G. (1985). Two decades of leadership in measurement and evaluation. *Journal of Counseling and Development, 63*(7), 436-439.

Shertzer, B., & Linden, J. (1979). *Principles and purposes of assessment and appraisal.* Boston: Houghton Mifflin.

Shimberg, B. (1982). *Occupational licensing: A public perspective.* Princeton, NJ: Educational Testing Service.

Smith, R.L., Engels, D.W., & Bonk, E.C. (1985). The past and future: The National Vocational Guidance Association. *Journal of Counseling and Development, 63*(7), 420-423.

Smith, R.L., Piercy, F.P., & Lutz, P. (1982). Training counselors for human resource development positions in business and industry. *Counselor Education and Supervision, 22,* 107-112.

Solomon, C. (1982). Special issue on political action: Introduction. *Personnel and Guidance Journal, 60*(10), 580.

Steinglass, P. (1979). Family therapy with alcoholics: A review. In E. Kaufman and P. Kaufman (Eds.), *Family therapy of drug and alcohol abuse.* New York: Gardner Press.

Sundel, M., & Sundel, S. S. (1975). *Behavior modification in the human services.* New York: Wiley.

Super, D.E. (1957). *The psychology of careers.* New York: Harper & Row.

Super, D.E. (1969). Vocational development theory: Persons, positions, and processes. *The Counseling Psychologist, 1,* 2-9.

Super, D.E. (1976). *Career education and the meaning of work.* (Monographs of Career Education). Washington, DC: Office of Career Education, U.S. Office of Education.

Super, D.E., Thompson, A.S., Lindeman, R.E., Jordaan, J.P., & Myers, R.A. (1979). *Career Development Inventory.* Palo Alto, CA: Consulting Psychologists Press.

Tiedeman, D.V., & O'Hara, R.P. (1963). *Career development: Choice and adjustment.* New York: College Entrance Examination Board.

Tolbert, E.L. (1974). *Counseling for career development.* Boston: Houghton Mifflin.

Trotzer, J.P. (1977). *The counselor and the group: Integrating theory, training, and practice.* Monterey, CA: Brooks/Cole.

Truax, C.B., & Carkhuff, R.R. (1967). *Toward effective counseling and psychotherapy: Training and practice.* Chicago: Aldine.

Truax, C.B., & Carkhuff, R.R. (1964). The old and the new: Theory and practice in counseling and psychotherapy. *Personnel and Guidance Journal, 42,* 860-866.

Tyler, L.E. (1969). *The work of the counselor* (3rd ed.). Englewood Cliffs, NJ: Prentice Hall.

Vacc, N.A., & Loesch, L.C. (1983). Research as an instrument for professional growth. In G.R. Walz & L. Benjamin (Eds.), *Shaping counselor education programs in the next five years (Conference Proceedings, Association for Counselor Education and Supervision),* (pp. 25-38). Ann Arbor, MI: ERIC Counseling and Personnel Services Clearinghouse.

Vacc, N.A., & Wittmer, P.J. (1980). Prologue: Special populations. In N.A. Vacc and P.J. Wittmer (Eds.), *Let me be me: Special populations and the helping professional* (pp. 6-12). Muncie, IN: Accelerated Development.

Wagman, M., & Kerber, K.W. (1984). Computer-assisted counseling: Problems and prospects. *Counselor Education and Supervision, 24*(2), 142-154.

Weikel, W.J. (1985). The American Mental Health Counselors Association. *Journal of Counseling and Development, 63*(7), 457-460.

Westervelt, E.M. (1978). A tide in the affairs of women: The psychological impact of feminism on educated women. In L.W. Harmon, J.M. Birk, L.E. Fitzgerald, and M.F. Tanney (Eds.), *Counseling women* (pp. 1-33). Monterey, CA: Brooks/Cole.

Wetzel, L., & Ross, M.A. (1983). Psychological and sociological ramifications of battering: Observations leading to a counseling methodology for victims of domestic violence. *Personnel and Guidance Journal, 61*(7), 423-427.

Wheeler, P.T., & Loesch, L.C. (1981). Program evaluation and counseling: Yesterday, today, and tomorrow. *Personnel and Guidance Journal, 59*(9), 573-577.

Whiteley, J.M., & Resnikoff, A. (Eds.) (1978). *Career counseling.* Monterey, CA: Brooks/Cole.

Wiggins, J.D., & Weslander, D.L. (1986). Effectiveness related to personality and demographic characteristics of secondary school counselors. *Counselor Education and Supervision, 26*(1), 26-35.

Williamson, E.G. (1939). *How to counsel students.* New York: McGraw-Hill.

Williamson, E.G. (1950). *Counseling adolescents.* New York: McGraw-Hill.

Wilson, E.S., & Robinson, E.H. III. (1985). Association for Humanistic Education and Development: Leadership and diversity. *Journal of Counseling and Development, 63*(7), 416-419.

Wittmer, P.J., & Loesch, L.C. (1986). Professional orientation. In M.D. Lewis, R.L. Hayes, and J.A. Lewis (Eds.), *An introduction to the counseling profession* (pp. 301-330). Itasca, IL: Peacock.

Wittmer, P.J., & Myrick, R.D. (1974). *Facilitative teaching: Theory and practice.* Pacific Palisades, CA: Goodyear.

Zahner, C.J., & McDavis, R.J. (1980). Moral development of professional and paraprofessional counselors and trainees. *Counselor Education and Supervision, 19*(4), 243-251.

Zunker, V.G. (1981). *Career counseling: Applied concepts of life planning.* Monterey, CA: Brooks/Cole.

INDEX

INDEX

A

Abused persons
    trends in counseling 190
Accountability 97
    counseling 35
Accreditation
    approved programs 61
    by other agencies 61
    denial of approval 60
    full approval 60
    procedures 59-60
    provisional approval 60
    self-study 59-60
    site visitation team 59-60
    three-person review committee 59
Adjustment problems
    figure 5
Adler, A. 71, 233
Affective domain
    assessment 94-5
Affeman, M. 181, 235
American Association for Colleges of
  Teacher Education (AACTE) 21
American Association for Counseling
  and Development (AACD) 16, 19, 24,
  52, 210, 215
    Ethical Standards 33, 215-7
    Foundation (AACDF) 200
    governance structure 199
    international branches 200
    state branches 200
American Association for Marriage and
  Family Therapists (AAMFT) 61, 206, 215
    clinical member status 206
American College Personnel Association
  (ACPA) 20, 28, 52, 198
American College Testing Program
  (ACT) 91
American Correctional Association 27
American Educational Research
  Association (AERA) 197
American Mental Health Counselors
  Association (AMHCA) 24, 28, 52, 198

American Personnel and Guidance
  Association (APGA) 21
    ethical standards 223-30
American Psychological Association
  (APA) 61, 197, 215
American Rehabilitation Counseling
  Association (ARCA) 22, 52, 198, 206
American School Counselor Association
  (ASCA) 22, 50, 178, 198
American Vocational Associaton
  (AVA) 197
Analysis
    applied behavioral 75
    statistical 169-73
    type of measurement scale 170
Anderson, B.S. 216, 218, 236
Applied behavior analysis 75
Appraisal
    definition 86
    individual 10
Apprenticeships 138
Approach
    decision 121-24
    developmental 132-5
    direct contact 138
    matching 118-21
    personality 125-32
    practitioner-scientist 16-7
    scientific 17
    sociological 124-5
Assessment 85-112
    acceptable evidence 102-3
    accountability 97
    affective domain 94-5
    after counseling 108
    anecdotal records 104
    attitude 96
    beginning of counseling 107
    behavior rating scales 104
    checklist 104
    client's behavior, *figure* 110
    cognitive-domain 90-94
    convenient measures 109
    definition 85
    derive meaning 109-11

dichotomy 86
during counseling 108
empirical counseling 96-102,
102-11
event recording 104
frequency counting 104
goal 86, 105
guidelines 102-11
improvement of counseling 97
in counseling 86-96
interval recording 104-5
meaningful 105-7
outcome 87
personality 95-6
prior data 104
process 98-102
purposes 87-9
record conditions 108-9
repeat measures 108
see tests
sensitive 105-7
several measures 105
target concern 102-3
three wishes 103
traditional 86-96
typical day or week 103
use observation 103-4
Association for Adult Development and
Aging (AADA) 24, 198
Association for Counseling and
Development (AACD) 197-200
Association for Counselor Education
and Supervision (ACES) 50-1
Commission on Standards and
Accreditation 50
Association for Counselor Education and
Supervision (ACES) 21, 198
Association for Humanistic Education
and Development (AHEAD) 21, 30,
52, 198
Association for Marriage and Family
Therapy (AAMFT) 197
Association for Measurement and
Evaluation in Counseling and
Development (AMECD) 22, 29, 52, 198
Association for Measurement and
Evaluation in Guidance (AMEG) 22
Association for Multicultural
Counseling and Development (AMCD)
23, 52, 198
Association for Non-White Concerns

in Personnel and Guidance (ANWC) 23
Association for Religious and Value
Issues in Counseling (ARVIC) 23,
198
Association for Specialists in Group
Work (ASGW) 23, 52, 198
Attributes
personal, *figure* 15
counselor, *figure* 15
Avocational
definition 115
Axelrad, S. 132, 235

B

Bandura, A. 122, 125, 233
Bardon, J.I. 12, 13, 233
Barlow, D.H. 14, 102, 105, 174, 233
Bartlett, W.E. 23, 233
BASIC ID 76
Behavior
change 35
Behavior Rating Scales 104
Belkin, G.S. 1, 11, 13, 233
Benjamin, L. 239
Bennett, V.C. 12, 13, 233
Bergland, B.W. 122, 233
Berne, E. 80
Bindman, A.J. 144, 233
Birk, J.M. 240
Blake, R.R. 155, 233
Blocher, D. 144, 233
Bloland, P.A. 155, 233
Bonk, E.C. 20, 238
Bordin, E.S. 126, 127, 233
Brammer, L.M. 139, 234
Branch Assemblies
regional 198
Brayfield, A.H. 120, 121, 234
Burnout prevention 212
Business and industry
trends in counseling 181-2

C

California Association for Counselor
Education and Supervision (CACES) 51

problem-solving activity 155
process 143, 150, *figure* 145
program-centered 149
purposes 143
relationship conditions 144-5
steps, interacting 150
training-workshops 146-8
Consultee-centered
    administrative consultation 149
    consultation 149
Consulting 216, 229
Contributions
    by counselors 212-4
Corey, G. 68, 234
Correlation coefficient 172-3
Council for the Accreditation of
    Counseling and Related Educational
    Programs (CACREP) 9, 49, 51, 52-3,
    54-5, 58, 59, 60, 61, 199, 201,
    202-5, 213, 234
Council on Rehabilitation Education
    (CORE) 61
Counseling 195-220
    accountability 35
    act in opposition to trends in
        society 29
    career 135-40
    clarify the situation 100-1,
        figure 99
    counselor preparation 33-4
    definition 1
    determine the focus 98-101,
        figure 99
    developmental 179
    Ethical Standards 33, 215-7
    evolution 19-35
    group 66-8
    identify activities 101,
        figure 99
    improvement 97
    individual 66-8
    initiate plan 101-2, *figure* 99
    legal aspects 217-9
    mental health 2, 31, 53
    point of view 1-18
    political involvement 34
    preventive 179
    profession today 30-5
    professional 1-18
    professionalism 195-220
    programs 33

public relations 34-5
reflects needs and trends in
    society 28-9
relationship 216
relationship with empiricism 29
remediative 179
research 157-75
school 3
scientific methods 16
specialties 2
theories 32
trends 177-94
Counseling and Human Development
    Division 197
Counseling Psychology 197
Counselor
    assumptions for professional 8-15
    born or made 38-40
    burnout prevention 212
    characteristics 38-40
    contributions 212-4
    credential 201-9
    difference from other mental
        health specialists 3-8
    differentiated 26-7
    fulfill societal needs 27-8
    identifiable 25
    mental-health 7
    practitioner-scientist 15-8
    preparation 37-59
    preparation programs 33
    professional 3-8, 25
    professional development 209-12
    scientist 13
    selection criteria 40-3
    skills in scientific inquiry 16
    unique 25
    use of technology 211-2
Counselor preparation
    counseling 33-4
    programs 33
Countertransference 71
Counting
    frequency 104
Courage 12
Cox, W.E. 24, 234
Cramer, S.H. 115, 116, 117, 118, 122,
    123, 128, 135, 139, 140, 236
Credentials
    certification 201-7

counseling concepts 192-3
Family Educational Rights and Privacy Act of 1974 219
Field theory perspectve 81
Field trips 138
Fitzgerald, L.E. 240
Forrest, D.V. 181, 235
Foundations
  social and cultural 10
Frank, V. 82
Fredrickson, R.H. 124, 235
Freud, S. 19, 69, 126, 235
Freudian psychoanalytic theory 69-71
FUTURE I 138

G

Gelatt, H.B. 123, 235
Gelso, C.J. 173, 175, 235
Genders
  trends in counseling 189-90
Genuineness 12, 73
Gestalt therapy 81-2
Gifted, intellectually
  trends in counseling 188
Ginsburg, S.W. 132, 235
Ginzberg, E. 132, 235
  decision-making 132
  phases 132
  proposition 132-3
  stages 132
Gjernes, O. 23, 237
Glasser, W. 78-9
Goldman, L. 174, 213, 235
Graduate Record Examination (GRE) 42, 89, 91
Gross, S.J. 191, 235
Group
  counseling 66-8
Group dynamics 10
Grunwald, B.B. 193, 235
Guidance Information System (GIS) 138
Guidelines for Doctoral Preparation in Counselor Education 51
Guidepost 199
Gysbers, N.C. 114, 235

H

Harmon, L.W. 240
Harren, V.A. 122, 238
Harris, T.L. 39, 238
Harris-Bowlsbey, J. 211, 235
Hayes, B.A. 181, 182, 236
Hayes, R.L. 240
Hayes, S.C. 14, 102, 105, 174, 233
Health Maintenance Organizations (HMOs) 181
Healy, C.C. 117, 235
Helping
  relationship 10
Helwig, A. 23, 237
Herma, J. 132, 235
Herr, E.L. 21, 24, 115, 116, 117, 118, 121, 122, 123, 124, 128, 134, 135, 139, 140, 233, 235, 236
History
  lessons from 25-30
Hock, E.L. 16, 236
Holdsworth, R. 236
Holistic-health proponents
  trends in counseling 191
Holland, J.L. 129, 236
  classification system 130
  hexagonal model, *figure* 131
  RIASEC model 130-1
  therapy 129-32
  types 130-1
Hollis, J.W. 33, 42, 45, 192, 211, 236
Holmes, Oliver Wendell 25
Homeostasis 193
Hopkins, B.R. 216, 218, 236
Hopson, B. 69, 236
Hoyt, K.E. 136, 236
Human growth and development 9-10
Human Resource Development (HRD) 181-2

I

Id 70
Identified patient (IP) 193
Individual
  counseling 66-8
Information
  about clients 118-21

Measurement and evaluation 216
Median 171
Mehrens, W.A. 90, 92, 214, 237
Membership
    associate 197
    classifications in
        organizations 197
    life 197
    regular 197
    student 197
Mental health
    consultation 148-9
    counseling 2, 31, 53
    delivery continuum, *figure* 5
Meyer, D. 23, 237
Military Educators and Counselors
    Association (MECA) 24, 198
Miller Analogies Test (MAT) 42, 91
Miller, E. 173, 237
Milliken, R.L. 11, 237
Minkoff, H.B. 22, 237
*Minnesota Multiphasic Personality
    Inventory* (MMPI) 106-7
Mitchell, A.M. 123, 236
Mitwelt 83
Modality profile 76
Mode 171
Model
    affective 81-84
    behavioral 72-5
    client/person-centered 73-4
    cognitive 77-81
    community based 137
    employer based 137
    experienced based 137
    home based 137
    neobehavioristic stimulus-
        response 75
    psychoanalytic 69-73
    rural/residential 137
    school-based 136-7
    theoretical 68-82
    traditional assessment 86-96
Mouton, S.S. 155, 233
Muro, J.J. 214, 234
Murphy, H.B. 38, 238
Myers, J.E. 188, 237, 238
Myers, R.A. 135, 239
Myers, R.S. 188, 237
Myers-Briggs Type Indicator (MBTI) 107
Myrick, R.D. 151, 152, 237, 240

N

Nachmann, B. 126, 127, 233
National Academy of Certified Clinical
    Mental Health Counselors (NACCMHC)
    200, 203, 205-6, 215
National Association of Appointment
    Secretaries (NAAS) 20
National Association of Counselor
    Supervisors and Counselor Trainers
    (NAGSCT) 49
National Association of Deans of Women
    (NADW) 20
National Association of Guidance
    Supervisors (NAGS) 21, 49
National Association of Guidance
    Supervisors and Counselor Trainers
    (NAGSCT) 21
National Association of Placement and
    Personnel Officers (NAPPO) 20
National Association of Student
    Personnel Administrators (NASPA) 20
National Board for Certified
    Counselors (NBCC) 199-200, 202-7,
    208, 213, 215
National Career Development
    Association (NCDA) 20, 52, 198
National Catholic Guidance Conference
    (NCGC) 23
National Certified Career Counselor
    (NCCC) 205
National Certified Counselor (NCC) 205
National Council for Accreditation of
    Teacher Education (NCATE) 61, 201
National Council for Certified Career
    Counselors (NCCCC) 203, 205
National Employment Counselors
    Association (NECA) 198
National Employment Counselors
    Association (NECA) 22-3
National Rehabilitation Association
    206
National Vocational Guidance
    Associaton (NVGA) 20
Needs
    hierarchy 127
    Maslow 127
Nelson, R.O. 14, 102, 105, 174, 233

Thompson, A.S. 135, 239
Tiedeman, D.V. 113, 133, 238, 239
  career development 133
  developmental approach 133
Time sampling 104-5
Tolbert, E.L. 115, 116, 133, 239
Tort 218
Training-workshops
  approaches 146-8
  consultation 146-8
Trait-and-factor approach 118-21
  definition 118
  information use 120
  informational 120
  motivational 120
  readjustive 120
Transactional analysis (TA) 80-1
Transcendere 83
Transformation 193
Trends
  business and industries 181-2
  colleges and universities 179-80
  community agencies 180-1
  counseling 177-94
  elementary school 179
  elementary-school children 185-6
  in clientele 184-193
  legal systems 183
  preschool children 185
  private practice 183-4
  religious congregation 182-3
  secondary schools 178-9
  settings 178-84
  where counselors work 178-84
Trends in counseling
  abused persons 190
  business and industry 181-2
  colleges and universities 179-80
  community agencies 180-1
  elementary schools 179
  elementary-school children 185-6
  ethnic minority groups 188-9
  genders 189-90
  gifted, intellectually 188
  holistic-health proponents 191
  legal systems 183
  older adults 187-8
  people, talented 188
  persons, abused 190
  persons, in mid-life 187
  preschool children 185

private practice 183-4
problems, family 192-3
problems, marital 192-3
problems, sexual 192
religious congregation 182-3
secondary school 178-9
secondary-school students 186-7
substance abusers 190-1
Trotzer, J.P. 67, 68, 239
Truax, C.B. 12, 13, 239
Trust 11
Tyler, L.E. 64, 239

U

United States Office of Education
  (USOE) 136
Unwelt 83

V

Vacc, N.A. 189, 203, 204, 213, 214,
  237, 239
Validity
  external 166-7
  internal 164-6
Values, personal 122
Variables
  research 167
Vocation
  definition 114-5
Vocation maturity 135
Vocational Bureau of Boston 20
Vocational development
  definition 116
Vocational Preference Inventory 131
Vocational Rehabilitation Act (VRA) 22

W

Wagman, M. 211, 240
Walz, G.R. 239
Wantz, R.A. 33, 42, 45, 192, 211, 236
Weikel, W.J. 24, 240
Weslander, D.L. 39, 240
Westervelt, E.M. 189, 240
Wetzel, L. 190, 240
Wheeler, P.T. 47, 115, 237, 240
Whiteley, J.M. 117, 236, 240
Wide Range Achievement Test 106
Wiggins, J.D. 39, 240
Williamson, E.G. 87, 118, 121, 240
Wilson, E.S. 21, 240
Winder, C.L. 16, 236
Wittmer, P.J. 151, 189, 195, 202,
239, 240
World War II era 22

Y

Yalons, I. 82

Z

Zahner, C.J. 39, 240
Zunker, V.G. 115, 134, 138, 240
Zytowski, D.G. 123, 236

Nicholas A. Vacc, Ed.D.

Nicholas Vacc, Professor and Chairperson of the Department of Counseling and Specialized Educational Development at the University of North Carolina at Greensboro, received his doctorate in counseling from the State University of New York at Albany. He is a National Certified Counselor and serves as Examination Consultant for the National Board for Certified Counselors, Inc. He is a member of American Association for Counseling and Development (AACD) and the American Psychological Association (APA) and a Fellow in the American Orthopsychiatric Association. Nicholas' special interests include teaching counselor education, doing clinical supervision, and serving as a consultant in the professional practice of counseling. He recently taught courses and consulted in New Zealand, and regularly conducts in-service training and supervision workshops for counselors and other mental-health professionals. Prior employment experience includes work in residence life, counseling with veterans and their dependents, and directing a university counseling center.

Nicholas is a former editor of the journal *Measurement and Evaluation in Counseling and Development* (formerly known as *Measurement and Evaluation in Guidance),* a past chairperson of the AACD Council of Journal Editors, and a former President of the North Carolina Association of Measurement and Evaluation in Counseling and Development. He has authored or co-authored more than 50 articles in professional publications.

Larry C. Loesch, Ph.D.

Larry Loesch, Professor and Graduate Coordinator in the Department of Counselor Education at the University of Florida, received his doctorate in counselor education from Kent State University. He is a National Certified Counselor and serves as Examinations Coordinator for the National Board for Certified Counselors, Inc. He is a member of the American Association for Counseling and Development (AACD). Larry's special interests include teaching counselor education, doing clinical supervision, and consulting in the professional practice of counseling. He regularly conducts training workshops for counselors, other mental-health professionals, and personnel in public and private agencies. His prior employment includes work in residence life, secondary school teaching and counseling, and computer programming.

Larry is a co-recipient of the 1983 AACD Research Award, a former President of the Association for Measurement and Evaluation in Counseling and Development and of the Florida Association for Counseling and Development, a past editor of *Measurement and Evaluation in Guidance,* a previous chairperson of the AACD Council of Journal Editors, and a recipient of the 1986 Association for Measurement and Evaluation in Counseling and Development Exemplary Practices Award. He currently is an editorial board member for the journal *Counselor Education and Supervision* and Secretary of Chi Sigma Iota, Counseling Academic and Professional Honor Society International. He has authored or co-authored more than 70 professional publications.